COURAGEOUS COUNSEL

Conversations with Women General Counsel in the Fortune 500

COURAGEOUS COUNSEL

Conversations with Women General Counsel in the Fortune 500

Find your own path &
go courageously!

Kara Baysinger

By Michele Coleman Mayes and Kara Sophia Baysinger

With a foreword by Judge Judith S. Kaye

ISBN: 978-0-615-44478-9

The opinions expressed in this book are those of the authors and the sources cited throughout
and do not, in any way, reflect on the companies or firms for which they work.

"And by the way, in the new code of laws which I suppose it will be necessary for you to make, desire that you will remember the ladies and be more generous and favorable to them than your ancestors. Do not put such unlimited power in the hands of husbands. Remember, all men would be tyrants if they could be. If particular care and attention is not paid to the ladies, we are determined to foment a rebellion, and will not hold ourselves bound by any laws in which we have no voice or representation."

—ABIGAIL ADAMS, IN A LETTER TO HER HUSBAND, JOHN, THE FUTURE U.S. PRESIDENT, 1776

"You may not always have a comfortable life, and you will not always be able to solve all of the world's problems at once, but don't ever underestimate the importance you can have because history has shown us that courage can be contagious and hope can take on a life of its own."

—MICHELLE OBAMA, SPEAKING TO THE YOUNG AFRICAN WOMEN LEADERS FORUM, 2011

To our sisters whom we will never meet, but hope to teach and inspire, even mentor, with this book, and to all good women and the men who surround and support them—may we be them; may we know them; may we help them; may we raise them.

—MICHELE COLEMAN MAYES AND KARA SOPHIA BAYSINGER

Gloria Santona

Carol Petren

Dorian Daley

Sara Moss

Pamela Carter

Christine Edwards

Anastasia Kelly

Teri Plummer McClure

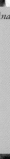

Carrie Hightman

Cathy Lamboley

Amy Schulman

Kim Rucker

Mary Ann Hynes

Lauri Shanhan

Sandra Leung

Vickie O'Meara

Andrea Zopp

Louise Parent

Sara Moss, Vickie O'Meara and Sandra Leung by Steven Freeman

WHAT'S NEXT?

a paved but perilous road

Do you believe in destiny—that some things are just fated to happen? How else can one explain the extraordinary coincidence of my weeklong medical convalescence and the arrival of the invitation to write a foreword for *Courageous Counsel*? The invitation was flattering, but became utterly irresistible as I was quickly engrossed in the manuscript. The week flew by, for which I thank not only the authors but also every single one of the book's subjects, whom I have come to know through their photographs, biographies, and stories.

Now knowing these remarkable women as I do, I can tell you for sure that destiny is one thing *Courageous Counsel* is most definitely not about. Hard work, persistence, dedication, mentoring, risk taking, never giving up? Yes to all of the above. But cruising to the position of general counsel in the arms of Destiny? No way. "Time waits for no one," in the words of Michele Coleman Mayes. Better believe it.

Having been a lawyer for nearly 50 years (gulp!), and a woman far longer than that, I love reading women's stories of success in our noble profession. It continues to shock me that, even in the justice system, still we struggle for equal opportunity in the judiciary and the bar, and that our progress toward diversity is so new and so slow. Just think where our world has come in the past 30 years—technologically, scientifically, medically—as we celebrate the rise of each immensely talented woman into top positions within our "justice" system and our society. All of this is powerfully and beautifully portrayed in *Courageous Counsel*, in numbers and commentary. But that is not what so quickly captured my mind and my imagination.

It's the unique focus of the book that excites me: women general counsel, women top legal officers of the mega-corporations that today dominate the headlines and the fabric of our society. For a 1962 law school graduate, a "miracle" litigation associate hired back then by the prestigious law firm of Sullivan & Cromwell, this is absolutely breathtaking. It's not that I didn't see this gradually happening around me—several of the featured individuals are my friends. It's just that the composite picture multiplies the phenomenon beyond description, and is downright inspiring. But there's more.

What I saw during my own initial years as a practicing lawyer was the drift of departing associates—all male—into the corporate-client world, firms assiduously nurturing those relationships, which held vast promise for future engagement as outside counsel. What I saw in *Courageous Counsel*, coincident with the arrival of women, was the evolution of the general counsel role, from gatekeeper-cop farming out the legal work, to corporate moral compass, decision-making fulcrum, mainstay of trust with investors and others, a highly visible, accountable fiduciary steering the ship and shaping strategy alongside the CEO and CFO. Great insights into the changed corporate world.

So, I necessarily ask myself, how much of this evolution is attributable to the mere passage of time—like melting glaciers—and how much of this is attributable to the arrival, in significantly increasing numbers, of women, people whose life experiences if not innate attributes may be vastly different? To be frank, I've asked myself this same question as I have watched the nationwide rise of women chief judges (the position I recently vacated in New York), similarly rethinking the way courts do their business.

Even the most jaded among us, I think, would have to answer that critical question: "Clearly it's both." So much for what lies behind.

What now? What of the future? There are indeed lots of thoughtful answers to these questions throughout the book, things to think about for those contemplating the journey. What I find most encouraging are not the A to Z answers—it's the A to Z names and (smiling) faces of the battle-scarred survivors, tangible evidence that we have made it to the office of general counsel. We are there, in our own voices and our own dress; we are there to perform outstandingly, there to mentor, assist, and advise. We are there—powerfully positioned to effect lasting change in the profession—in our choice of outside counsel. But no doubt about it, the barriers, agonies, risks, and double-binds remain very much alive, perhaps even more so in today's challenging economy.

What next? The road is now paved but still perilous. For me this book is exquisitely timed and exquisitely titled. I look forward to being part of the many discussions it undoubtedly will kindle about the hopefully brighter future for women in the legal profession and throughout society.

—JUDITH S. KAYE
Former Chief Judge of the State of New York
Of Counsel, Skadden, Arps, Slate, Meagher & Flom LLP
New York City

HOW THIS BOOK CAME TO BE:

many paths to take

We initially envisioned this book as a straightforward account of the rise of women general counsel in Fortune 500 companies, tracking and mapping their ascendency against the backdrop of changing social, cultural, business, and other environmental factors over the past four decades.

That growing numbers of women have successfully fulfilled the increasingly important and influential role of chief legal officer since 1979 seemed a persuasive document on its own. After all, prior to 1979, when Mary Ann Hynes became the first female general counsel of a Fortune 500 company, women were substantially invisible in the legal profession as a whole.

However, we soon realized that there was a richer narrative opportunity at hand. While our account of their collective rise stood to be a meritorious chronicle in its own right, the more illuminating—and impactful—approach by far would be to entrust the storytelling to our intended subjects themselves.

We knew clearly that we would be encountering a special group of women, as much as a special group of lawyers—in the Fortune 500, there is only room for 500 top lawyers at a time—and that there would be so much that we could learn from them. This awareness in turn became the spark and inspiration for how we would architect the book, and how we would invest it with intrinsic meaning and benefit. By opening its pages to firsthand accounts of their journeys to the top, we could capture, preserve, and impart an unprecedented trove of lessons learned and knowledge gained to past, present, and future generations of women lawyers who wanted to be legal leaders in the corporate world.

Who were their early role models? Why did they choose the law as a career? What steps did they take to advance their plans and dreams? Where did they go, and how did they get there? From their early childhoods on, we wanted to capture the stories and experiences that present their true *curricula vitae*, or courses in life. In addition to learning key biographical details, our approach was to interview our subjects on three specific topics that we saw as the essential components of success in the field: mentoring, risk taking, and requisite (along with the extraordinary) skills and attributes.

By setting these stories in an interweave of social, cultural, and historic contexts—including a review of how women have advanced in the U.S. legal system from the mid-1600s to the present—and supporting research, statistics, and expert commentary, we hoped to arrive at some conclusions about what it takes for a woman to become general counsel of a Fortune 500 company.

An exciting, daunting prospect, yes, but we immediately sensed its constraints and limitations. Over time—and never more so than now—the role of the general counsel has evolved into one of the most vital positions in corporate America. In today's risk-laden environment, it has also become one of the boardroom's most vulnerable positions—the barbed nexus where ultimate responsibility for guarding against legal, compliance, regulatory, and reputational risk sits. But could we really get these distinguished, accomplished leaders to talk or reveal much beyond the details of their resumes? To our surprise, the answer, happily, was yes.

Recognizing the challenge of trying to meaningfully interview all the women who have served as Fortune 500 general counsel from 1979 to present, we decided instead to go for representative groupings across time and by industry and geography. We divided the women into three "waves," comprising the pioneering first wave of 1979 to 1996; the second, "pre-critical mass" wave from 1997 to 2001; and then the third and current wave, from 2002 to the present. Their individual life and career journeys would take us around the United States—between past assignments and current positions, we knew we would have a robust mix of industries and recognizable corporate names.

Road map in hand, we began the outreach process, introducing the concept and extending invitations to our initial target list of some 30 women. In creating this list, we identified candidates we believed would be most comfortable talking about their experiences. In our view, this was the project's great unknown, even its potential stumbling block. Instead, it turned out to be the book's greatest surprise and reward, starting with near-unanimous acceptance of our invitation to be in the book.

The real magic happened, however, when we began the interview process.

Assisted by five women partners from SNR Denton—Leslie Davis, Linda Chaplik Harris, and Natalie Spears in Chicago; Robin Edwards in San Francisco; and Peg Hall in Dallas—we soon found that we weren't so much conducting interviews as we were engaging in conversations. Some women we knew, some we were meeting for the first time, but in speaking with virtually all of them, we found our early concerns about comfort levels and zones to be unfounded.

Surprisingly revealing, our conversations in person and by phone routinely exceeded the time allotted and the parameters set. There were "off-the-records" aplen-

Along the way, we were able to harvest and share a great deal of knowledge and a great many lessons, just as we had hoped to in creating the book.

ty, experiences and challenges necessarily off-limits for this book or any forum, but from a list that would grow to more than 40 past, present, and likely future Fortune 500 women general counsel, we went panning for gold and struck riches every time. Along the way, as you will discover reading the enlightening, inspirational, triumphant stories that follow, we were able to harvest and share a great deal of knowledge and a great many lessons, just as we had hoped to in creating the book.

Two takeaways resonated with us most: There is no one path for aspiring chief women chief legal officers—few paths are linear or actually ever plotted—and if we had to name the one quality shared by the women in this book, it is unequivocally the quality of courage.

This, then, is their book. These are our conversations with and about courageous counsel, and more than just offering conclusions about the qualities and experiences that it takes to be a legal leader in business, we are also able to offer a road map and a toolkit for today's women lawyers—for all their advances to date, still walking the narrow (but improving) line between social progress and traditional attitudes—to be the pioneers of tomorrow.

Your own path awaits. Go courageously.

—MICHELE COLEMAN MAYES
Chicago

—KARA SOPHIA BAYSINGER
San Francisco

August 2011

Chapter 1

HOW WE GOT HERE:

change agents

The number of women general counsel in the Fortune 500 has more than doubled since 1999. Still, there's a long road to travel.

f legendary American lawyer and civil libertarian Clarence Darrow were alive today, he would surely regret once telling a group of women lawyers this: "You can't be shining lights at the bar because you are too kind. You can never be corporation lawyers because you are not cold-blooded. You have not a high grade of intellect. I doubt you could ever make a living." This coming from the famously progressive Darrow, whose own mother, Emily, was an early advocate of women's rights.

Wind forward to 2011, and women "corporation lawyers" have certainly over-turned Darrow's cold-blooded verdict. According to the Minority Corporate Counsel Association's 2011 annual survey of women general counsel in Fortune 500 companies, 101—or 20.2 percent—of these top legal officers are women. As the MCCA itself once noted, "serving as general counsel of a major corporation is perhaps the apex of achievement for any lawyer in America….Although the United States has thousands of qualified lawyers, only a select 500 can hold this position for the largest public companies in the country—the Fortune 500."

Even for the Fortune 500's first women general counsel, among them Maud Mater (Freddie Mac, 1982), Louise Parent (American Express, 1993), Rebecca Kendall (formerly Rebecca Goss, Eli Lilly, 1995), Sara Moss (Pitney Bowes, 1996) and the first ever woman general counsel at a Fortune 500 company, Mary Ann Hynes (CCH Inc., 1979), such ascendancy was far from an obvious option at the outset of their careers. While all states, albeit many begrudgingly, were finally admitting women to the bar by 1914, it took all U.S. law schools until the 1970s to drop their gender barriers, along with such excuses as lacking sufficient toilet facilities for women. Even with the door open, however, entry was slow: in 1972, women comprised just 7 percent of conferred law degrees, compared with 44 percent in 1997 and nearly 50 percent today. And while women steadily made inroads at law firms through the first seven decades of the 20th century, the concept of women as senior-level corporate counsel remained virtually unknown during this same period. Notable for being the first woman to clerk at the U.S. Supreme Court, Alaska-born Lucile Lomen (1920–96) was a distinctive exception: during her 35-year career with General Electric, from 1948 to 1983, she held several important positions in the law depart-

The People's Work

As a little girl, **Pamela Carter** found herself in the crucible of history. The year was 1966. The scene: Dr. Martin Luther King's protest march into the all-white housing areas near Marquette Park in Chicago. Carter was there, amid the bottle and rock throwing—and the presence of the KKK. "I remember seeing them in their white satin robes, and being shocked that people would take such great care and pride into making garments that were symbols of hate and subjugation," she recalls.

Carter would find lasting inspiration in Dr. King and with the courageous, unwavering people with whom she marched that day. "It was a time of such strife, with so many people wanting to see me fail," says Carter. "I experienced the full impact of public scorn from those who did not believe in racial tolerance or suffrage. All I knew, though, was that I too wanted to help people, and that's why I pursued my Master of Social Work along with my law degree—not because of money or any intention to work in a corporate environment, but because I wanted to do the people's work."

ment, including counsel for corporate affairs. For the first wave of women general counsel of the Fortune 500, though, the top legal spot was clearly not sharply in the framework as they began their careers.

In today's highly regulated, potently risky corporate world, the role and responsibilities of general counsel have attained an acute new meaning; that 101 women currently fulfill this visible, critical position makes their arrival as corporation lawyers undeniable. In what we will call the "first wave" of female ascendancy to the general counsel role, the period between 1979 and 1996, eight women, beginning with Mary Ann Hynes, became Fortune 500 general counsel. In the second wave, or "pre-critical mass" phase from 1997 to 2001, another 12 women became general counsel. And from 2002 to 2011, the third and current wave, women steadily achieved critical mass as chief legal officers, with 2011's all-time high of 101 more than double the 44 recorded in the MCCA's first survey in 1999.

Women general counsel have arrived, but their pursuit of full equality as corporate legal leaders clearly has miles to go: 20.2 percent, after all, remains far shy of parity. In a 2010 radio interview, Dorian Denburg, general attorney, Network Operations, for AT&T and president of the venerable and influential Chicago-based National Association of Women Lawyers from 2010 to 2011, noted that "50 percent of graduating law students are women, yet only 15 percent were equity [profit-sharing] partners...general counsel of corporations, or tenured law professors." She added in the

> "As lawyers, [women's] seductive wiles would cause juries to acquit the guilty and reward the undeserving."
>
> —BABCOCK

same interview that "we must continue to eliminate disparity and persistent barriers that hinder the retention and promotion of women attorneys."

There remains a significant gender gap in the legal profession as a whole. Headquartered in New York, Catalyst is a highly respected global advocacy and research organization devoted to the advancement of women in professional leadership roles, with many Fortune 500 CEOs serving on its board. According to research cited in Catalyst's 2010 "Women in Law in the U.S." report, women made up 32.4 percent of all lawyers in the U.S. in 2009; given a constant rate of change, Catalyst estimates that "it will take more than a woman lawyer's (born in 2010) lifetime to achieve equality."

Parity by, say, 2095, seems an awfully long road ahead—especially given all the trailblazing to date—but if several more generations must pass before women achieve equality as general counsel and across the profession, what will it take to get there? As we would come to learn in interviewing the women general counsel featured in this book, there is no one path to the top, but many, just as there is no neat formula for success, but a distinct set of attributes, characteristics, and skills employed in varying degrees and different combinations. If there is any one answer, it is in maintaining the courageous spirit that has helped the women featured in this book and all their "sisters in law" to blaze the 20.2 percent trail to date—a spirit we find embodied in a comment made by four-time Fortune 500 general counsel Anastasia Kelly. After her first stint at Fannie Mae, and before taking tenures at MCI WorldCom and AIG, she accepted the general counsel job at then-troubled Sears, Roebuck and Co. in 1999. The job required that she and her family relocate to Chicago, a notion resisted at first by her children. As Kelly relates, her husband, encouraging the kids to be supportive of their mother, promoted the move as "Mom's Excellent Adventure."

It's a phrase that perhaps can be borrowed to define the continuing drive for equality. As we will explore later in the book, "Mom" power cannot be denied: several women general counsel interviewed for this book expressly link mothering and family skills to success in the corporate and legal suites. While women are "excellent" in law and in legal leadership, perhaps their highest esteem is defined by the optimism of every woman lawyer—from the earliest pioneers forward—who believed she could make it in the profession. And the quest continues to be an "adventure" in every sense of the word, loaded with intrigue, risk, pitfalls, setbacks, battles, conquests, and triumphs—one that began in earnest in 19th-century America.

"Horror and Disgust"

In Darrow's late 19th-century America, women lawyers faced fearsome ideological barriers: there were but inklings of gender equality before the law, let alone gender equality in the law. In *Beyond Her Sphere: Women and the Professions in American History*, Barbara Harris writes that "Practicing law was even more incompatible with

19th-century ideas about women than was practicing medicine. Female doctors could claim that their careers were natural extensions of women's nurturant, healing role in the home and that they protected female modesty by ministering to members of their own sex. By contrast, women lawyers were clearly intruding on the public domain explicitly reserved to men."

Barbara Babcock is a preeminent women's legal historian and a pioneer in her own right. In 1972, she became the first woman appointed to the regular faculty at Stanford Law School; she is also the first woman to hold an endowed chair at the school and its first emerita. In 1995, Babcock teamed up with Stanford Law School's reference librarian, Erika Wayne, to create the online Women's Legal History Biography Project, a comprehensive collection of student papers and other resources dedicated to the stories of pioneering women lawyers. In her review of Virginia Drachman's 1998 book *Sisters in Law: Women Lawyers in Modern American History*, Babcock identifies a central 19th-century concern that "time spent 'fore the justice seat' would unsex women not only by removing them from their proper sphere but also by degrading their finer natures." Or that women "would skew the process," meaning that "as voters and jurors, they would favor the best-looking man, or be swayed by sympathy rather than principle. As lawyers, their seductive wiles would cause juries to acquit the guilty and reward the undeserving."

The "intrusions" were not without precedent. The first recorded woman in the U.S. legal system was Margaret Brent (1601–71), an English emigre of privilege and means best known for arguing before the Maryland Assembly in 1648 for "vote and voyce." Yet, while proclaimed by some modern feminist scholars (and disputed by other commentators) as the original feminist and woman lawyer, Brent (who also appeared in about 100 land-related hearings before the provincial courts of Maryland and Virginia) did not exactly inspire a movement. Save extraordinary individual moments—as in 1797, when an African-born Vermont woman named Lucy Terry Prince, enslaved in the U.S. and liberated via marriage, successfully argued a property dispute before the Supreme Court—the ensuing two centuries would see little progress for women before the bar. Come 1869, though—one year after Darrow began practicing law—those "inklings" began materializing into slightly greater possibilities.

In 1869, Iowa became the first state in the union to admit women to the practice of law; on June 15 of that year, Iowan Arabella "Belle" Mansfield (1846–1911) became the first woman formally admitted to practice law in the U.S. She may not have been the country's first official woman lawyer; scholars suggest that honor may belong to another Iowan, Mary Magoon, an unlicensed practitioner reportedly enjoying a thriving trial practice at the same time. Nevertheless, though she would never actually practice law, it was Mansfield who officially took this landmark first step for female lawyers.

The year that the first woman suffrage law in the U.S. was passed in the territory of Wyoming, 1869, also reportedly saw Lemma Barkaloo from Brooklyn, New York,

> "The story of my triumphs will eventually disclose that though the battle has been hard-fought, it was worthwhile."
>
> —FOLTZ

The Minority Corporate Counsel Association:
Onward and Upward

Richardson: Corporate counsel are changing "the face" of the profession.

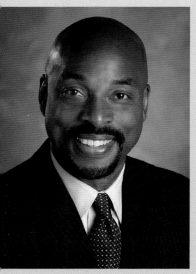

Johnson: Conducted the first survey of women general counsel.

As an attorney in the law departments of Hewlett-Packard and Empire BlueCross in the early '90s, Lloyd M. Johnson Jr. says he saw "opportunities to accelerate diversity by disseminating information about best practices in a systematic way."

Stirred to action, he envisioned a national organization that would "galvanize support for diversity practices through the sharing and cross-pollination of best practices and success stories." Johnson went coast-to-coast on a networking, fact-finding, and consensus-building mission. "I knew that I needed clear evidence that there was a pathway to lasting success in achieving diversity goals," he says—and, finding overwhelming support for his idea, he founded the Minority Corporate Counsel Association in 1997.

Focused on empowerment like few other organizations, Washington, D.C.-based MCCA has since made landmark strides in its ongoing mission to "advance the expanded hiring, retention, and promotion of diverse attorneys in legal departments and the law firms that serve them."

MCCA has made women a focal point of its pioneering research, a comprehensive body of survey-based reports, feature stories, case studies, and data-driven analysis that continues to contribute greatly to the organization's influence. In 1999, MCCA began charting the rise of women general counsel in the Fortune 500 by inaugurating a survey then known as the Survey of Women in Corporate Law. Introduced in the August 1999 issue of *Diversity & the Bar,* MCCA's influential bimonthly magazine, the first survey, then co-

sponsored by Winston & Strawn, counted 44 women chief legal officers.

Enhanced by vivid portraits of women general counsel in action—Sandra Leung, Jennifer Vogel, Catherine Lamboley, and this book's co-author, Michele Coleman Mayes, are among the many women who have been profiled to date—the goal of the survey then, as now, is to develop practical insights about career strategies women can apply to improve their own opportunities for professional advancement in the corporate legal function. The numbers alone tell a story of progress: by 2011, in the 11th edition of this annual benchmark, now known as the MCCA Survey of Fortune 500 Women General Counsel, that number had passed 100.

Mixing news, advice, and insight, *Diversity & the Bar* itself is a powerful, awareness-raising vehicle for women and other diverse legal professionals, a fact highlighted by ALM President and CEO William Pollak in MCCA's 10th anniversary video, released in 2007: "There is no question that the message of *Diversity & the Bar* has gotten through to the general counsel of major corporations around the country. We know that the organization's goals have been heard."

Now counting more than 200 corporate law departments as members, many in the Fortune 500, MCCA has played an integral role in "getting corporate counsel to look as diverse as the rest of the world," says former MCCA Executive Director Veta Richardson. "Working with the law firms they retain, corporate counsel continue to change the face of the legal profession."

become the nation's first female law school student, completing just one year of classes at Washington University in St. Louis before passing the Missouri Bar. She began practicing in 1870, only to die shortly thereafter from typhoid fever.

And it was 1869 again when Myra Bradwell (1831–94) passed the Chicago Bar exam, only to be denied admission by the Illinois Supreme Court because she was married (to a judge, no less, though husband James was on her side). Bradwell was primed for the challenge, though: as founder of the *Chicago Legal News*, she advocated vigorously for women lawyers in her regular "Law Relating to Women" column. Taking her case to the Supreme Court, Bradwell argued that under the 14th Amendment, she was guaranteed, as a U.S. citizen, the privilege of pursuing a profession. The Court was unmoved, with Associate Justice Joseph Bradley disapprovingly writing, "The natural and proper timidity and delicacy which belongs to the female sex evidently unfits it for many occupations of civil life....The paramount destiny and mission of women are to fulfill the noble and benign office of wife and mother. This is the law of the Creator."

Another age-old dilemma between the sexes is the assertion that women are better listeners than men. The scientific jury may still be out on that one, but while aspiring 19th-century women lawyers heard perfectly well what Darrow, the Supreme Court, and society at large were saying, an intrepid few listened instead to their own convictions. An exemplar in this regard, Bradwell appealed and eventually won the right to practice. The bravura she inspired in other women sat poorly with the establishment. In *A History of American Law,* Lawrence Friedman writes of "the horror and disgust evoked by these few brave, stubborn women." Unlike Brent, though, Bradwell's actions would prove influential. "Because of *Bradwell [v. Illinois],*" writes Babcock, "there are hundreds, maybe thousands, of vivid particular stories, with their displays of nerve and courage, personality and character, idealism and eccentricity."

Charlotte E. Ray (1850–1911) was another shining light. Reportedly convinced that Howard University's Law Department would be reluctant to admit her as a woman, Ray applied as "C.E. Ray," using her initials to mask her gender. Whether she was trying to outsmart the system by effecting a male persona à la Portia in Shakespeare's *The Merchant of Venice* is the subject of some scholarly debate (it has been argued that Howard University, in fact, did not discriminate against women at the time, and, furthermore, that the use of initials on application forms was a general practice among blacks), but accepted she was—and though certainly surprised to find that C.E. Ray was a woman, the school did not deny her enrollment. After graduating in 1872, she was admitted to the District of Columbia Bar that same year, reportedly becoming the first woman admitted to the practice of law in the District of Columbia while also becoming the first black woman, and only the third woman, admitted to practice law in the United States.

Another pioneer, Belva Lockwood (1830–1917), was a model of persistence. Denied a diploma after graduating from the National University Law School, she

A 1931 proposal to admit women to the bar's clubhouse was denied in part because of male "disgruntlement."

appealed successfully to the school's president *ex officio*, no less than the president of the United States, Ulysses S. Grant. Then in 1876—three years after the Supreme Court's ruling against Bradwell—she was denied admission to the Supreme Court Bar. Undeterred, she took the matter up with Congress; her lobbying would result in the 1879 "Act to relieve certain legal disabilities of women" and make her the first woman at the Supreme Court Bar, thereafter going on to a distinguished legal career.

And then there was Indiana-born Clara Shortridge Foltz, the "First Woman of California." Her application to the Hastings College of Law in San Francisco was famously rejected on the grounds that "...it's a well known fact that the rustling of a woman's skirts distracts the minds of male students," leaving Foltz to sue for her right to attend the school. Then, after becoming the first woman to pass the California Bar exam in 1878, she confronted the state law admitting only "white males" to the bar. Foltz prevailed once more, writing a state bill substituting "person" for "white male" and thereby becoming the first woman admitted to the California Bar. Foltz would blaze a trail for women over the ensuing six decades; her numerous accomplishments included authoring the law providing for public defenders and, at the age of 81, in 1930, becoming the first woman to run for governor of California.

Reflecting on her life, Foltz wrote, "Everything in retrospect seems weird, phantasmal, and unreal. I peer back across the misty years into that era of prejudice and limitation, when a woman lawyer was a joke...but the story of my triumphs will eventually disclose that though the battle has been long and hard-fought, it was worthwhile." Foltz, who died in 1934, would never know quite the prescience of these words, for despite the innumerable gains over her lifetime, the battle—as Babcock once noted, "state-by-state, territory-by-territory"—for gender equality in the law, and in society as a whole, was far from won.

"Disgruntlement of the Majority"

Foltz was familiar with Bradwell, Lockwood, and her other peer pioneers. Babcock notes the "flurry of press attention" generated when any new woman joined the bar in the 1870s and 1880s, each story generally mentioning the "others." So, while there was not a women's lawyer movement at the time per se, the word was getting out, the momentum was building—and women lawyers continued to make strides going into the 20th century.

While the 1870 U.S. Census recorded (likely inaccurately) only five women lawyers in the country, that number rose to 75 in the 1885 Census and then 1,010 in the 1900 count. As their numbers rose, women lawyers began to organize. In 1886, lawyer and suffragist Lettie Burlingame founded the first professional organization for women lawyers, The Equity Club at the University of Michigan. The club provided a nurturing support network in its four years of existence; in *Sisters in Law*, Drachman quotes one member as asking, "[W]hat can be so refreshing to an aspiring soul...as to be simply understood?"

Organized by the Chicago-based activist "Queen Isabella Association," the first-ever recorded "congress of women lawyers" took place at the 1893 Chicago World's Fair. Present at the gathering, Belle Mansfield was heralded as the woman "who had opened the way for them all" 24 years earlier; by one scholar's account, this "congress" of some 30 women represented the more than 200 women admitted to state bars since Mansfield's groundbreaking acceptance in 1869.

Barred from all-male D.C.-area law schools, Ellen Spencer Mussey and Emma Gillett founded the women-centric Washington College of Law in 1898. While also admitting men, this landmark institution, today the American University Washington College of Law, was the first ever to have a woman dean and the first to graduate an all-female law school class.

Then, in 1899, a group of 18 women lawyers in New York City gathered to form The Women Lawyers' Club. In 1911, "Club" became "Association," and in 1923, with members across the U.S., the body became known as the National Women's Lawyers Association. Committed to fostering diversity and advancing women in the legal profession, the National Association of Women Lawyers, as it is now known, has been at the forefront of change since its inception, playing a significant role in obtaining women's rights in the suffragette movement, improving child labor and minimum wage laws, and securing a woman's right to keep her name after marriage and to serve on juries. Today, NAWL is the only national women's bar association with both individual and organizational members in all 50 states, its membership (men included) uniquely drawn from law firms, corporations, government, nonprofits, and law schools.

The early 20th century brought more milestones. In 1918, Judge Mary Belle Grossman and Mary Florence Lathrop became the first two women lawyers admitted to the American Bar Association. In 1920, the 19th Amendment guaranteed women the right to vote in federal elections. It might have appeared that the days of "horror and disgust" were fading as women also began moving into the U.S. judiciary. In 1928, Genevieve Cline became the first woman federal judge; appointed in 1934 by President Franklin D. Roosevelt, Florence Allen became the first woman on the federal appellate bench.

A true pioneer was Russian-born Soia Mentschikoff (1915–84). Raised in New York City from the age of three, Mentschikoff graduated from Columbia Law School in 1937 and then embarked on a distinguished career as a legal scholar and educator in which she established several firsts for women in the law. Among her achievements: co-drafting the Uniform Commercial Code with her husband, Columbia Law professor Karl Llewellyn; becoming the first woman partner at a major Wall Street firm in 1944, at the remarkable age of 29; joining the faculty of Harvard Law School in 1947 as its first female professor, at a time when the school did not accept female students; and thereafter becoming the first woman law pro-

Required: a "pioneering spirit, thorough preparation, special ability, and determination."

fessor at the University of Chicago, the first woman to be elected president of the American Association of Law Schools, and one of the first women ever mentioned as a judicial nominee for the Supreme Court.

Equality, however, was still far off. In 1931, *Time* magazine reported that a proposal to admit women members to the "marble-and-brocade clubhouse of the exclusive Bar Association of New York City" was denied in part over the "potential disgruntlement of the male majority," an echo of that "rustling of a woman's skirts" argument that initially kept Clara Foltz from the Hastings College of Law. The echo grows fainter in this excerpt from a 1958 U.S. Department of Labor publication called *Employment Opportunities for Women in Legal Work*, but, as noted by the curators at Columbia University's Arthur W. Diamond Law Library, "hints of inequitable work assignments for women lawyers" are unmistakable: "Women lawyers employed by law firms often have duties that include legal research rather than client contacts and trial work in court." And this, from the publication's concluding paragraph, that any woman considering a legal career will need to have a "pioneering spirit, thorough preparation, special ability, and determination." Echoes, again, of Myra Bradwell, Belva Lockwood, and the pioneers of the 19th century—women still had to be pioneers almost 100 years later. For all the progress, mid-20th-century women lawyers were still "clearly intruding." What would it take, as Babcock writes, "to change the profession so that it truly accommodates women"? One thing, she offers, would be an "astonishing increase in the number of women lawyers." Another, the advent of feminism: "For the movement to progress beyond self-interested promotion and even beyond a quest for formal equality, it must place women at the center of thought and action."

Both of these drivers would kick into high gear around the time the women who would come to redefine the office of general counsel were coming of age.

The Wheel Turns

Born between 1946 and 1967, these women, the legal leaders featured in this book, grew up amid the second significant step in the evolution of feminism in the U.S. The first stage of the movement, dating to the Seneca Falls Convention of 1848, was about achieving suffrage. That goal was largely realized via the passage in 1920 of the 19th Amendment—but suffrage would prove divisive for women lawyers. "Most women lawyers believed that the [federal amendment] would almost instantly change their professional status," writes Babcock, noting that, "they viewed the vote as empowering women lawyers and as therefore enhancing their status and respect...."

In fact, the opposite happened. With suffrage actually changing little in the way of professional advancement, women trended toward "sex-neutral professionalism" over feminism, seeking credibility as lawyers, not as women. The result, writes Babcock, "was the first real divergence between feminism and professionalism."

"I knew that I had to create the opportunity for myself to succeed."

—MADRID

This would not help move women lawyers forward as a gender: overall, during the period between 1920 and the late 1960s, women were still stuck in the "access without advancement" gear. Even the access was unremarkable. The 1920 Census showed 1,738 women lawyers in the U.S., a gain of only 728 since the 1900 count. By 1960—a time booming with echoes of 19th-century ideology—only 3 percent of U.S. lawyers were women. In her book *When Everything Changed*, Gail Collins portrays 1960s American culture as one in which "women are meant to marry and let their husbands take care of all the matters relating to the outside world." Among Collins' wealth of anecdotes: the dean of Harvard Law School, hosting a dinner for the "handful" of women students (future Supreme Court Justice Ruth Bader Ginsburg among them), started the evening off by asking the women "to explain what we were doing in law school taking a place that could be held by a man." Harvard Law School, by the way, did not admit women until 1950, almost the last law school in the country to do so.

Assuming women could even get a job (as Collins puts it: "Since it was perfectly legal to discriminate on the basis of sex, there was no real comeback when employers simply said that no women need apply."), advancement opportunities were painfully thin. Writes Collins: "A report on women in management by the *Harvard Business Review* in the 1960s said there were so few of them, 'there is scarcely anything to study.' The idea that men were supposed to be in charge went beyond conventional wisdom; it was regarded by many as scientific fact." According to Collins, conditions were no better in law firms, where women lawyers "were nudged into behind-the-scenes work like real estate and insurance law."

It was high time for a new brand of feminism, a vigorous acceleration of the movement that would move beyond the vote into changing social attitudes and equalizing legal and social rights for women. Their collective consciousness fueled by books such as Simone de Beauvoir's *The Second Sex* (1949) and Betty Friedan's *The Feminine Mystique* (1963), women moved toward liberation. United under slogans such as feminist activist Carol Hanisch's "The Personal Is Political," women organized to take on the establishment. Stalled for decades, the wheels of progress began to turn once more, quickening along with the victories. In 1963, President John F. Kennedy signed the Equal Pay Act into law, abolishing wage disparity based on sex. In 1966, the National Organization of Women was founded, followed by the launch in 1970 of its sister organization, NOW's Legal Defense and Education Fund (later renamed Legal Momentum). Two years later, 1972 was a watershed year for women: Katharine Graham became the first woman CEO of a Fortune 500 company (The Washington Post Co.); Catherine Cleary became the first woman director on General Motors' board; Title IX was enacted; and Congress passed the Equal Rights Amendment (though it has never been ratified). In 1973, the Supreme Court made its landmark privacy ruling on behalf of women in *Roe v. Wade*; that same year Billie Jean King defeated Bobby Riggs in the nationally televised "Battle of the Sexes" tennis match.

Perry Mason provided many Americans with their very first glimpse at what being a lawyer might mean.

Making the Grade

Fay Chapman has always adhered to the principle of "doing my best to succeed." It was not easy in the beginning. In high school in Ventura, California, she pursued college prep classes. Walking into algebra, the teacher told her she was in the wrong room—"home economics is next door." At UCLA, figuring that a professional degree was the way around the secretarial pool, she set her sights on medical school. Despite "sailing through" chemistry, she failed to get the requisite "A." "The professor gave all the A's to the men so they could avoid the draft," she says.

Shifting her focus to law, a scholarship enticed her to William & Mary. She did not stay long. "My first week there, I overheard a guy talking about how besides the two women, the black guy, the blind guy, and the guy in the wheelchair, integration was otherwise fine." Chapman transferred to the more welcoming New York University Law School, graduating in 1972. "I was getting pretty tired of being a groundbreaker, but back then, you just had to keep trucking."

It was also a woman who provided one of the signature moments of the 1974 Watergate hearings, when Congresswoman Barbara Jordan—a lawyer by training who grew up in an impoverished neighborhood in Houston—gained national attention and prominence in calling for the impeachment of President Nixon. Women would continue to gain ground through the '70s and into the '80s (as Elizabeth Holtzman did in 1972, when she became the youngest woman ever elected to Congress), and it was against this backdrop that the future women general counsel of the Fortune 500 came of age. Interestingly, a century after Belle Mansfield had officially lifted the bar for women, it was neither the influence of pioneering predecessors nor the heady gender reforms of the day that ushered them into the profession—for most, personal rather than political factors were the draw.

In the Door

At her 2009 confirmation hearings, Supreme Court Associate Justice Sonia Sotomayor named fictional TV defense lawyer Perry Mason as her inspiration to go into law. It was a resolute, confident decision, cast in childhood: "I was going to college and I was going to become an attorney, and I knew that when I was 10. Ten. That's no jest."

Sotomayor was not alone in harking to actor Raymond Burr's commanding portrayal of the highly skilled and eminently just Mason. Originally a 15-minute radio show, *Perry Mason* became one of the most enduring and popular franchises of television's early days, running weekly from 1957 to 1966 on CBS. The program came in second (behind *L.A. Law)* in the American Bar Association's 2009 survey of the "25 Greatest Legal TV Shows" of all time, with the *ABA Journal* writing that "Raymond Burr's Perry Mason provided many Americans with their very first glimpse at what being a lawyer might mean."

This was certainly the case for several women general counsel interviewed for this book, with Carol Petren, former general counsel of CIGNA, and Sandra Leung, general counsel of Bristol-Myers Squibb since 2007—interestingly, both in the third wave—among those naming *Perry Mason* as an influence. Rebecca Kendall (then Goss), whose 25-year legal career at pharmaceutical leader Eli Lilly and Co. included five years as general counsel for U.S. pharmaceutical operations and eight years as general counsel for the company, graduated from high school the year that *Perry Mason* went off the air. She recalls finding appeal in the Mason character. "I had kind of formulated this idea that I wanted to be a lawyer, though not with any realistic clue of what lawyers did," she recalls. "Watching *Perry Mason* helped give me some insight into what being a lawyer was all about. I remember thinking to myself, hey, I kind of like this guy."

Kendall's avid scholarship, focused on topics including government, history, politics, and current events, would help sharpen her understanding of the law beyond the compelling image presented by Mason, as would the benefit of a key mentor, a local judge, who helped guide her decision making toward the law as she prepared to leave high school. Still, Kendall's chosen pursuit of the law was an unlikely choice coming out of an era when a woman's place was decidedly in the home. In 1959, when Kendall was attending elementary school in rural Brazil, Indiana, *Time* ran a cover story that noted that whereas "a few years ago, it took the housewife five-and-a-half hours to prepare daily meals for a family of four, today she can do it in 90 minutes or less—and still produce meals fit for a king—or a finicky husband."

For women in the first general counsel wave, coming to terms with being a lawyer was far from an apparent choice, and unlike Sotomayor, few of our corporate legal leaders-to-be knew they wanted to be lawyers at age 10, let alone be general counsel. For most, the decision process would be evolutionary, typically cemented somewhere between their high school and post-collegiate years. Ranging from the casual to the circumstantial to the deliberate, their entry into the law sprang from a variety of motivations.

Janet Kelly, for example, weighed other options before deciding on the law. Destined for the top legal spots at Sara Lee, the Kellogg Company, and currently ConocoPhillips, Kelly has vivid childhood memories of her father going to law school at night, recalling especially the "big deal" luncheon on the day he was sworn in to the Illinois Bar. These strong impressions aside, Kelly went through Grinnell College as a history major "exploring about a thousand different career possibilities." When graduation "snuck up on her" in 1979, she applied, too late, to several doctorate programs in medieval history. Living at home for a year while working, unhappily, in a

> "I felt I would have the power to make a difference if I were a lawyer."
> —MOSS

retail buyers training program, she took the LSAT exam. Seeing a more stable path in law, Kelly enrolled in Yale Law School in 1980.

Of course, there are more deliberate approaches, such as Pamela Carter's response to the profound social experiences of her upbringing, but surprising perhaps is that few women interviewed for this book ascribe their motivation to enter the law to outright feminism or the pursuit of a feminist agenda. That said, feminism was a deciding factor for Sara Moss, general counsel of Pitney Bowes from 1996 to 2003 and now chief legal officer at The Estée Lauder Companies Inc.

Growing up on Long Island in the 1960s, Moss always assumed she would be a teacher or a nurse. Marrying her Yale Law School-bound husband right after she graduated college and relocating to New Haven, Connecticut, Moss started out as a history teacher—but in the intellectual milieu of Yale, often in the company of law school wives, she found herself moved by the feminist currents of the day. "Feminism was everywhere, and new constitutional underpinnings were being formed, such as in *Roe v. Wade*," she says. "I realized that I could make a difference." Working for the Teacher's Union with a focus on women-related issues, Moss began to understand how the interplay of law, human nature, and power could really help effect social change. "I felt I would have the power to make a difference if I were a lawyer," she says. Following her husband to New York after graduation, she enrolled at the New York University School of Law. During the summers she worked at the Center for Law and Social Welfare Policy, representing welfare mothers in class action lawsuits, and did a clinical program with Legal Aid.

After graduation, she followed her husband, first when he took a job in Buffalo, New York, and then, after his relocation, back to Manhattan. Once she was finally settled, she was confronted with the challenge of finding a job. She had passed up an offer from Legal Aid, thinking she would be living in Buffalo, and though she was interested in working at the ACLU Women's Center, the organization's lack of funding made the choice impractical. Law firm employment was not on her radar screen, but a chance meeting with an acquaintance who was working at a major Manhattan firm led to an interview and a job. Although she had no corporate law experience, she got the job because, as the hiring partner eventually concluded, "we know talent when we see it."

Also notable for her gender-centric perspective on getting into the law is Louise Parent, executive vice president and general counsel of American Express since 1993. After her father passed away when she was a child, Parent learned a lasting life lesson about courage and self-reliance from her mother. "She told me that life may not always work out as planned, and that you have to be ready to adapt," recalls Parent, calling her mother "an absolute role model." Parent was also influenced by a woman lawyer who worked in her hometown of Wilton, Connecticut. "She was a solo practitioner with a reputation for great work," remembers Parent, "who also had time to spend with her family and to play tennis."

"Life may not always work out as planned... you have to be ready to adapt."

—PARENT

It was a compelling vision of law as a career with balance, one that stayed with her while attending all-women Smith College from 1968 to 1972. In a 2009 interview with *Super Lawyers*, Parent called Smith "one of the best experiences of my life, honestly, because it was so dedicated to women doing everything….Women were the math majors, women were the pre-med majors, women ran the student government, women ran the newspaper—women did everything. And the belief was—why not? Why wouldn't a woman be able to do absolutely everything?" Distinctively one of the few women interviewed for this book who referenced the Women's Liberation Movement as an influencing factor, Parent said that reading *The Feminine Mystique* while at Smith cemented her decision to become a lawyer. "A light bulb went off," she says. "I knew that I wanted to have a career, not a job."

Immersion in the social issues of the day brought Cathy Lamboley, who served as Shell Oil's senior vice president, general counsel, and corporate secretary from 2000 to 2007, to the law. Raised in rural Wisconsin in the 1960s, Lamboley recalls a "political awakening" while attending the University of Wisconsin at Madison. A natural introvert, Lamboley, her social consciousness stirred by Vietnam, back-street abortions, and other concerns, found her voice in protest, marching amid the clamor and tear gas. Influenced by her teacher mother, she decided upon the "noble occupation" of teaching, starting off in a middle school in 1972. Answering the higher need to be independent and to be challenged—and to connect with people who were interested in politics and issues—she went to law school, graduating from the University of Texas at Austin in 1979.

For other women, resolute self-determination in the face of obstacles—or lack of options—was the driver. The example of first-waver Fay Chapman, who would go on to become general counsel of Washington Mutual, illustrates the pragmatic, unequivocal attitude necessary for advancement in the late 1960s, when career opportunities for women were still limited. Attending UCLA as an undergraduate during the Vietnam War, her goal was to attend medical school, motivated as she was to get "credentialed in some way" so that she would not be "pigeonholed" in the secretarial pool or some other closed-end area. Though she "sailed through" chemistry, she failed to receive the "A" she expected, which would have stood her in good stead in her quest to attend medical school. "When I asked the professor why," she recounts, "he said that he had to give all the A's to the men so that they could avoid the draft. Medical school, therefore, was a non-starter, so law was my next best bet."

For Linda Madrid, the obstacles were cultural. Now a senior client partner in the legal division of global recruitment leader Korn/Ferry International, Madrid's distinguished legal career included being a commercial litigator at Sidley & Austin, serving as general counsel to two financial companies, Riggs Bank and Carr America Realty, and being a senior vice president and deputy general counsel with Fannie Mae. Growing up in Phoenix in the late '60s and early '70s, Madrid encountered socio-economic and cultural limitations early on. "The hardest part was trying to envision

> "[My father] very much wanted me to go to law school. Feeling rebellious, I would have none of it."
> —MCNAMARA

GC Succession at Pitney Bowes:
Postmaster Generals

Moss, Mayes, and O'Meara

Perhaps surprisingly, Fortune 500 women general counsel infrequently cross corporate paths. In two exceptional cases, though, a trio of women served as successive general counsel—at Gap Inc. (see page 53), and at global mailstream technology company Pitney Bowes.

Invited by a recruiter, Sara Moss visited Pitney Bowes in 1996 thinking it would be good business development for her law firm. Instead, she became general counsel, successfully defending two multimillion-dollar cases right out of the gate. It was a "fabulous" experience—until 9/11. As she remembers it, "I was in Connecticut; the awful separation from my kids that day crystallized my need to be back in New York."

Moss knew exactly who would replace her—Michele Coleman Mayes. "I first met Sara when, as a law firm partner, she pitched business to us at Colgate-Palmolive," recalls Mayes. "Several years passed before we saw each other again, mainly at networking events, and while we never worked together, we had real chemistry. It was a bond based on similar values and life experiences." Moss was so sure, in fact, that she told then-Pitney Bowes CEO Mike Critelli not to put the GC position out for search. "I put Michele's name on top of that list," says Moss.

Then chasing the general counsel spot at Colgate-Palmolive, Mayes realized that the odds of the job opening up were pretty slim—so she interviewed with Pitney Bowes, won the job, and left, with Moss providing transitional support.

"Sara left a great legacy, but I wanted to create my own path," says Mayes, who did that over the next four years. "Then came the executive recruiter call beckoning her to Allstate Insurance, where she now holds the GC post.

Replacing her was former Army Captain Vicki O'Meara, a public service-driven legal leader whose early career experiences included working on the Superfund legislation while in the Pentagon and involvement with the Iran-Contra hearings while working in the White House Counsel's Office. Following subsequent postings as deputy general counsel for the EPA and assistant attorney general for the Department of Justice, O'Meara led the global environmental practice group at Jones Day before becoming GC and then president of U.S. supply chain solutions for Ryder Systems Inc.

Recruited by Pitney Bowes for her business and regulatory acumen, O'Meara took over as GC in 2008, and has since been promoted to executive vice president and president, Pitney Bowes Services Solutions, plus head of global government relations and postal affairs functions.

"I did not follow a linear course toward becoming general counsel," says O'Meara, reflecting on her global regulatory work and other successes at Pitney Bowes, "but I consider it among the best jobs going. You have the opportunity to practice at the highest level, there's the excitement of building and changing things, and you are afforded a significant role in the company's strategy and success."

Steven Freeman

that which did not exist within our community—we did not see women as lawyers, let alone Latina women." As a promising student and engaging personality, though, Madrid heard now and then that she should be a lawyer, and her vision began to take shape. "Whether it was going to be law or something else," she recalls, "I knew at least that I had to create the opportunity for myself to succeed."

The influence of parents, family members, and teachers figures significantly in several of our stories, though sometimes with a surprising twist. Growing up, the last thing Anne McNamara wanted to be was a lawyer—remarkable for a woman who would become one of the highest-ranking female executives in the airline industry, serving as senior vice president and general counsel for AMR Corp. and its subsidiary American Airlines from 1988 to 2003. "My father would have loved to have been a lawyer, but he couldn't afford college. So he very much wanted me to go to law school. Feeling rebellious, I would have none of it. I alternately wanted to be a career diplomat, a political science professor, a secretary (like my mother), or even a make-up artist—anything but a lawyer," she says. But her father, who died when she was 14, had planted a seed, which, along with the influence of a professor at Vassar College, inspired her passion for the law. She entered Cornell Law School in 1970 not wanting to be a lawyer per se, but in "pursuit of the intellectual challenge."

For Andrea (Andy) Zopp, it was more about charting her own path. Formerly executive vice president and general counsel of Chicago-based utility Exelon Corp. and now president and CEO of the Chicago Urban League, Zopp was 17 years old in 1974 when her lawyer father, a general practitioner and corporate counsel, became a judge in their hometown of Rochester, New York. Less in rebellion than in the spirit of independence, she determinedly opted for medicine over law. "Then I met organic chemistry, and realized I was not going to medical school," recalls Zopp with a laugh. Her hardworking mother, a member of Rochester's first class of women police officers and on the force briefly, was a major influence. "Be able to take care of yourself financially," she advised her daughter, "and do something you care about." Ironically, that "something" would be the law after all. After interning with New York Congressman Frank Horton, an environmentalist focused on energy policy, Zopp became intrigued by how laws made in Washington were translated into everyday life. With her mother "in full cheerleader mode" behind her, Zopp's next stop was Harvard, where she earned both her undergraduate and law degrees.

For first-waver Pamela Strobel, going into the law was a straightforward family affair. Strobel, who became general counsel for electric utility giant Unicom Corp. and its chief subsidiary, Commonwealth Edison Co., in 1993, had a powerful reference point for becoming a lawyer: her grandfather George was chief justice of the Illinois Supreme Court. While "Papa George" passed away when Strobel was a child, his influence would prove epiphanous on her 21st birthday. Celebrating with her parents at a jazz club, the conversation turned to her future. "My father told me how much I reminded him of Papa George," relates Strobel, "and that was all the direction I needed to go to law school." Her father, David, a pediatrician, was another important force in her life. "He raised me to believe that women could do anything," says Strobel. As the lasting legacy of her pioneering grandmother, Beryl Bristow, Papa George's wife, this mantra would be Strobel's guiding force, too. A member of the first female graduating class at the University of Illinois, Bristow was the first woman at the university to receive a master's degree in physics (and Latin, too). And there would be an element of pre-destiny in her subsequent career, for in 1919 Bristow went to work as a researcher at Commonwealth Edison, the same company where Strobel would become general counsel one day. Bristow passed away in 1999 at the age of 102, but for Strobel, she will always be "a reference point for what women were capable of doing, despite the cultural norm."

Whatever their motivations, the female students of the late 1960s and early 1970s, unlike their pioneering predecessors a century earlier, did not have to mask their gender or sue to get into law school. These were still raw times for female law students, but the collective law school door was finally open, and this access would only improve heading into the 1980s and 1990s, fulfilling Babcock's call for an "astonishing increase in the numbers of women lawyers." In 1984, *Time* ran a story called "Law: Getting a Piece of the Power" that noted that while 30 percent of the associates in the largest U.S. law firms were female, women made up only 5 percent of the partners. Nevertheless, the story went on, "the mere pressure of numbers should guarantee some progress: there are now 93,000 women among the nation's 612,000 lawyers." Progress indeed: an ABA study in 1996 concluded that the "single development that has changed the face of the profession most visibly over the last several decades is the large-scale entry of women into the profession." As first and second wavers left law school and headed into the workplace, though, it was clear that many challenges remained ahead—often pejorative and prejudicial in nature.

Ugly Encounters

Ironically, that same *Time* article in 1984 also included mention of a major Atlanta-based law firm, described by anonymous former associates as a "Southern gentleman's club," where female summer associates had reportedly been asked to enter an office wet T-shirt contest. Wind the clock forward to 1995—one year before its encouraging report on women's "large-scale entry into the profession"—and the ABA found troubling evidence of a still-gaping gender divide. In its survey-based "Unfinished Business: Overcoming the Sisyphus Factor," the ABA reported that judges and bailiffs in mid-sized towns in New York and Florida were still calling women attorneys "baby" and "honey," and furthermore, referring to them by their first names while addressing males by their titles.

Often, stark realities awaited women in law firms. Teri Plummer McClure, now senior vice president of legal, compliance, and public affairs, general counsel, and corporate secretary for UPS, recalls an "eye-opening experience" as a young associate in the early '80s. "There was a nice African-American woman attorney there who took me under her wing," says McClure. "I never learned the substance of it, but she was having challenges at the firm. Then one day she called to tell me that she was leaving right there and then, and then she was gone. Nobody at the firm said anything—it was total radio silence. Her name stayed on her door for months until one day it was not there, and that was that. Not another word." McClure believes that the fact that the woman—who would go on to a successful legal career elsewhere—was the first African-American woman in the firm was a contributing factor. "It was either the firm's expectations of her or vice versa," she says, "but I never saw the same response when white male associates came and went. For her to just disappear and then have the silence that followed was pretty shocking."

Starting out in a white shoe firm in Manhattan, Fay Chapman remembers a "horrible" rotation with a partner in the municipal bond department who confined her work to indexing closing books. "He thought that women should be secretaries and nothing more," says Chapman. That was in 1972; in 1988 Pamela Strobel had an uglier encounter still. At the time, she was working for Isham, Lincoln & Beale, a venerable Chicago firm with a traditionalist culture that was unwinding an ill-fated merger with a more aggressive firm. Loyal to the Isham firm, Strobel elected to stay on—until hearing an influential partner tell somebody on the phone that "pretty soon they're gonna admit dogs." He was talking about women getting admitted to a top Chicago business club—and as a result, Strobel reversed her decision.

Having graduated in the top 5 percent of her class at The George Washington University Law School in 1981, Anastasia Kelly asked the general counsel of Martin Marietta—where she had worked on pension and benefit planning since 1974—if he wanted to hire her for the law department. "He told me I was bright and would make a great addition," says Kelly, "but that they already had a woman." Remembering the incumbent woman as "a pain in the butt," Kelly believes "that was how all women lawyers were viewed" at the time.

Untoward advances were not uncommon. As an associate at a law firm in the South, one future woman general counsel had to deal with men who "could not get past the fact that you're an attractive and smart woman." She would end up gaining respect within the firm by refusing to work with a lecherous litigator, or as she put it, "bolting the lech." Egregious, too, was the "major" sexual harassment of one of our interviewees by a senior law firm partner early in her career. "The law was less developed back when it happened, so I really did not see it clearly as sexual harassment at the outset," she recalls. "It took time for the situation to evolve into something hideous, by which time I felt I could not handle it anymore." For the woman in question, who prides herself on being able to handle anything, the matter became a subject of embarrassment, which in turn prevented her from speaking

■

In the first wave, "general counsel historically played the role of gatekeeper."

—HANSON

up. Once she did, however, "the firm was fabulous in how it responded," and while she feels that the situation did not hamper her career, "it certainly made me love practicing at the firm less."

What would it take for women lawyers to overcome these and myriad other encounters with discrimination, prejudice, and entrenchment? A significant change in attitude would come from corporations, where changes in the business environment would dramatically redefine the role and responsibilities of legal leadership and, in turn, engender new board and management perspectives on women in the general counsel role.

Litmus Tests

Catherine Nathan has a straightforward explanation for why there were so few women in the first Fortune 500 general counsel wave, the period we have defined as 1979 to 1996. "There were simply not enough female candidates, and besides, the general counsel position at that time was not as desirable as it is now," says Nathan, a lawyer and New York partner with global executive search firm Spencer Stuart and founding member of the firm's Legal Search Group. "All the prestige was on the law firm side, and going in-house was regarded with less esteem." Formerly in law and investment banking before becoming a partner at global recruiting firm Heidrick & Struggles, Lee Hanson describes the first-wave era as a time when "the best people went for the glamour of big law firm partnerships, and general counsel historically played the role of gatekeeper."

The traditional general counsel role generally looked inward, with leadership largely confined to the legal department itself and responsibilities typically extending little further than advising the corporation on standard legal issues or farming out work to outside law firms. Often physically removed to a separate wing of the office and kept at arm's length from the actual business brainstorming and decision-making processes, corporate lawyers were generally relegated to a gatekeeping and policing role, fulfilling the unenviable role of naysayer—their job was to find reasons why fully cooked business ideas should not be served to the marketplace. Their relationship with the CEO was similarly constrained—not an integrated, collaborative deal, not the role of trusted business advisor and *consigliere*, but mostly one that consisted of keeping the dragons off the CEO's back.

That was then. The role would evolve, and while not immediately becoming more glamorous, it certainly became more business-focused. "Senior corporate leaders began realizing that the general counsel could play more of a critical, strategic, integrated role in the business," says Julie Goldberg Preng, a former practicing attorney who is now managing director of legal at Korn/Ferry International. Accelerating this awakening were some distinct operational and attitudinal shifts in corporate America. Among those highlighted by Preng: the changeover of compliance from an internal

> "Risk management favored the rise of women in the general counsel role."
>
> —PRENG

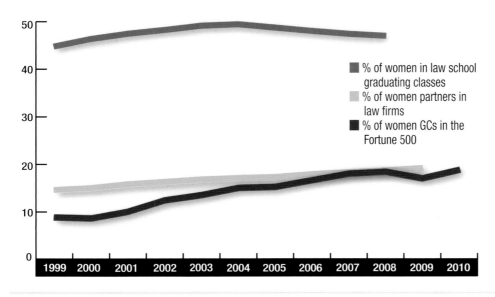

For over a decade now, women have achieved roughly equal parity in law school and entry into the legal profession. That's the good news. There's still far to go once the climb begins, though; while the percentage of women general counsel in the Fortune 500 has more than doubled since 1999, like their law firm peers, they're stuck around the 20 percent ceiling.

Sources: American Bar Association, The National Association for Law Placement, Minority Corporate Counsel Association

audit function into a strategic role; the growing awareness that a healthy, diverse culture keeps good talent bound to an organization, while also serving as the glue between employee engagement and revenue growth; and most acutely, the sharpening of the regulatory function in the post-scandal Sarbanes-Oxley era. Accordingly, the view of what the general counsel could do changed as well. "Instead of looking for people to simply shuffle legal matters off to outside law firms, senior executives began looking for legal leaders who could help make better business decisions and find creative solutions to business problems," says Preng.

As part of this transition, general counsel would increasingly be called upon to be "persuaders." In a 2007 interview with *Metropolitan Corporate Counsel*—five years after the introduction of Sarbanes-Oxley and just as the storm clouds of the global meltdown were gathering—Thomas J. Sabatino Jr., then executive vice president and general counsel of Schering-Plough Corp., characterized the evolved role of the general counsel as "persuasive counselor" this way: "The general counsel often sits at the fulcrum of decision making in a corporation, especially where he has a deep understanding of the business dynamics and challenges that drive the corporation. He is frequently in the best position to see both the opportunities and risks of a given business decision, and he can give the CEO, other members of senior management, and the board a balanced view and advice. The general counsel is also frequently seen as a moral compass for the organization—helping to ensure that the organization 'does the right thing,' not just the legally acceptable thing. This behavior reinforces a corporation's commitment to good corporate governance and compliance and amplifies the right 'tone at the top.'"

The evolution of the general counsel role would take something of a Darwinian turn in the still-reverberating aftermath of the global economic crisis. The circumstances that birthed Sarbanes-Oxley were onerous enough, but the legal and regulatory climate generated by the Great Recession has made corporate governance and risk management more complex and unforgiving than ever. The handling of risk in the corporation and in the general counsel role evolved—some might say mutated—from simply reporting on risk (from 1979 to around the mid-'90s, or essentially parallel with what we are calling the first wave of women general counsel); to identifying, monitoring, and managing risk (2001 to 2007); and, from 2008 to the present, to actually predicting and managing risk.

Consequently, the chief legal job now unequivocally *faces outward*, with the general counsel visible—and often accountable—to many more audiences than before. As the moral compass or "conscience" of the corporation, today's general counsel is no longer at arm's length from the business, but familiar and in close contact with all of its working parts. This is now expected by the CEO and the board and is vital for the overall health of the corporation. Like a doctor, the general counsel must monitor and examine legal, ethical, governance, and compliance issues for overt or lurking risk to the body corporate. To continue the medical analogy, when an affliction strikes, the general counsel must be ready to perform immediate triage to assess and remediate the situation before it reaches crisis proportions. Protecting the interests of the corporation is the top priority for general counsel today: with shareholders, regulators, and investors watching, the only acceptable bill of health today is a clean one.

As the requirements of the general counsel role changed, so did the definitions of what worked—and especially, what no longer worked—in corporate legal leadership. Among the key new leadership attributes: political savvy; emotional intelligence; fielding and prioritizing multiple inputs without getting overwhelmed; keeping a calm, cool, and collected head in times of crisis and keeping it all together; an ego-free, consensus-focused approach to strategy, decision-making, hierarchy, and other considerations. As boards and senior executives began awakening to this new leadership model, it would also steadily emerge as an unforeseen game-changing advantage to women lawyers on the rise.

"Co-Ed Common Sense"

For the past 25 years, Joan Williams has been a leading voice in reshaping the debates over gender, class, and work-family issues. Williams, who is Distinguished Professor of Law and 1066 Foundation Chair at University of California, Hastings College of the Law (where Clara Foltz was not allowed to matriculate), is also the founding director of the Center for WorkLife Law at Hastings, as well as director of the Project for Attorney Retention, a leading organization in helping the legal profession advance and retain women, and offer work-life balance to men as well as women.

She is also a prolific and highly influential writer. Along with many oft-cited law review articles, Williams has authored or co-authored five books, including her prize-winning *Unbending Gender: Why Family and Work Conflict and What to Do About It* in 2000, and, in 2010, *Reshaping the Work-Family Debate: Why Men and Class Matter*.

In her view, the gender differences—actually, gender pressures—that have traditionally defined men's and women's places in the leadership framework have in fact favored the rise and acceptance of women in the modern general counsel role. "One of the strengths that women have in this role is that they're not under the kind of gender pressures that men face," says Williams, identifying competitiveness as the ethos that has traditionally shaped the male leadership persona. "Conventional masculinity is involved in the constant signaling of who is higher on the hierarchy, which can encourage men to take bigger risks than are justified from a purely business standpoint," she explains. "This tends to make you less of a team player and good listener and diminishes the premium on emotional intelligence because the whole point of the exercise is to authoritatively show who is the king of the hill."

Williams is quick to acknowledge that the king of the hill approach is not the only masculine code and that many men resist the pressure of this ethic. Nonetheless, in the hyper-competitive world of finance and big business, it tends to be the default masculine mode. "But it is just not a style that works very well anymore," says Williams.

In late 2009, Williams wrote the following on the *Huffington Post* blog she writes with Sharon Meers: "What's needed is more thoughtfulness about how to free certain work cultures from masculine bravado. The result will be a lot more co-ed common sense." In effect, that "thoughtfulness" has been ushered in by changes wrought upon the business environment, and consequently, upon the role of general counsel, to the natural benefit of women, who have long faced their own version of gender pressure.

"By default alone, women have traditionally been under the pressure of not putting themselves ahead in the pecking order, but rather, assuming a more attentive, helpful, emotionally intelligent role," says Williams. "These are the sort of things they were expected to do, but now, these same qualities are seen as being very effective for corporate legal leadership." Women, she continues, "tend not to get confused or tripped up on issues of ego and hierarchy and order, and as a result of not being under the same pressure as men to play this particular set of games, find themselves particularly well suited for the role of the modern general counsel."

Relieving conventional gender pressures and finding the balance of "co-ed common sense" will likely benefit both women and men as legal leaders—and the corporation itself. In their 2010 book, *The Female Vision: Women's Real Power at Work*, authors Sally Helgesen and Julie Johnson start from the premise that "what women

"If you don't assert yourselves, you will certainly lose opportunities."

—HIGHTMAN

see—what they notice and value and how they perceive the world in operation—is a great, underexploited resource in organizations." Based on a full-scale research study of senior women leaders supported by the National Council for Research on Women, Helgesen and Johnson deliver the general conclusion that women, seeing the world via a distinctive lens, possess an "observational style" that "tends to be broad and wide-ranging, while men tend to focus more narrowly on what they perceive to be the task at hand." They add that "women are continually scanning their environment for information, whereas men are more apt to restrict their observations to what a specific set of actions requires."

In his foreword to *The Female Vision*, acclaimed author and executive coach Marshall Goldsmith asserts, "Most of the problems that led to the recent economic meltdown occurred in organizations dominated by men." Goldsmith goes on to propose that "perhaps organizations that embraced more women in strategic roles and recognized their broader vision would not have experienced the same degree of crisis." As the book's authors are careful to acknowledge, there are also bottom-line-focused women and sensitive men in corporations. There is no doubt, however, that historically, women's broader vision has gone unrecognized in the workplace, and therefore, as *The Female Vision* argues, corporations have shortchanged themselves along with women.

While the still-evolving awareness—and acceptance—of their suitability for the general counsel role was certainly a step in the right direction, women still faced gender-related pressures related to exerting power and influence and meeting steep standards of image and perception. For starters, they would have to "interrupt" the old way of doing things as the basis for defining their own place, identity, and credibility within the existing order and operating framework of firms and businesses.

Women Interrupting, Sharing Power

Ida Abbott is a leading authority on professional development and advancement for women in the law. Co-founder and director of the Hastings Leadership Academy of Women at the University of California, Hastings College of the Law, Abbott practiced law for 20 years at a large international firm, specializing in complex litigation and running the firm's professional development and pro bono programs. In 1995, she became a consultant focused on helping professional service firms, professional associations, and corporations develop, manage, and retain legal talent.

Published in 2010, her latest book, *Women on Top: The Woman's Guide to Leadership and Power in Law Firms*, addresses the subject of leadership within the framework and structure of law firms, but the lessons are easily translated to the corporate law department and the role of general counsel. In her introduction to the book, Abbott asks, "Why do we need a book on leadership for women in law firms?"

One could pose the same question for women lawyers in corporations—why indeed? The answer, quite simply, is that in today's risk-laden environment, the general counsel must be an absolute leader. She or he must be able to get all of the lawyers in the corporate law department rowing in the same direction. When there is a serious triage situation, she or he must first persuade the CEO and the board of the necessity and urgency of responding and then lead the way in resolving the matter. Personifying the conscience of the corporation, she or he must lead by example; in a job that has gone from passive to proactive, she or he must lead all the time and all the way.

Part and parcel of leadership are power and influence. While these terms may seem interchangeable, they are, in fact, distinct, and it is the deft use of each, as separate attributes, that is crucial if women are to be successful as general counsel. Power, as we are using it here, is the authority granted by dint of position, title, or other organizational means. Power dictates who reports to whom, where official decisions rest, and who has authority over budgets, hiring, and internal operational functions. Influence, on the other hand, describes the intangible, authoritative effect of power: think of power as an energy source and influence as its output. Influence means using the power at one's disposal to affect who listens and who is motivated to act or not to act. Influence is based on relationships and interpersonal skills, including the ability to discern what others need, value, and aspire to.

While clearly in the arsenal of the women vying for and being appointed to the general counsel position, power alone does not a successful leader make. It takes power plus the influence it generates to create real leadership.

Jim Kouzes, co-author of *The Leadership Challenge* and *Encouraging the Heart*, writes that "Influence is central to leadership. Without the ability to mobilize others, the smartest people with the grandest visions will accomplish nothing." Another persuasive writer on the subject of influence is B. Kim Barnes, president and CEO of Berkeley, California-based Barnes & Conti Associates Inc., an independent learning and organization development firm. In the well-titled first chapter ("What We Have Here Is a Failure to Influence") of her acclaimed book, *Exercising Influence*, Barnes discusses the value of influencing skills: "In the real world, a good idea doesn't necessarily sell itself. People don't always share the same values, priorities, and vested interests, even though they work for the same company, share a profession, or live in the same community or household. If you want to be successful as a leader, manager, colleague, friend, spouse, parent, or partner, you must be able to achieve results through the effort and support of others."

As Barnes also writes, "Influence enables you to build the relationships you need to get results inside or outside the formal power structure of your organization." All perfectly sound in theory, except that for women to be influential, they have to find their own place on the power grid. How? The answer lies in interruption.

In March 2010, Carrie Hightman, executive vice president and chief legal officer of Indiana-based Fortune 500 energy company NiSource Inc., spoke about career success steps for women at the annual meeting of the DePaul University Women's Network. She opened by addressing one of the more pernicious corporate gender

> "I replied that I didn't realize you had to see my legs for me to be dressed appropriately."
>
> —MADRID

dynamics: the damned-either-way, double-bind dilemma faced by women in law and other professional arenas. "Assertive women tend to be seen as competent but not personable or well-liked, while women adopting a more stereotypically feminine style are liked but not seen as having valued leadership skills," Hightman said.

Not that Hightman has ever allowed herself to become ensnared in the competence versus likeability Catch-22. A self-described extrovert, she has advanced her career by speaking up, sitting in the front row, and "running counter to the traditional and antiquated notions that have held women back for decades." It's part of what she calls "mastering the art of interruption," and for Hightman, it's a golden rule. Remember the 19th-century establishment's frown on women lawyers "intruding on the public domain explicitly reserved to men"? Hightman is all for stepping in and speaking up. "Ladies," she told the DePaul assembly, "if you don't assert yourselves, you will certainly lose opportunities. You have to ask for things to get them." Madeleine Albright, the first woman Secretary of State, was one such "master" of the art. "Interrupt," she once emphatically stated. "If you've got a good idea, don't feel like you've got to be polite and wait your turn. Men don't."

But what about the real world, where the aggressive, interrupting woman is the disliked woman? Certainly back in 1971—the year that 22-year-old Anastasia Kelly, the first woman to ever work for the "overeducated, oversexed" all-male Airline Pilots Association, "got her (Boston) Irish up" with management after learning what her non-exempt status meant in terms of pay and benefits—the "interrupting girl" was unwelcome. "They did not want me around the office," recalls Kelly, "because they did not know what to do with me."

Speaking up and interrupting, of course, were not culturally available to women back then. Today, however, it is certain traditional masculine leadership behaviors—such as pounding the table or unilaterally giving orders—that are culturally out of place. A woman does not have to act imperiously or autocratically to "interrupt" effectively: in the modern context, where handling risk and avoiding crises are paramount, her voice actually carries just the right authority. In many ways, a woman's less forceful—but no less firm—approach to establishing authority mirrors the difference many commentators see between how men and women view accomplishment. UPS General Counsel Teri Plummer McClure believes that, in general, women approach accomplishment in a more objective, matter-of-fact way. "Taught to be competitive and sell themselves, men tend to take credit for things they are supposed to do anyway, turning the expected into the extraordinary," she says. "Women, on the other hand, will see doing the same thing as part of the job." Or, as one past female general counsel expressed in confidence, "if men could have babies, we'd never hear the end of it."

As Joan Williams explains, these differences can be ascribed to the gender pressures on both men and women: men are under pressure to show they are king of the hill, while women are under pressure to show they are helpful to those around them without getting too hung up on ego." While women in general may not have

Williams' depth of insight into this particular nuance of gender dynamics, the subject of gender differences relating to influence and power has been a long-running dialogue.

For example, in 1999, nine highly placed women lawyers—six of them in-house at corporations and three at law firms—convened in New York City to talk about the concept of power as it related to women in the legal profession. Organized by *Corporate Counsel* magazine, the roundtable included three of the women featured in this book: co-author Michele Coleman Mayes, then deputy general counsel, international and corporate, for Colgate-Palmolive Co.; Susan Lichtenstein, then associate general counsel for AT&T spinoff Ameritech Corp.; and Francesca Maher (now Edwardson), then senior vice president, general counsel, and secretary for United Airlines and general counsel for UAL Corp.. Each offered a distinct point of view on the gender divide over power, such as this from Mayes: "Men, as a gross generalization, will tell you how good they are or…how powerful they are. They don't wait for somebody to anoint them. I had a woman partner who once said to me that when her male partner came back from lunch, he bragged about the fact that he'd crossed the street safely. Everything was worthy of discussion. Women consider it being boastful rather than making themselves visible."

For Lichtenstein, it was a matter of "real irony," as she explained that day: "When it comes to power, men have always understood that it is all about relationships. I mean, what do you think is happening on the golf course except that they are building relationships? The irony is, we are good at relationships, and traditionally we are the ones who are sitting in our offices thinking that if we just do a really good job, the phone is going to ring, and we will somehow be recognized by whomever is on high, and power will be dropped down on to us."

And then this from Maher, on how men and women view achievement, and ultimately power, in the office. In the male-dominated workplace, she explained, value was historically placed on individual contributions, according to the association with male definitions of outcomes or measures. If the old way was "that was my idea that got implemented," Maher saw a different direction taking hold, one in which teamwork was becoming more important. "Women have been far more comfortable saying, 'I have been part of the team,' or 'I helped spark the idea that ended up being the ultimate outcome,'" she said. "Women have always been more comfortable with shared power than men." Continuing, Maher added, "As the workplace changes and begins to capitalize on the contributions of both men and women, that kind of behavior by both genders will continue to be rewarded and ultimately will be a stronger measure of success."

Those were their views just a decade ago. How do these women feel about the power dynamic today? Maher may sum it up when she says, "Wow. Who was I to think I could forecast changes in workplace dynamics? I think I've mellowed over the last decade. Today I'd say that it's important that women learn how to showcase their

> "Walking the line between appearing confident…without coming off as strident remains hard."
>
> —HANSON

talents and achievements, and that it's also important that employers recognize and reward team performance. Talent retention and development are critical, and this just won't happen if the stars don't shine. But they can't shine so brightly that the rest of the team is left out in the cold. Women and employers have both become better at this over the last 10 years. It remains a work in progress." Mayes agrees that there is work to be done. "Unfortunately, my view has not changed a great deal," she says. "Too many women still find it uncomfortable or awkward to talk about their impact and contributions—using the pronoun 'I.' (I once observed that a male colleague of mine would not have been able to complete a sentence if it were not for the pronoun 'I'). Are there exceptions to this generalization? Yes, but there always were. We are far too reticent when it comes to taking credit and demanding what we want (even if this signals that the negotiations will now begin)."

Women still have to interrupt to be heard. However, Hightman is careful to distinguish interrupting from say, interjecting or talking over others—there is an art to interrupting at the right time. "As women, we are traditionally taught from an early age that a woman's place is by her man, in the background, taking orders, and most of all, never asserting herself," she said. "But in today's world, in order for a woman to get ahead, she can't remain in the background. She needs to be confident in her ability to speak her mind and ask for what she wants." And in the general counsel role, of course, the velvet must come with some steel linings. In addition to serving as general counsel for Ameritech, Lichtenstein was general counsel of Tellabs and health-care giant Baxter International before joining medical technology company Hill-Rom as senior vice president of corporate affairs and chief legal officer; she was also general counsel to former Illinois Governor Rod Blagojevich for a year. She credits her mother, once a sniper in the Israeli Army, with instilling in her the no-nonsense, fearless attitude that distinguishes her legal leadership. "Your No. 1 priority can't be being everyone's best friend," she says. "Sometimes you have to make—and communicate—hard decisions."

How women communicate verbally is just one part of rebalancing the power, influence, and leadership equation; historically subject to even greater scrutiny is how women dress and act.

"The Proper Alignment"

Iconic Italian actress Sophia Loren once famously commented, "Sex appeal is 50 percent what you've got and 50 percent what people think you've got." Fine for on-screen sirens, but in the arch climate of image and perception in the corporate and legal worlds, this math would set off alarms.

Linda Madrid remembers the first time she wore a pants suit to work. "After looking me up and down, the CFO said he didn't realize the company had a casual day. I replied that I didn't realize you had to see my legs for me to be dressed appro-

Future Cast

How did **Susan Blount**, then an attorney in Prudential Financial's commercial real estate division, feel when her supervisor tapped her shoulder and said that she could be the company's general counsel someday? "Thrilled and incredulous," says Blount, who would rise through a series of leadership positions, including chief investment counsel and corporate secretary, en route to being named the company's chief legal officer in 2005.

That "tap" was also a wake-up call. "If you want to be general counsel, he told me, you need to start thinking about your career differently," Blount relates. "It was not something that I had even thought about before that day, but from then on, I became more open to opportunities that would expand my experience." One such opportunity was her integral role in Prudential's demutualization process, which would factor in her appointment as general counsel. Taking the initiative remains one of her core disciplines, and a key message for young lawyers.

"Regardless of where you are, never stop learning, and do not limit yourself to a singular specialization," says Blount. "Breadth of experience is what counts—and always seek feedback to make sure you are on track."

priately." Madrid also relates that in 1982, the Commonwealth of Virginia mandated that women wear a skirt and hose to the bar exam—or they were not permitted to take the test.

Dress and appearance have long figured in the (mis)perception equation. Picture this: as a young Sidley & Austin corporate associate in the early '90s, Kim Rucker, today senior vice president, general counsel, and corporate secretary for Avon Products, went to her first practice group lunch dressed in a brightly colored suit. She entered the conference room to find herself in a room full of men in dark suits. "I thought for a moment, I'm not sure what is going through their minds...whether I was ready for them or whether they were ready for me."

In dressing for success by asserting her femininity, or at least not cloaking it, Rucker does not recall this as a negative moment; if this raised eyebrows in 1993 though, it would have raised consternation in earlier times. "The women of the first wave not only stepped onto the men's playing field, they stepped into their clothes," says Preng. Recalling the then-mandated look of "no pants, traditional male suit, and big silk bowtie," she says that even today, women cannot afford to let their guard down. "You have to dress the part every day. Women suffer from the risk of not being taken seriously much more acutely than men do based on their appearance."

What is the right look for women lawyers and general counsel aspirants, both on the way up to the top and then once there, in support of that position of power,

Frank Veronsky

influence, and leadership? While there is always room for personal style, it's a matter of properly aligning dressing for the part and for what's expected, dressing to show professionalism and confidence, and dressing as a statement of one's individual self. "Look at least as well put together as the standard in the organization where you are interviewing," says Martha Fay (Marty) Africa, partner at renowned global attorney search firm Major, Lindsey & Africa. "While it is good to have personal style, don't take risks with it. Candidates should also be mindful of the cadence of their voice and watch for subconscious behaviors, such as hair-twirling and affectations."

For women, perception can be unforgiving. As a young associate at Mayer, Brown & Platt in the early '80s, Francesca Maher felt that as a woman, she had to "dress perfectly, make the right impression, work incredibly hard, avoid mistakes—and be perfect at everything." It's a sentiment echoed by Rucker. "On the path to general counsel, or any powerful job, there are many opportunities for women to get it wrong. For men, it tends to be upside all the way, but a woman does something wrong and watch how quickly she is judged."

Getting the "stature part" right was uniquely challenging for the first wave of women general counsel, states Heidrick & Struggles partner Lee Hanson. "Walking the line between appearing confident and presenting the appropriate level of gravitas without coming off as overly aggressive and strident remains hard for women, and was especially so for the pioneers," says Hanson. "Without any peers or precedents to refer to, women in the first wave went in needing highly honed political and social skills to be able to navigate very tricky waters."

Balancing Acts

Veta Richardson served as executive director of the Minority Corporate Counsel Association from 2000 to 2011. Under her leadership, MCCA, founded in 1997, made great strides in its mission to advance the expanded hiring, promotion, and retention of diverse attorneys by legal departments and the law firms that serve them, with its definition of diversity encompassing gender, race/ethnicity, sexual orientation, disability status, and generation. Before embarking on a career in nonprofit/bar association management, Richardson was in-house counsel to Sunoco Inc., joining the company upon graduation from law school in 1986. "In the mid-'80s, women were still finding their voice and finding their place in a corporate environment," recalls Richardson, who became president and CEO of the Washington, D.C.-based Association of Corporate Counsel (ACC), the world's largest association of in-house counsel, in July 2011. "As women, we tried very hard to play the game like men played the game, yet to acknowledge how our differences could actually be turned into strengths."

Saluting the first-wave pioneers who "really forged a path and were able to open doors for others because of their success," Richardson also saw a changing corporate

> "Today's general counsel has to be laser-focused and maintain a real clarity of analysis."
>
> —AFRICA

environment that was accepting women. "I think that the corporate environment is more receptive to women than other legal environments such as law firms because corporations measure people by their ability to work with people, to be consensus-builders, and to create results." Generally speaking, she continues, "these are skills that many women possess, and so being in the right environment allows them to really shine and use those skills to the fullest."

Among the most significant of these skills—attributes really—is emotional intelligence. "Women traditionally have been assigned the emotion work of being attuned to the needs and comfort level of those around them" says Joan Williams. "That training pays business dividends."

In the chapter entitled "Broad-Spectrum Notice," *The Female Vision* authors Helgesen and Johnson note the meaningful distinction between how men and women notice things, or how "men tend to focus deeply and narrowly on a single perception or task, whereas women's attention is often simultaneously engaged by many different things." Right there, you might think "multitasking"—more on that to follow—but in terms of the female vision, women generally tend to be "first-class noticers."

Why is this so, and why does it matter in the workplace, or more specifically, in the role of general counsel? As the authors explain, the first answer is rooted in "women's domestic experience, socialization, and evolutionary development," which collectively "have accustomed them to monitoring emotional cues, anticipating what others might need, and making subtle adjustments in order to avoid potential conflicts." Which in turn answers the second half of the question: through acculturation, women have become adept at sensing risk, reading and discerning the emotional states of others, and effectively handling crisis situations. Skilled at building relationships, write Helgesen and Johnson, "women's tending and befriending behaviors give them emotional resilience and decrease their susceptibility to stress."

This does not mean that women are all things to all people in an organization, and that leads us back to the subject of multitasking. As wives, mothers, and professionals, women, especially in today's hectic world, may be required to be the world's greatest multitaskers, but this is not in the job description for chief legal officer. Quite to the contrary, in fact. "Multitasking?" asks Africa. "Not if you want to do the job properly. Today's general counsel has to be laser-focused and maintain a real clarity of analysis."

Noble as doing it all may seem, multitasking is an activity for domains other than today's risk-threatened Fortune 500 law department: as Roman philosopher Publilius Syrus observed back in 100 B.C., "To do two things at once is to do neither." More recently, Dr. Jim Loehr, co-founder of the Orlando, Florida-based Human Performance Institute, a Johnson & Johnson company focused on campus- and client-based training programs in what it calls "Energy Management technology," wrote that "Human beings, sorry to say, can focus fully on only one thing at a time. When people multitask, they are not fully engaged in anything, and partially disengaged in everything." The authors of *The Female Vision* are similarly

> "Women's tending and befriending behaviors give them emotional resilience and decrease their susceptibility to stress."
>
> —HELGESEN AND JOHNSON

opposed to multitasking, especially for women focused on establishing leadership in the workplace. "Many women regard their capacity to multitask as a badge of honor, yet doing so significantly detracts from being able to function at the level that implementing one's vision requires," they write. Citing recent scientific evidence that calls multitasking "the thief of time," they note that "when we make the decision to multitask, we are in essence agreeing to diminish the value of our contribution..." and "...our ability to project authority...." This can have an especially pernicious effect on women, the authors conclude, since women "must often work consciously to develop a leadership presence."

That said, we see another school of thought on multitasking, based on our interviews for this book. Avon Product's Kim Rucker, for example, swears by her ability to multitask; so does Dorian Daley, senior vice president, general counsel, and secretary of Oracle Corp. "Being general counsel is the ultimate multitasking position," says Daley. "With so many things going on at once, you have to be able to manage priorities and perform triage really, really well." So while on the one hand, yes, multitasking can be the "thief of time," it can also significantly enhance the general counsel's ability to switch from task to task while always maintaining laser-focus on the task at hand. The key, as we discuss in Chapter 5, sorting out the semantics, is to "be able to focus intensely on one thing for a short period of time, and then quickly shift to another task with the same singular, defined focus." Some call this "quick shift" the essence of multitasking.

Another balancing act for women harks back to that divide between feminism and professionalism that started in the 1920s: put lawyering first, ahead of being a woman or a feminist. As Anne McNamara once told *The National Law Journal*, "I do not think it is appropriate for a general counsel to let their own personal agenda substitute for what's in the company's best interest." Yet there is still room to be a woman—and being a woman has its advantages. As a litigation associate in an Atlanta-based firm, third-waver Laureen Seeger, now executive vice president, general counsel, and chief compliance officer of San Francisco-based McKesson Corp., said that being a woman in a man's world, especially in the South, created "a lot of tools in her arsenal." As with instances where judges would let her argue first, she often found that "it was difficult for some men to say no to a woman."

Gloria Santona, general counsel of McDonald's and with the company since 1977, recalls the "double-edged sword" of the early days. "I think I was noticed more as a woman, and that was a good thing," she says, adding that she "has always been true to herself as a woman." As a woman on the sword's other edge, however, Santona still felt that she "had to shine and be better than men." Anastasia Kelly, one of many women who got called "little honey" in court, adopted this sanguine view as she rose through the ranks: "I realized early on that it was less about my being comfortable with men and more about making them comfortable with me.

There are differences between men and women, and that's OK, but back when I was coming up, or at least according to my view of what it took to get ahead, sometimes it comes down to developing a thick skin, being tolerant and flexible, and figuring out how to use what you've got in front of you to your own advantage, the old female manipulation and all."

■　　■　　■

Blazing trails, opening doors, and overcoming obstacles, women lawyers have been leveraging advantages and interrupting disadvantages for more than four centuries now—but just how have they made their way up the corporate legal ladder and into legal leadership in business and in the Fortune 500 over the past three decades, or since Mary Ann Hynes became the first woman general counsel of a Fortune 500 company in 1979? One quick answer is simply to say that in their respective eras and as individuals, these are exceptionally talented, driven, and courageous women. Overcoming once formidable and still considerable odds to become powerful, influential leaders in powerful, influential jobs at the top of America's most powerful, influential companies, they are undeniably women with a difference. But the true heart of their remarkable ascendance lies in their personal stories, where we find very recognizable, very human, and often truly humble and modest tales of aspiration, drive, self-development, and achievement. Within these stories are contained myriad lessons and inspirations, enough to provide hope and confidence to women lawyers today. Is there a discernible, tangible formula for success? Somewhere in there, yes, composed of essential factors that we explore throughout this book. But amid the generalizations and career advancement basics and individual talents and aptitudes, we found nuances, juxtapositions, and departures and deviations from the expected that revealed myriad differing on-ramps and routes to the top. If the success formula for women general counsel in the Fortune 500 has a natural center of gravity, however, it is found in an approximate balance of three major factors: mentoring; risk taking; and personal and professional skills, attributes, and characteristics. As the personal stories that form the core of this book will show, these are the common elements in 33 otherwise very different, individual paths to the top.

As we discussed in this chapter, the redefinition of the general counsel role and what it takes to be an effective legal leader in today's radically altered corporate environment has profoundly transformed and enlightened the understanding of women's effectiveness as chief legal officers. Once, the general counsel was little more than the corporate gatekeeper, generally kept at arm's length from the business. Then the role changed, and with risk analysis and risk management now priority one for the corporation, the emotionally intelligent woman, historically in the out-group because of gender pressure, is increasingly being seen by corporate executives and boards (recruiters, too) as possessing the right match of attributes and characteristics for the general counsel role.

To answer the natural question that arises from this new reality—are women now better suited to the general counsel role than men?—right up front, our focus and intent in this book are not on making the case for women versus men, or saying that women are better than men, or advancing an agenda for feminist elitism, but on setting forth the strong and compelling case that women are eminently qualified and able to lead the increasingly challenging and complex corporate legal function. This is a book about women and women lawyers, and while we will not shy away from talking about gender differences, we ultimately arrive at talking about what it takes to be a legal leader in business, period. When interviewing general counsel candidates, Marty Africa looks only for a telltale clue when asking about risk: "Some candidates become paralyzed, others have great responses…but I see no gender difference in the ability to answer that question."

Over the next three chapters, and in the tinted sections that run between all six chapters, we present a rich tapestry of life and career experiences and insights from 45 past, present, and future women general counsel, along with industry insiders, including leading executive recruiters with frontline insight into the field. Starting with Chapter 4, which deals with the skills and attributes necessary for legal leadership in business as told by the women themselves, we move toward understanding precisely what it takes to succeed in this area, along with developing a road map and toolkit for success that we hope readers of this book, and especially the courageous women counsel of today and tomorrow, can use on their own "excellent adventures."

As with many of life's endeavors, professional or otherwise, our women's stories often start with having—or, perhaps more important, making—friends in the right places.

Discomfort Levels:
The Double-Bind Dilemma

There is no doubt that women can lead. Developed over six years, national survey results published in The White House Project's comprehensive "Benchmarking Women's Leadership" report from November 2009 find that

American women and men are "overwhelmingly comfortable" with seeing women in the highest positions of leadership. In law and nine other major sectors, including business, academia, politics, and the military, a growing body of prominent research is validating the suitability of women's "risk-smart" leadership qualities. According to the "Benchmarking Women's Leadership" report, "Women tend to include diverse viewpoints in decision making, have a broader conception of public policy, and are also more likely to work through differences to form coalitions, complete objectives, and bring disenfranchised communities to the table."

This is precisely the consensus-driven, "risk-smart" approach demanded by today's general counsel role. From profits to the "quality and scope of decision making," it is also good for the corporate bottom line: a recent Catalyst study shows that Fortune 500 companies with high percentages of women officers experienced, on average, a 35.1 percent higher return on equity and a 34 percent higher total return to shareholders than did those with low percentages of women corporate officers.

Comfort level and proven capability, yes; leadership parity and wage equality, no. Mirroring the current Fortune 500 general counsel percentage, women presently account for just 18 percent of leaders across sectors—and earn 78.7 cents to every dollar earned by a man.

As The White House Project asks: "If so many Americans are comfortable with women leading in all sectors, then why are we so far from that goal?"

Where women in the law are concerned, this question has been a long-running concern of Catalyst, the acclaimed research organization founded in 1962, at the beginning of the modern U.S. women's movement, to help women advance in the workforce. In 1996, Catalyst released a groundbreaking study defining the barriers and success factors for women in corporate America, following that up with another study in 2003. Then, in 2007, Catalyst released a report called "Damned If You Do, Doomed If You Don't," which found that women, while eminently qualified to lead, still face a persistent barrier it calls the "double-bind dilemma." It's the trap that women corporate and legal managers know all too well—the "nagging sense that whatever you do, you can do no right."

Catalyst found three specific predicaments—which it calls double-bind dilemmas—facing women leaders: extreme perceptions of women as too soft, too tough, or never just right; the "high-competence threshold" of higher standards and lower rewards that women face versus men; and the old "competent but disliked" conundrum, whereby women are perceived as competent or likable, but rarely both. Catalyst sees these "punishing" predicaments (see table, below) as creating "an invisible barrier to women's advancement."

Among the women leaders surveyed by Catalyst for this report, 69 percent identified the prevalence of Predicament 1, with 39 percent and 46 percent, respectively, identifying Predicaments 2 and 3 (interviewees commented on one or more predicaments).

Talking openly about the issue, using clear and effective communications, and establishing clear visibility are among the strategies suggested by interviewees to deal with the overall double-bind dilemma. "Ultimately," writes Catalyst, "it is not women's leadership styles that need to change but the structures and perceptions that must keep up with today's changing times. Companies versed in negotiating complex social and financial interactions must help employees see that stereotypes, like first impressions, are mutable—and not truths cast in stone."

This stone resists easy sculpting; years of chipping away, and still the equal female within remains trapped. In a 2009 *New York Times* op-ed piece, Joanne Lipman, a former *Wall Street Journal* deputy managing editor, proclaimed, "FINALLY! I hear we're all living in a women's world now." She was being facetious. Citing statistics including women making up half the workforce and mothers being the major breadwinners in 40 percent of families, Lipman asked, "Great news, right? Well, not exactly.....The truth is, women haven't come nearly as far as we would have predicted 25 years ago. Somewhere along the line, especially in recent years, progress has stalled. And attitudes have taken a giant leap backward." Her answer echoes the spirit of this book: "If we can change the conversation about women, the numbers will finally add up. And that's what real progress looks like."

The Invisible Barrier *(according to Catalyst)*

PREDICAMENT	HOW IT LEAVES WOMEN IN A DOUBLE-BIND
1. Extreme and equally undesirable perceptions	When women leaders act in ways that are consistent with gender stereotypes (e.g., focus on work relationships and express concern for other people's perspectives), they are viewed as less competent leaders, as too soft. When women act in ways that are inconsistent with such stereotypes, however (e.g., act assertively, focus on work tasks, display ambition), their behavior is judged as too tough, even unfeminine.
2. Higher standards but lower rewards	When it comes to proving leadership capabilities, women are subjected to higher standards than men. They have to work harder to show the same level of competence and have to confront more trade-offs than their male counterparts in order to lead effectively.
3. Competent but not liked	Women who adopt a "masculine" leadership style are viewed more negatively. Although they might be viewed as competent because of their leadership style, they also receive more negative evaluations of their interpersonal skills than women who adopt a "feminine" style. Hence, even acting in counterstereotypical ways has potentially harmful consequences for women leaders and may negatively impact their work relationships and access to social networks.

DATA

Chapter 2

MENTORING:

the rose trellis

As many women general counsel have discovered, having a champion at your side can serve as a powerful career starter—and career accelerator. But mentorship takes many forms.

**f**or some women general counsel, the earliest mentorships began at home. As attorney general for the state of Indiana from 1993 to 1997, for example, Pamela Carter became the first black woman in U.S. history elected to that position. In 1997, she joined global power leader Cummins Engine as general counsel, and now serves as president of Cummins Distribution Business. Her introduction to the law as a small child, by her grandfather, the orphaned son of slaves, is strikingly poignant. Despite completing law school and passing the bar, he was not allowed to practice because of his color. Yet he managed to be an inspiration

to his young granddaughter, reciting portions of *Blackstone's Commentaries*—the authoritative writings of Sir William Blackstone that serve as the basis of U.S. common law and include references speaking out against slavery—to her from memory. Galvanizing on the one hand, this also provided her with an early, sharp exposure to the effects of racism, but, Carter recalls, "he always was careful to make sure I understood that there was no room for hate."

Carter's story points to the essence of mentorship: a person whose words, actions, or legacy—in this case all three—anchors in the heart and mind of another a compass for navigating her future endeavors. In her book *The Lawyer's Guide to Mentoring*, Ida Abbott writes that "a mentor is a person who helps a lawyer develop professionally to achieve the lawyer's desired professional goals, and mentoring is the process by which the mentor and protégé work together to identify and help the protégé work toward those professional goals." The concept, explains Abbott, is as old as time itself: The terms are derived from the relationship between Mentor (an earthly incarnation of the goddess Athena) and Telemachus (Odysseus' son) in Homer's *The Odyssey*.

In the classical construct, continues Abbott, "mentoring has been described as a one-on-one relationship between an all-powerful elder teacher and a neophyte who is taught, nurtured, and protected." The modern version, in law and other spheres, is significantly more multifaceted and far less hierarchical, where the one mentor is

Early Bird Special

Janet Kelly gifted herself a key mentor through her own diligence. After graduating from Yale Law School in 1983, Kelly became an associate at prominent M&A and business litigation firm Wachtell, Lipton, Rosen & Katz in New York. True to her Midwestern work ethic, Kelly arrived at the office early every morning. Taking notice was founding partner Martin ("Marty") Lipton, of "poison pill defense" fame from the 1980s. That she was at work ahead of her peers was hard to miss—their offices were adjacent. "He gave me great work *because I was there*," says Kelly. Lipton, along with then-partner and now firm co-chairman Daniel Neff, became lifelong mentors, both substantively and in terms of her career advancement. "They watched out for what I was ready for next," says Kelly, "and have remained mentors since." Her advice on seeking a mentor? "You need to figure out what you can offer that nobody else can."

replaced by many mentors; the elder teacher is, more often than not, a peer or even a junior; and the long term can be relatively transitory. Practically anyone in one's orbit can serve as a mentor, with as many possibilities outside the workplace as inside, and as Abbott's table listing 19 different mentor roles and functions demonstrates (see page 55), the range of mentoring interactions has expanded as well. The classical construct of one-on-one mentoring is also evolving as technology continues to advance. Through e-mail, social media, and other electronic means, mentors no longer necessarily have to see their mentees to be effective.

The positive association of mentoring and other work-related dynamics makes it a career imperative for women in the law. From 1993 to 2003, Sheila Wellington served with distinction as president of Catalyst. In her 2001 book, *Be Your Own Mentor,* Wellington wrote that "Mentors are more important to career success than hard work, more important than talent, more important than intelligence. Why? Because you need to learn how to operate in the work world and mentors can teach you how. The dictionary will tell you that a mentor is 'an experienced and trusted counselor.' At work, that translates into a person who can hook you up with the experiences and people you need to move ahead and tell you how to handle them. Mentors can show you the ropes. And pull strings."

From ally and confidante to supporter and nurturer, mentors, drawn from any of life's orbits, can take many forms, with even tangential, indirect mentorships produc-

> **"He was careful to make sure I understood that there was no room for hate."**
> **—CARTER**

Mentoring Glossary:
The Five Dimensions of Mentoring

Phillips: Overlapping mentors

In an interview with Lloyd Johnson Jr., MCCA founder and publisher emeritus of *Diversity & the Bar*, Sandra Phillips, then assistant general counsel and section chief for products litigation (and later senior vice president, associate general counsel, and chief litigation counsel) at Pfizer Inc., shared some of her thoughts on mentoring. Her vision of five different dimensions of mentoring—often with individual mentors fulfilling one or several roles simultaneously—clearly embodies the collective mentoring experiences of the women interviewed for this book.

The Champion: The person who makes it his or her personal business to sing your praises to others and help you navigate the maze of your organization's internal politics.

The Technical Advisor: One who helps with the technical aspects of the job, from research and writing to presentation skills.

The Navigator or Strategic Advisor: Often someone outside your organization, a person who helps advise you over the course of your career.

The Personal Mentor: A friend or confidante who knows you perhaps even better than you know yourself and can therefore provide a perspective that no one else can.

Peer-to-Peer Mentors: Friends, associates, or colleagues that one finds in professional associations or networking groups such as MCCA and the DuPont Minority Lawyers Network.

ing reliable life and career coordinates. For people confronted with adverse personal or professional circumstances that might make advancement of ambitions or goals seem unattainable, mentors can be real agents of change and transformation. Above all, though, a mentor is someone whose adoption and attention must be earned, for mentorships ultimately reward a demonstrated or perceived show of promise, of commitment, of ambition. Mentoring may describe a one-on-one relationship, but it is definitely a two-way street.

Influential business writer Marshall Loeb, formerly managing editor of *Money* and *Fortune* magazines and an authority on mentoring and professional leadership, once described mentors as one's "board of advisors." It's a concept we embrace, as do many of the women we interviewed for this book. Avon Products General Counsel Kim Rucker, for example, holds in the highest esteem the assembly of friends, family, and colleagues who have mentored her in some way throughout her life, not seeing this group of people so much as a board of advisors but as a network.

Almost to a woman, our interviewees recall the mentors who made a difference. When she was starting out as an associate in a small law firm, for example, Teri Plummer McClure, who today oversees global legal, compliance, and public affairs activities for UPS, was given instruction in meticulous legal writing by a woman attorney at the firm. "That was probably one of the best experiences I had, and it was certainly one of the most valuable tools that I learned," says McClure. Same story from Suzanne Bettman, general counsel of print services giant RR Donnelley & Sons: as a young associate at Kirkland & Ellis, she had the value of good drafting "pounded into me" by a woman partner.

And, as women general counsel such as Linda Madrid and Rucker (see sidebar, page 50) have discovered, having a champion on your side can serve as a powerful career starter and career accelerator.

Unremarkably perhaps, given their traditional dominance of the corporate and legal leadership structure, it was men far more than women who mentored women as they moved up the ladder to general counsel. In 1992, while she was an associate with Morrison & Foerster, Michelle Banks, now general counsel for Gap Inc., took an opportunity the firm provided to work in Japan. There, it was an aggressive male Japanese legal executive who became one of her most valuable mentors. His advice to "figure out what you want and go get it" has guided her career. Later, after she had joined the legal department at Gap Inc., the role of mentor would be played by a woman, Lauri Shanahan, who groomed Banks to be her successor as general counsel and helped to transition her into the role, which Banks assumed in 2006 (see sidebar, page 53). Still, Banks came to an early reckoning on male versus female mentors: "While I do not feel that a mentor has to be a man or a woman to be effective," she says, "the lack of female mentors and role models early in my career was an inflection point. Men, far more than women, were the ones stepping up to mentor me."

There are notable exceptions, of course. During her time as general counsel for Dean Witter, Christine Edwards regularly met in New York with American Express General Counsel Louise Parent and future JP Morgan General Counsel Rachel Robbins (now vice president and general counsel for Washington, D.C.-based International Finance Corp., a member of the World Bank Group) to share work and life stories. "There were very few women general counsel at that time, especially in financial services," recalls Edwards, "and so it was invaluable to be able to talk to these other women about substantive issues and generally what it was like out there."

In a similar vein, the one-time leading women lawyers of the airline industry, Francesca Maher of United Airlines and Anne McNamara of American Airlines, enjoyed a mentoring-based relationship, with McNamara serving as a sounding board and coach for Maher. Maher (now Edwardson) in turn lauds her "great support network of gal pals," a group of friends and professional women drawn from various walks of life.

> "Men, far more than women, were the ones stepping up to mentor me."
> —BANKS

The 20-Minute Career Accelerator

Avon Products General Counsel **Kim Rucker** grew up fascinated by how the law defined people—historically and currently—and their participation in the economy. "The law had defined blacks as fractionally human and women as having less power," she says, "and this gave me a burning passion to understand the constitutional, economic, and other impacts of the law." Laser vision and hard work saw Rucker through Harvard Law School and into Chicago's Sidley Austin—where a blood-and-guts senior partner would kick her career into high gear. While withstanding comments like, "Harvard Law was good before they let women in," Rucker chose an all-night work session to take a stand. "Starving, I insisted that I had to eat," she recalls. "Over that senior partner's objections, I took a 20-minute food break." One moment of rebellion, a lifetime of respect. "After that, he gave me unprecedented mentoring and career-making access to clients. He was one of the first among the many special, career- and life-changing mentors who have blessed me."

Like Maher, the women we spoke with while researching this book identify mentorship as a vital element in their career progression—and accordingly, many have embraced the opportunity to pay it forward by becoming mentors themselves.

Champion. Navigator. Technical advisor. Personal friend. Peer group. Whether relying on one or more of these major mentorship categories—and in Andrea Zopp's case, all of them—the women GCs of the Fortune 500 have blossomed like roses on the trellis of mentorship (for more on key categories of mentorship, see page 48).

The Full Range

As if they were coordinates on a map, mentors mark Andrea Zopp's rise to the top. Finding a few people of influence but no mentors at Harvard Law School, her mentoring experience began in earnest with her first job, clerking for U.S. District Judge George N. Leighton in the Northern District of Illinois. "He loved the law, he treated his clerks like family, and he was a natural teacher," says Zopp, remembering Leighton's dedication to educating her on the legal system and lawyering and courtroom skills. It was also after law school that she started meeting black women of influence, notably famed federal Judge Constance Baker Motley and Barbara Jordan, the first black woman to serve in the U.S. Congress from the South. "OK, they exist," Zopp thought at the time.

Two years of watching criminal trials with Judge Leighton opened her eyes. "I saw defense attorneys in constant reactive, damage-control mode, whereas the prosecutors were in charge and calling the shots." Seeing the opportunity to "make an impact as a prosecutor," she applied to the U.S. Attorney's office in Chicago. "I got a call one day from an assistant U.S. attorney there," says Zopp, "who said, 'We gotta talk.'" That attorney was Ann Claire Williams, a future federal appellate judge. Impressed by Zopp's resume, Williams guided her through the interview process, and, like Leighton, would go on to be a lifetime friend and mentor.

Zopp describes the culture of the U.S. Attorney's office—where future novelist and SNR Denton partner Scott Turow was a colleague—as mentor-like in its own right. "There was a focus on molding the younger attorneys into the best prosecutors they could be, and so I benefited from having many technical advisors," she says. Her boss, Anton Valukas, now chairman of Jenner & Block, was especially supportive of diversity and opportunities for women, and, in praising and eventually promoting her, provided her with "a real confidence boost."

In 1990, after a short stint at a Chicago law firm, Zopp was hired by Cook County State's Attorney Jack O'Malley to run the narcotics bureau of what is the second-largest prosecutor's office in the U.S. Promoted thereafter to first assistant state's attorney—the first woman ever in the job—Zopp made her name by prosecuting Congressman Mel Reynolds in a sex scandal case.

Making a difference all the way was O'Malley's mentorship. "My job there was like being general counsel of a big law firm, managing over 100 attorneys," she says. "Jack taught me management skills, how to build a budget, how to establish a fair and equitable compensation structure—and the value of using my intellect to do what I thought was right, even if it was not popular." It's a skill she values to this day. "He taught me that how you deliver news is often more important than the news itself. I learned that you can deliver bad news if you deliver it the right way."

After O'Malley lost his reelection bid in 1996, Zopp became a commercial litigation partner at Sonnenschein (now SNR Denton) in Chicago, staying there until 2002. While she liked civil litigation, the call of her "proactive" prosecutorial instincts and management experience was hard to ignore. Learning of an in-house opening at the Sara Lee Corp., she called then-Deputy General Counsel Roderick (Rick) Palmore. "The rest is history," says Zopp, referring to the subsequent series of ascending deputy and full general counsel moves that would take her from Sara Lee to the Sears Holding Corp. and then to Exelon in 2006 as senior vice president of human resources. "I was new to business and far from the courtroom when I joined Sara Lee," reflects Zopp, "but it was Rick, now general counsel of General Mills, who helped get me started and who has since served as an incredible mentor in every possible way."

Zopp's view on mentoring is unequivocal. "From deep, long-standing relationships to passing moments, mentoring comes in many forms," she says. "You need to

"It was invaluable to talk to these other women about substantive issues and what it was like out there."
—EDWARDS

be open to them wherever they are and whenever they come, and be able to grasp and absorb their full range in order to really reach your potential."

An Investment of Trust

Of all the mentor categories, having a champion at the wheel has taken women general counsel the most places. Whether parents, teachers, employers, peers, partners, or clients, the personal or career champion can be the ignition switch, drive train, and accelerator that transform cold starts or stalls into fast-track, open-highway opportunities.

When third-waver Laureen Seeger's parents balked at the idea of her going to law school, her high school guidance counselor stepped up to champion her interest. "The relationship with my counselor began when she gave me a career assessment test," explains Seeger, who grew up in Milwaukee and graduated high school in 1979. "The results showed I was cut out for law or for art, and since I could not draw a thing, she began encouraging me to participate in law-related studies and activities, such as a mock-political program called Badger Girls State." An accomplished student, Seeger gained enough credits to graduate high school in three years; the counselor introduced her to Quarles & Brady, a law firm with an office in Milwaukee, where Seeger, needing to make money for college, worked much of the following year as a legal secretary. And when Seeger's parents, with nine other children to support, worried about the financial implications of her going to law school, the counselor persuaded them of their daughter's aptitude, capabilities, and potential. "She was a wonderful woman who truly cared about me," says Seeger, who also received substantive mentoring and personal encouragement from her boss at Quarles & Brady. "He told me I was very bright and recommended that I go to law school at either the University of Wisconsin at Madison or Harvard," continues Seeger. Harvard being too expensive, she chose Madison—and by continuing to work at Quarles & Brady, semester breaks included, Seeger paid her way through law school and graduated debt-free.

Driven to succeed in the face of cultural and socioeconomic challenges, Linda Madrid did her part as a student: her stellar grades earned her one of eight places in the first wave of a program for gifted students at her 4,000-student inner-city high school in Phoenix. Making this rare opportunity truly click was her counselor, Bernie Horowitz. "He was a phenomenal mentor, and a major part of why I went to college," says Madrid. From figuring out finances to guiding Madrid and her family through the process, Horowitz did it all. "He encouraged recruiters to meet me, he arranged for dinners, he even bought me bus tickets and convinced my mother to let me go visit schools on my own." His efforts paid off in Madrid's acceptance to Bowdoin College in Maine, but after one year at the distant liberal arts school, it was time to come home: her father had passed away, and she felt isolated as the school's sole Latina. Finding a better fit at Arizona State University, she would discover another champion there. "ASU was beyond my family financially," says Madrid, "but

The Necessary Steps
Bridging the Gap

Currently in the spotlight as the influential wife of California Governor Jerry Brown, Anne Gust, now Anne Gust Brown, was an executive at global retailer Gap Inc. from 1991 to 2005, including four years as general counsel. As recounted by Lauri Shanahan, who succeeded Gust as GC in 1998 and then later as chief administrative officer, Gust made a persuasive first impression.

"A friend had told me of a potential opportunity at Gap," relates Shanahan. "Anne was the first person I talked to there, and I was immediately struck by her business savvy, openness, and sense of humor. She did not seem lawyerly at all." In a subsequent interview with Gap founder, the late Don Fisher, Shanahan told him she much preferred the business side and that her interest in being a lawyer was waning. "I told Anne that I really thought I had blown it with Don," says Shanahan, "but she just laughed, and I accepted the job offer that followed."

That was in 1992, and in what would evolve into a very close friendship, Gust guided Shanahan into the job. "The culture at Gap was uniquely stable and refreshing, with a strong focus on taking risks and relying on your gut," says Shanahan. "Anne developed people in the moment and believed in letting people shine. She didn't hesitate to push you out of your comfort zone." Gust saw Shanahan's managerial potential even when Shanahan herself did not, and helped drive her toward success. "There were no hidden agendas with Anne," continues Shanahan. "Anne was all about authenticity and integrity and open debate on how to solve problems and keep the business aligned and moving forward. She taught me how to handle the tough issues and conversations, and ultimately, to believe in myself as a leader."

Invested with the spirit of Gust's leadership, Shanahan would in turn help develop her successor, Michelle Banks, in a near replay of her own story with Gust. "At first, Michelle saw herself as an individual contributor and not the team leader," says Shanahan. "Seeing her great integrity and terrific legal mind, I knew she could be more. My challenge was to set her up to want that bigger role." To help Banks realize this vision on her own, Shanahan pushed Banks into unfamiliar work and responsibilities. "It was a journey we took together, and as she expanded her perspective, as I had with Anne, she began having fun and seeing new possibilities," says Shanahan, who left Gap in 2008 to serve on corporate boards and establish her own investment consultancy.

"When I first joined Gap in 1999, becoming general counsel never crossed my mind, in part because I had figured that Lauri would be there for the long term," recounts Banks, who took over the general counsel role from Shanahan in 2006. "Lauri was in my court all the way, though. Once she had decided that she wanted me to be her successor, she took all the necessary steps to ensure that I got the exposure, the credibility, the credit, and all the things I needed to be a viable candidate. Even after I got the job, she took the time to guide the transition of responsibilities to me. She was my first female mentor, and the quintessential guide."

Michelle Banks succeeded...

Lauri Shanahan, who succeeded...

Anne Gust Brown, now first lady of California

the dean of students, Dr. Leon Shell, kindly provided me with the Dean's Pocket Scholarship. Combined with my other scholarship, this allowed me to complete my studies, and Dr. Shell remained an active mentor throughout my time there." Learning of Madrid's interest in the law, Judge Marilyn Riddle, an alumna of her sorority at ASU, championed and encouraged Madrid from the sidelines, including making introductions and writing glowing reference letters for her. Completing this critical series of early mentorships were her professors at Georgetown Law School's Center for Applied Legal Studies. "They helped me understand my skills and the difference I could make as a lawyer," says Madrid. "With their mentoring I became a lawyer—and knew that I could be very passionate in representing others." Above all, her mentors helped Madrid to believe. "Within my family and my community, there was little vision on opportunities in the outside world. My mentors represented a true investment of trust."

Flights of the Navigators

Georgetown Law professors also provided solid foundational mentorship to Louise Parent, who attended the school from 1972 to 1975, when women represented one-fifth of the enrollment. "Don Schwartz and Jeff Bauman taught a clinical program [for Georgetown] at the SEC, and it was unlike any professorial relationship I had experienced before," says Parent. "They truly brought us in, inviting us to their homes, ensuring we had a good experience at the SEC, and giving us great work assignments." Crediting them with sparking her substantive interest in corporate law, Parent says that the professors also shepherded her through the law firm interview process, "providing the encouragement and confidence to pursue whatever I wanted to do."

Emboldened to pursue securities law, she went to work for Donovan, Leisure, Newton & Irvine, a Manhattan litigation firm with a small corporate practice. It was to be an uninspiring experience for Parent, who found herself at odds, she says, with the irrational work hours, with the repetitive document work, and with only being able to see tiny slices of big deals. Then, on a Saturday night, with one eye on the stack of documents before her and the other on the full moon rising over the Empire State Building, she had an epiphany: "It was my birthday, and this was the last place I wanted to be. There had to be a better way." One headhunter call and leap of faith later, and she was at American Express, "at the bottom of the pile and as happy as could be." Like the relay of a baton, she would find another professorial-style mentor at the company where she was destined to become the legal leader—then-General Counsel Gary Beller. "He believed strongly in the value of in-house lawyers and that the American Express law department should have the best in-house team," says Parent. "I learned so much from him substantively in terms of negotiating, how to navigate and manage my career, and in terms of trying new things and expanding my horizons."

By establishing herself as a leader early in her career, Pamela Carter drew a

> "There is a difference between being assigned a mentor and developing a relationship with one."
>
> —KENDALL

Exploring All the Possibilities

While this table, adapted from Ida Abbott's article "Mentoring Plays a Key Role in Retaining Attorneys of Color," published in *Law Governance Review* in 1998 and reproduced in her 2000 book *The Lawyer's Guide to Mentoring*, may be somewhat dated and refer specifically to women of color in law firms, it remains a comprehensive, relevant, and universal guide to the evolution of the mentoring role from a one-on-one relationship to a flexible, accessible, high-utility—and indispensable—professional development and career advancement tool.

Roles and Functions of Mentors

ROLES	FUNCTIONS
Host	Welcomes protégés to the firm, introduces them to others
Bridge	Acts as a link to the firm for work, support, administrative information
Protector	Provides support, runs interference
Guide	Explains the firm's political issues and unwritten rules
Champion	Advocates for protégé's promotion within the firm
Social Director	Helps individuals get involved in the firm's social affairs
Teacher	Teaches legal and practice skills
Role Model	Demonstrates appropriate behaviors and attitudes
Coach	Provides feedback, monitors performance and experience, encourages professional growth, gives "stretch" assignments
Career Counselor	Advises about work assignments, career decisions, professional dilemmas
Troubleshooter	Helps with problems
Sounding Board	Listens to ideas, proposals, plans
Confidante	Listens to individuals express doubts and fears
Enhancer	Builds confidence
Business Source	Connects individuals to networks, business contacts
Sponsor	Opens doors to business, community, outside opportunities
Publicist	Promotes individual outside the firm
Friend	Forms personal and social bonds
Catalyst	Makes things happen, inspires action, looks for new possibilities

"The mentor and protégé work together to identify and help the protégé work toward [her] professional goals."

—ABBOTT

Stretch to Fit

Her career has spanned four postings as corporate general counsel: at Ameritech Corp., Tellabs Inc., Baxter International, and, since 2010, Hill-Rom Holdings Inc. Along the way, **Susan Lichtenstein** enjoyed one of the ideals (and certainly one of the requisites) for today's top legal officers: a close, intuitive relationship with the CEO. "Dick Notebaert first took serious notice of me because of a presentation I had given on the perils of misbegotten e-mails when we were at Ameritech together," says Lichtenstein. "This led to my working more closely with him and, eventually, to his asking me to become general counsel of Tellabs."

Working alongside the "always accessible, always decisive" Notebaert was like "a graduate course in management every day," she continues. "He gave me the kick to do things that were good for my career, often outside of my comfort zone." She went "kicking and screaming" into one outside board appointment—but it was Notebaert's way of giving her board-level experience, part of his dedication to her overall development as a public company general counsel. "He believed in investing in people," says Lichtenstein.

number of mentors and supporters behind her. Dedicated to "doing the people's work," Carter devoted 15 years to social work before earning her law degree from the Indiana University School of Law in 1984 (see sidebar, page 11). After honing her litigation skills at Baker & Daniels in Indiana, she became a securities enforcement attorney for the state of Indiana. In 1992, after serving as chief of staff for Indiana Governor Evan Bayh (whom she names as a mentor), she successfully ran for Indiana attorney general, becoming the first black woman elected to the position in the history of the United States.

Under her leadership, the office would gain national acclaim for its superior briefing wins before both the Indiana State Supreme Court and the U.S. Supreme Court, along with the notoriety of the 1992 Mike Tyson rape case. Infamy was also the hallmark of Carter's "brutal" election campaign, one saturated with racism, gender bias, defamation, and character assassination. Her opponent put unflattering pictures of her on billboards to remind everybody that Carter was black; lies and lawsuits were among the many landmines laid in her path. Carter fought back, going everywhere and talking to everyone, "so that people could measure me as a person." Her level-headed strategy proved triumphant in a 52 percent majority win—and then, in a topic that goes to the heart of how women are perceived as general counsel, Carter says she discovered for the first time the true meaning of power.

"It is amazing how visibility and power can draw people," she says. "While not having a true mirror for myself to know if I was doing right or wrong during and after the election, I found myself increasingly approached by people—older white males, specifically—who came forth in a mentoring way. There was a wise old doctor, for example, who took a liking to me and wanted to help. He and others provided an echo for me in terms of getting my bearings and shaping my direction." Once elected, she drew a different crowd—some about-facers among her most ardent opponents. "There is an affinity for power that transcends relationships in this country," continues Carter. "Once you are perceived as having power, people want to get close to you—now it's no longer personal, but about the power."

How Carter would go on to manage this power—including her handling of the Tyson sex case, which brought her back into the same vitriol that had characterized the election—is perhaps the quintessence of what distinguishes women from men and makes women so well suited for the general counsel role today. "My goal was not to seek attention for myself or to use the office as a career stepping stone," says Carter, "but to do right by the situation and be the voice of the people." Among the people who saw Carter in the spotlight and heard the call: J. Irwin Miller, chairman of the Cummins Engine Co. and the executive who would eventually hire Carter and serve as a valuable mentor on her way up the company's corporate and legal ladder.

Golden Archer

No matter who you are, in whatever you may pursue in life, the influence of a mentor or role model is nearly unavoidable. Yet, as for every rule, there are exceptions, as in the case of Gloria Santona, general counsel of McDonald's Corp. Unique among our interviewees for this book, she describes her career path as largely self-navigated.

In a company where consistency rules—not just across the counters of more than 31,000 restaurants in over 100 countries, but at every level and in every department throughout the organization—Santona has excelled at globalizing the law department. "Whether in Singapore, China, or Chicago, McDonald's is the same business," she says. "Taking the idea that our lawyers essentially face similar problems around the globe, we took the approach of 'globalizing' our legal knowledge and then sharing it to the collective benefit."

This is just one example of Santona's precise, analytical, consensus-driven approach, one that she has been crafting since joining McDonald's law department straight out of the University of Michigan Law School in 1977. What makes her method especially noteworthy is that she has advanced herself essentially by serving as her own champion, navigator, and technical advisor.

"It evolved into a rewarding co-mentoring experience, which we both appreciated."
—KELLY

Ambitious and self-directed since childhood, Santona set her sights on being a doctor, drawn by two defining desires: intellectual challenge and working with people. A math and science whiz, she majored in biochemistry at Michigan State— only to be disappointed when she didn't get into the medical school of her choice. With her original plan scuttled, she took a labor relations job at the General Services Administration, where she met a lawyer who thought she might enjoy the law and encouraged her in that direction. "He was not a mentor per se," she explains, "but he definitely planted the idea." As it turned out, it was the right idea—she found in law what she had been looking for in medicine.

At a friend's suggestion, Santona interviewed with McDonald's and was offered a job. From the outset, she would prove adept at learning and adapting by observing how things got done, relying more on influence and inspiration than on direct mentorship to move ahead. "There was no formal training—it was a matter of learning on the job," she says, adding, "I pride myself on being able to self-teach and to know what resources to use and how to use them efficiently and effectively." Asking questions was a big part of her approach; from outside counsel to her direct superiors, Santona put herself under the wings of the people with the knowledge.

Starting out in the corporate law department, where she was the fourth woman and fourth minority on a team of 13, Santona first worked on securities and other corporate work. She describes her first boss, the man who had interviewed and hired her, as a "good safety net" in terms of being a reliable go-to resource when she had questions; she also learned a great deal from Jim Listak, a senior lawyer with whom she worked on large financing deals. Gathered with representatives from top-tier law firms on one such deal, she demonstrated her self-assuredness by proposing some creative math for a complex repayment provision. She was roundly ignored (though when a male lawyer articulated the same formula later in the day, the assembly embraced it), but more meaningful payoffs were ahead: about four years in, she was invited to take on the corporate transactional work herself.

Again, it was sink or swim, and once more, Santona turned to her colleagues. "Jack Greenberg, who came in as the new CFO, gave me invaluable lessons on the finance side, while the head of the legal department, Don Horwitz, taught me the legal and negotiating skills on the deal side." Santona takes a pragmatic view of mentoring. "Assigning mentors in a formal, structured way is much less effective than allowing the process to happen organically and naturally," she says. She put this philosophy to great use at McDonald's. "There was this tremendous synergy among me, Jack, and Don that translated into heightened responsibility and exposure for me within the organization, including interacting with the board." Ever the student, she learned from outside counsel on both sides, read voraciously, and continued to absorb information from her colleagues, "thriving in the lack of structure." It is an approach that served her well. Appointed general counsel in 2001, Santona is a widely respected member of the company's senior leadership team.

"I pride myself on being able to self-teach and to know what resources to use."

—SANTONA

Passing the Torch

Reflecting on her three-decade climb up McDonald's corporate ladder, Santona today "takes great satisfaction in helping younger lawyers develop." Along with Pamela Carter and many other current and past women general counsel, Santona embraces the opportunity to mentor others. Whatever the polarity, though, most women agree with Santona that "organically grown" is more nutritious than "artificial" mentoring. Starting out in 1975 as a staff attorney at Elanco Products Co., the agricultural subsidiary of Eli Lilly, Rebecca Kendall (then Goss) says that she was "incredibly fortunate" to have Elanco's managing attorney, Dale K. Lewis, as her first boss. "He took a real interest in helping me understand how things worked and guiding me in the law, and we hit it off personally, becoming quick friends," recalls Kendall. "I never felt like he didn't have time for me. I could ask him any question I wanted to, and he always made sure that everything was alright." They remain friends to this day. "Working with him was nothing short of a tremendously lucky break," says Kendall, "and he absolutely provided the model for me about what a supervisor ought to be." She believes in staying alert for role models and teachers who naturally present themselves. "In my experience, formal mentoring programs do not work very well," Kendall explains. "There is a difference between being assigned a mentor and developing a relationship with one."

An all-natural opportunity fell to Janet Kelly (see sidebar, page 47) when she joined the Kellogg Co. as general counsel in 1999. Distinguishing her example is that her mentee was the company's new CEO. "It was a time of new strategic direction for the company, and I was able to leverage my boardroom and transactional experience in helping guide the CEO while formulating many of the deals and acquisitions supporting the new strategy," says Kelly. "It evolved into a rewarding co-mentoring experience, which we both appreciated."

In that case, it was the general counsel teaching the CEO; for Sara Moss, when she was at Pitney Bowes, it was the CEO teaching her to be general counsel. "He had been a general counsel himself and knew where all the landmines and obstacles were," says Moss. "I asked that we meet once a week in the beginning, because I was new to the role and wanted to ensure that I understood all that was expected of me. He was an incredible role model and help to me."

Peer-to-peer mentoring also pays dividends. At the beginning of her career, Pamela Strobel enjoyed the devoted mentorship of former Illinois Governor Richard "Dick" Ogilvie, a partner at the Isham, Lincoln & Beale law firm where she worked. "Instrumental to my development as a lawyer, he made me realize that being a good lawyer is not only about writing good briefs and being in the library, but getting out of our shell, getting to know people in the community, and getting to understand business," Strobel says. At a cocktail party one evening, Ogilvie introduced Strobel as a "terrific lawyer" to Jean Allard, the acclaimed business lawyer who was one of the

> "I asked that we meet once a week...because... I wanted to ensure that I understood all that was expected of me."
> —MOSS

true luminaries of the Chicago legal community and who, in 1976, had become the first woman partner at Sonnenschein Nath & Rosenthal, now SNR Denton (see section on Jean Allard, page 61). "We immediately clicked, and she told me not to quit, to push ahead, because too many women gave up." They would meet again years later when Strobel became general counsel of Commonwealth Edison—where Allard, along with Sue Gin, was one of two female board members. "They threw themselves into helping me step into the general counsel role," says Strobel, "and have been great mentors ever since." Included in their support: getting Strobel admitted into the prestigious Chicago Network, where women from the highest echelons of Chicago's business, legal, and other communities gather.

It's a far cry from that day when Strobel overheard that male partner say, "Pretty soon they're gonna admit dogs," and proof positive of the power of door-openers and ambassadors in high places. Is there a way to the top without mentors? The answer is likely not. Santona's relatively free-form approach is probably not for everyone, but, according to her, even she had a safety net. Mentors, safe to say, are an indispensable part of developing the requisite skills, business sense, and political acumen for legal leadership in the Fortune 500, for which an airtight career-development and ascension plan is essential. But striving to be fail-safe does not mean going risk-free. While no woman interviewed for this book ever put on Icarus wings, all have taken risks on their flights to the top. In the next chapter, we'll examine the role of risk taking and various approaches to risk management.

Jean Allard:
The Grande Dame of Women Business Attorneys

Historically hard-nosed and proud, Chicago can be a tough town for any guy to succeed in law, business, or civics—let alone a woman. Jean Allard, the first woman to become a partner at Chicago's prestigious Sonnenschein, Nath &

Rosenthal law firm (now SNR Denton), stood tall in all three. Fittingly, she was the first recipient, in 1993, of an honor created by the Business Law Section of the American Bar Association in her name: the Jean Allard Glass Cutter Award.

Nominees for this annual award are exceptional female business lawyers who have made significant contributions both to the profession and to the Business Law Section and who have worked to advance opportunities for other women in the profession. Allard, for decades a mainstay of Chicago's

legal, corporate, and civic scenes and one of the city's most visible personalities, built her career on these very pillars.

Born in Missouri in 1924, she earned her law degree from the University of Chicago in 1953 and began her career as an antitrust lawyer at the venerable Chicago law firm Lord Bissell & Brook. After following her lawyer husband to Ohio, the couple returned to Chicago in the mid-'60s—and Allard then embarked on a trailblazing career where few women lawyers had gone before, starting with her appointment as the first female secretary and general counsel of a NYSE-listed company (though not part of the Fortune 500), auto parts manufacturer Maremont Corp., still in operation today.

In the early 1970s she became the first female vice president of the University of Chicago, in a business and finance role; in 1976, she joined Sonnenschein as the firm's first female partner; in 1979, she became the first chair of the prestigious Chicago Network, formed that year as an organization for the most highly placed women of achievement in the Chicago area.

As the *Chicago Tribune* succinctly observed in 1987, "Allard thrives on being first."

A powerful networker and civic leader,

ICON

"That's not how my generation did it. Passivity is not going to help."

—ALLARD

Allard was among the first women admitted to Chicago's elite male-bastion clubs and committees, while also serving as a director on the boards of public companies including Commonwealth Edison, ABN LaSalle Banks, and Axel Johnson Bank. And she never missed a chance to help other women lawyers advance in the profession.

Herself a Chicago Law School friend and mentee of acclaimed lawyer and educator Soia Mentschikoff (whose own pioneering half-century in law earned her the moniker "the first woman everything") Allard formally mentored and helped two of the women general counsel featured in this book—including Mary Ann Hynes, who became the first-ever woman general counsel of a Fortune 500 company when she assumed the role at CCH Inc. in 1979 (see page 144). "She was the grande dame of women business attorneys," recalls Hynes, "and a cherished mentor."

The other was Pamela Strobel, who was introduced early in her career to Allard at a cocktail party (see page 59) and would benefit thereafter from Allard's devoted friendship and mentorship. "She told me to push ahead for what I wanted and to never quit," says Strobel, who would go on to become general counsel at Commonwealth Edison (now Exelon), the largest electric utility in Illinois and one of the companies where Allard held a board seat.

In 1991, Allard left Sonnenschein to become president of Chicago's Metropolitan Planning Council, and the seventh woman to lead this influential organization since its founding in 1934. Now retired, her legacy endures as one of Chicago's—and the legal profession's—brightest beacons. "In a business world previously dominated by men, she has been 'the stranger' who broke barriers—and who now carries immense power, a term she hesitates to assume," wrote the *Chicago Tribune* of Allard in 1987, the same year the International Women's Forum honored her as "a woman who made a difference." Allard preferred leadership over power or influence as "the more accurate assessment of successful women," however. "Leadership to me is the effective use of your own time and the time of others in a goal-oriented task," she told the *Tribune*. "Women have not acquired the wealth, so leadership becomes a more meaningful measure of importance."

In another conversation about courage and confronting the glass ceiling, Allard discussed having the "right attitude" toward mentoring in a 1991 *ABA Journal* article, as instructional today as back then: "Younger women say they look around a room and feel uncomfortable because they don't see any other women there. That's not how my generation did it," wrote Allard. "Passivity is not going to help."

Chapter 3

RISK TAKING:

plot lines

"Real courage" is a key success denominator, one shared by so many women because they have been willing to go outside their comfort zones, to be risk takers.

or today's general counsel especially, there are few dividing lines between success and failure more acute than risk. At any given moment a lawyer's best friend or worst foe, risk can literally make or break a career. On the way up, young lawyers who play it safe can stall or fall short of the mark—as many women interviewed for this book acknowledged, the greatest risk to advancement can be in not taking risks at all. The benefits of risk taking can take time to develop and wear the shroud of uncertainty. But in the other main area of risk—on the job—unmasking this omniscient foe is

today's top priority. From career inertia to legal consequences as severe as a federal indictment, risk ignored is an invitation to trouble.

There was a time when being general counsel was a relatively uncomplicated affair. Before Sarbanes-Oxley, risk for a general counsel perhaps amounted to retaining the wrong law firm. That's an oversimplification, of course, but if the risks of yesteryear can be likened to shallow waters, then risk in the post-SOX era is oceanic in nature, capable of engulfing and sinking the corporate ship. Not only must today's general counsel have a strong hand in steering that ship, but as we noted earlier in the book, the role includes establishing and maintaining trust with shareholders, investors, regulators, and the marketplace in general; setting and personifying the corporation's moral compass; and performing triage when necessary—all activities invested with degrees of risk.

Natasha Innocenti leads the Northern California partner practice group for global attorney search firm Major, Lindsey & Africa. In her view, a general counsel must be able to balance the business objectives of the organization with the risks associated with achieving those objectives—an area in which she believes women have an edge.

"For many general counsel, the ultimate business decisions reside not with them but with the leadership of the company," Innocenti says. "Therefore, the successful general counsel must be prepared to handle situations in which taking a risk or combination of risks results in a bad outcome." Innocenti goes on to say that success is not necessarily derived from how many risks are avoided, but whether

Fear Is the Key

For much of her career, **Cathy Lamboley** had to manage the dichotomy of being a liberal, socially minded woman in a conservative male world. She marched for women's rights and other issues of the day as a college student in the late 1960s, but professionally, she had good reason to suppress her personal life and views. Five years into her career at Shell, she says, "my boss told me that I had better not make any mistakes." Part of that equation was fitting in. "So I wore the uniform, kept up with the sports pages, and left the politics at home, by way of making my colleagues comfortable with my presence." Then, an inflection point, where Lamboley took a calculated risk. "The company started looking at diversity as part of its long-term plan," relates Lamboley, "and that's when I decided to be my own person again." Casting aside her fear of career consequences, she did just that; it was, in a word, "freeing."

the upside of taking those risks outweighs the downside of the company getting it wrong every now and then. "To find that balance involves insight into the business, risk management skills, outstanding communication skills, and a trusted relationship with management and the board," she says. "Defining success in this way requires that the general counsel and the CEO (or the board) have a strong, trust-based relationship, and it is in establishing that kind of relationship that I believe many women have the advantage."

Indeed, for women lawyers, this heightened risk quotient in today's corporate environment has actually produced something of a silver lining—or hidden gold— in terms of new and improved access to the general counsel role. As Korn/Ferry International executive recruiter Julie Goldberg Preng pointed out in the first chapter, the name of the game for general counsel today is risk management and risk analysis—for which women, their emotional intelligence heightened by their place in the conventional leadership culture, are increasingly seen to be ideally suited. An environment that is inherently risk-laden or risk-threatened can be destabilizing to all those who operate in it, from the perspective of confidence, morale, willpower, or essentially any intrinsic operational or functional metric. To keep such an environment stable and calm requires a heightened sensitivity and attunement to, by analogy, internal weather conditions; as general counsel, if you aren't wise to temperature and baromet-

> **"The first risk I took was trying to be a lawyer... back when people didn't want women to be lawyers."**
> —CHAPMAN

Gut Check

Among the professional success traits identified in the 2010 book *The Risk Takers* is "trust your gut," something the authors call "particularly valuable in the most chaotic, fluid business environments, when you must make critical, high-pressure decisions at a moment's notice." That also happens to be one of **Anastasia Kelly's** guiding principles for success. "As my mother always said, listen to that little voice inside of you—ignore that voice and you can mess up really easily." Heeding her gut helped Kelly navigate turbulent times at MCI WorldCom and AIG. "How many corporate crises have there been where people made decisions they instinctively knew to be wrong?" she asks. "Instead of trusting their own judgment, people too often defer to what they believe everyone else is thinking." Especially when going before the CEO or the board, Kelly simplifies the argument this way: "When everyone is going to jump off the bridge and you don't think that is a good idea—you know you're probably right."

ric changes, you are going to miss the storm that soaks everybody. In real terms, that can mean getting fired or, worse still, getting indicted. In the turbulence of today's radically changed reality, entire boards or management teams can get taken out.

In Chapter 1, we talked about how women are "first-class noticers," an attribute rooted in "women's domestic experience, socialization, and evolutionary development." The same factors make women lawyers first-class risk takers, an activity that essentially defines the history of women in the law. If there is one straight line that can be drawn from 1648—when Margaret Brent argued for "a vote and voyce" before the Maryland Assembly—to the present day, it is the willingness of women to take risks. As former Washington Mutual General Counsel Fay Chapman recalls, "The first risk I took was trying to be a lawyer in the first place, back in the day when people didn't want women to be lawyers....Once you're over that one, the rest of 'em kind of pale by comparison. You're already in the soup."

Risk is in the blood of some women lawyers, particularly those women lawyers featured in this book. From the first wave to the present wave of women general counsel, "real courage" is a key success denominator—one shared by so many women precisely because they have been willing to stretch, to go out of their comfort zones, to be risk takers. As Preng says, "If you do not take risks, you will never know how far your skill set can go. Women who take risks are truly tested—they have figured out what they're really made of, and that in turn goes far in bolstering courage and creating confidence."

"Risk essentially is fear of the unknown," says Anastasia Kelly. "You are not always going to know where risks are or where they are coming from. But you have to be willing to take the risk in the first place—and then you step up to what happens when risk actually materializes."

That's an overview of the risk story once you reach the general counsel level—and then there are the risks you have to take to get there in the first place. When discussing the risks confronted by women on the road to becoming corporate legal leaders and general counsel, the women interviewed for this book said their journeys had forced them to confront three primary types of risk. First there were reputational and professional risks, most often associated with job choices—up, down, or sideways. There were relationship risks, in terms of how women lawyers manage and navigate the ladder when spouses, children, and family are involved. And there were more inward-facing risks, in terms of self-identity—as a lawyer—as career goals and visions were met and realized. For some women, the path to general counsel involved detours away from the law itself, calling into question, at least for a while, their sense of who they are and what they do.

Dealing with any one of these risks is challenging enough, but for many of our interviewees, as for many women entering the legal profession today, it was a matter of taking on all three. No matter the risk or risks, this unassailable conclusion emerged: If you want to be a leader in the corporate legal environment, you can't be risk-averse. Or, more emphatically stated, it takes real courage for women to become general counsel. That's how we arrived at the title for this book. The more personal stories we heard, and the more reflection on our own experiences that resulted, the more evident it became that courage was the defining characteristic we were looking for. As we discuss in more depth in Chapter 5, courage underlies and informs virtually every decision and action a woman must make and take on the road to the office of general counsel. As this chapter indicates, risk taking, of course, is synonymous with courage. Some of our interviewees came to this understanding slowly, others naturally and even instinctively. But, as their personal accounts reveal, decisions to take riskier paths even when safer roads were available invariably produced positive and more substantial results.

In this chapter's collection of stories, a key lesson lies in considering what might have come of these women's careers had they not taken risks along the way. While each story differs in the details, there is something uniform in the way that each of them uses risk taking to unlock doors or resolve career "inflection points"—pivotal moments that at first may have seemed to interrupt, deflect, even hurt career advancement, but they ended up being the difference in making it all the way. Like an arterial lifeline, risk taking sustains the climb up the career ladder—especially in its upper reaches, where opportunities and options grow thinner with each rung.

"If you do not take risks, you will never know how far your skill set can go."

—PRENG

Taking Risks "Sooner":
For Whom Does Time Wait?

Joanna Barsh and Susie Cranston, senior-level leaders as McKinsey & Company and co-authors of the groundbreaking book *How Remarkable Women Lead*, write that "Women who have made their way to the top have also taken risks—it is the best way to develop at an accelerated pace. [However], we have found that many women don't [take risks]. We wait until we have all the necessary skills or the full answer."

That's the thing about risk taking—it can be something of an impatient suitor. Certainly, there must be time for all due forethought and deliberation; risk must be weighed and calculated intelligently. But if risk is about taking advantage of an open window of opportunity, then he or she who hesitates or decides to play it safe will likely find that window closed.

Acclaimed linguistics and communications expert Dr. Deborah Tannen of Georgetown University has written many books on gender differences, including her best-selling *Talking from 9 to 5: Women and Men at Work*. In that book, she makes a key point concerning career advancement into leadership positions: "In many organizations, those making decisions about promotions into leadership positions look for leader-like behavior *as well as evidence of a desire to be promoted….*"

One reliable way to effectively demonstrate such desire is to take risks. In a brief published in MCCA's *Diversity & the Bar* magazine, leadership consultants Heather Bradley and Miriam Bamberger discuss using risk as a career strategy: "Taking risks demonstrates the leadership skills and professional judgment necessary to rise to the top of an organization. Even if you do not aspire to reach the executive suite, taking risks shows you have the strength and flexibility to handle more interesting, challenging work."

Bradley and Bamberger identify two common dimensions of professional risk. The first is "taking on assignments in unfamiliar areas, such as learning a new area of the law, working in a different business unit, or managing a new project." The second is "going outside your comfort zone," which they define as "acting in ways that are not natural or easy." The risks in both cases range from disappointment to failure, but as Bradley and Bamberger note, "there is also the possibility of rewarding payoffs: personal growth, increased confidence, and higher visibility—all of which position you well for advancement."

The greatest risk is in not acting at all. "No risk is right or wrong in and of itself," they write. "Calibrating a situation, taking intelligent risks, and landing on your feet provide evidence of leadership ability and sound judgment when advancement decisions are made." How long do you have to calibrate the situation and take the "intelligent" risk? And what are the consequences of waiting too long? As Michele Coleman Mayes has learned, "The only regret I've got is that I didn't take more risks sooner. Time waits for no one."

Platinum Cards

On three separate occasions, Louise Parent confronted career junctures where she had to choose between relative safety and risk. By choosing the riskier route each time, she earned her way to the general counsel role at American Express, which she has held since 1993. Her first move was a step down, the second sideways, and the third a real "hot potato." Each was risky, and each lacked a clear view of where it might take her, but each put her in the right place to move onward and upward. In Preng's view, Parent's rise is "iconic."

Parent's first move, described in the previous chapter, came in 1977, when she left a law firm associate job she had found uninspiring, narrow, and mind-numbing (but secure) to join the general counsel's office of American Express. While "happily at the bottom of the pile" there, she quickly began making strides. "Driven to be the best employer possible, the company focused on providing its employees with opportunities for growth, learning, development, and coaching," she recalls. "I knew that if I positioned myself to do the job to the best of my abilities, opportunities would naturally come."

She flourished at American Express. "It was reassuring to see the number of women in senior positions, and on the client side," Parent says, adding that she was encouraged, too, by the freedom and support to try new things. "We were in acquisition mode, which meant loads of work and chances to dive right in. All I had to do was raise my hand to get thrown into a wide range of jobs, roles, deals, and projects." No longer was she just getting tiny slices of the deal. "Now I was framing out the entire deal," she recalls with satisfaction.

It was a heady time for the company and for Parent. Her skills grew as she assumed a central role in an acquisition spree that included First Data Resources, IDS (now Ameriprise Financial), and Warner Amex Cable (now Time Warner Cable), to name a few. She gained the attention of the company's luminary executive team, among them Harvey Golub (later American Express's CEO) and Lou Gerstner (destined for RJR Nabisco and IBM), all the while cultivating a strong sense of self as a highly sophisticated M&A and corporate finance lawyer. Then came an inflection point that at first glance looked like a bump on an otherwise smooth road.

"Lou Gerstner and then-General Counsel Gary Beller pulled me aside and asked me what I wanted to do with my life," she says. "I told them I wanted to continue doing sophisticated work and wanted more responsibility. Their response was that I needed to change jobs." They offered Parent the general counsel role at First Data, the company's information services subsidiary operating in Denver and Omaha, Nebraska. Parent initially hesitated, thinking this looked like a risky lateral move to a non-core business. But Gerstner countered: "Now you're an expert. You need to learn other things and broaden your horizons." Parent got the message and accepted the position; it would turn out to be a "platinum card" for her career. In fact, paraphrasing a comment she

> "You are not always going to know where risks are coming from. But you have to be willing to take the risk in the first place."
> —KELLY

made in a 2009 interview with *Corporate Counsel* magazine, Parent believes that had she not taken the First Data job, she would not be general counsel of American Express today. "The work was infinitely more complicated and interesting than I had first imagined," she says. "All of a sudden I'm on an international deal with four U.K. sellers that took 18 months of back and forth and was substantively one of the most difficult transactions I've ever handled—and among the most exciting and satisfying."

Those three years at First Data would also give Parent, who had never been afraid to raise her hand in the first place, even more confidence to take on tough, risky assignments—and provided her with another risk inflection point. While she could have stayed at First Data after it went public in 1992, she instead accepted American Express's offer to move back to headquarters as deputy general counsel. She stepped into the role just as American Express was dealing with a soured Shearson investment in the bankrupt insurer First Capital. "It was a hot-potato project that nobody in the legal department wanted to touch," she recounts. "It was going to be an ugly, inglorious, stressful process, one of those deals that could have dragged down my personal fortunes with it—but it had to be done, and so I took it on." Parent's already stellar image went platinum plus. Praising her "pluck" for stepping up and managing such a tough assignment, Harvey Golub asked Parent to be general counsel.

"It does not necessarily have to be a promotion to be valuable to your career," she tells young lawyers today. "If moving laterally or even down gets you the experience or expertise that then helps you in the bigger picture, it is well worth considering. I firmly believe in gathering experience, not titles or rungs on a ladder."

Early-Mover Advantages

Christine Edwards was another determined risk taker. Destined to become the first woman general counsel on Wall Street, she used risk as an advancement strategy. Her example clearly demonstrates the risk mind-set: she used risk not only to resolve career inflection points but, in fact, to create career inflection points.

Edwards gave her career early traction with some calculated—but still risky—opening gambits. While pursuing an English degree at the University of Maryland, she worked part time at Sears, Roebuck and Co. in Washington, D.C. After she graduated in 1974, she joined the company's credit card division. While law was not initially in her plans, working with company lawyers on credit disclosure policies, consumer regulation, and other issues sparked her interest—and her first brush with taking risks. Driving from Washington to Baltimore four nights a week, she attended the evening division of the University of Maryland School of Law, completing her degree in four years. If that were not tasking enough, she had to do this under Sears' radar, since the company generally frowned on people improving their careers outside of prescribed channels. Only her immediate boss knew—and helped; since Edwards also had to work one night a week, he arranged for her to work on

> "It was one of those deals that could have dragged down my personal fortunes with it—but it had to be done."
>
> —PARENT

"I Could Have Failed"

One of 10 children—nine of them girls—born to Chinese immigrants, **Sandra Leung** experienced firsthand the problems of language barriers and limited finances. She chose the law so she could "speak for those individuals who could not speak for themselves." Finding her calling in the courtroom, in 1984 Leung became the first Asian woman hired by the Manhattan DA. Eight years of prosecuting juvenile crime, infant homicide cases included, some while she was pregnant, eventually took their toll. Tough-skinned as she was, her 1992 in-house move to Bristol-Myers Squibb was initially jarring, but little prepared her for assuming the corporate secretary role in 1999. "That was a risk," she says. "Unfamiliar with the position, I could have failed." That risk turned red hot in 2002 when the company faced federal charges over its accounting practices—putting Leung in the hot seat. In front of the SEC, the DOJ, shareholders, and the press, she handled the case superbly—and earned herself the general counsel role. Her advice: "Don't be afraid to take risks."

Steven Freeman

Fridays, her one night off from law school.

She threw her chips on the table in 1981 when an opening was created in Sears' Washington, D.C., office of governmental affairs. The new vice president had just been promoted to head the office and needed someone to replace himself. "It was totally off my career path in terms of the credit work I was doing and in violation of all the hierarchical standards at the company," she says, "but I told him I wanted the position he had just vacated. After all, nothing ventured, nothing gained."

The risk was real and substantial for them both. He was banking on an as-yet unproven talent—albeit hedged by her guarantee that he could fire her if she did not complete law school and pass the bar—while Edwards was putting her job, livelihood, and, perhaps, her future on the line.

But her investment in risk would pay off beautifully. Two years later she was promoted to director of government affairs for Sears' subsidiary Dean Witter Financial Services Group Inc., all the while gaining tremendous visibility within the senior ranks of the company and among politicians and agency heads. Washington discovered Edwards; by assuming yet another level of risk—taking on legal and regulatory battles outside of her comfort zone—Edwards discovered herself. "I found that I could be calm and measured in a crisis, with a capacity for

"Parachute Credentials"

Around 1980—before beginning a richly varied career that includes service in the Pentagon and the White House as a U.S. Army Captain (recommended for the latter by Vicki O'Meara, a fellow U.S. Army Captain at the time and also featured in this book), a major law firm partnership, and since 2002, the role of executive vice president, general counsel, and secretary for Starbucks Coffee Co.—**Paula Boggs**'s cadet training included parachuting out of airplanes. "I was afraid of heights," relates Boggs, "but I put together my faith in my training, my colleagues, and my equipment, and I went ahead and jumped."

Calling her airborne training one of her life's "most influential experiences," Boggs relies on her "parachute credentials" to this day. "Moving up requires some level of risk taking," she says. "By accepting and taking on risks—otherwise known as opportunities—you gain the confidence, the credibility, the peripheral vision, and that valuable deep breath to keep moving forward."

synthesizing ideas." This confidence bolstered her vision of a career in financial services, at the same time that her accomplishments were attracting the attention of senior management. In 1988, she was invited to become general counsel to the business unit of Discover Card.

"Taking the job was risky because it meant moving to Chicago, where I knew nobody—and we had two infants at the time," recounts Edwards, who was so immersed in banking and regulatory work at that time that she and her husband jokingly called their children the Glass-Steagall and CEBA (the very esoteric Competitive Equality Banking Act of 1985) babies. "But of course, it was such a great opportunity that I was not going to pass it up." Her instincts proved correct. Not only did the appointment ultimately lead to the position, making Edwards the first woman general counsel on Wall Street, but it also led to successive general counsel roles at Dean Witter, Discover & Co., Morgan Stanley Dean Witter, ABN AMRO North America, and Bank One Corp., assuring her status in the pantheon of financial chief legal officers.

Ironically perhaps, it was Edwards' later insistence on staying in Chicago that led to her leaving Bank One and, in a move that would set her apart from many of her peers, leaving the corporate world for a law firm partnership. "Staying at Bank One—which was on a merger path and ended up being headquartered in New York—wasn't a good option for me," she says. "By that point, Chicago was home. I called the managing partners at five law firms, decided on Winston & Strawn, and the rest is history."

Parent and Edwards both faced situations where they knew they had to make a change: the risk of staying put was greater than the risk of taking action. For Parent, it would have meant staying stifled as an associate, shuffling documents. While Edwards was doing fine at Sears early on, earning five promotions in five years, she knew that the next promotion was going to be to collections manager, and she simply could not see herself doing that. Anastasia Kelly, no stranger to managing risk through her damage control roles at Sears, MCI WorldCom, and AIG, has a distinct point of view on the question of taking action versus sitting still. "When it's time to make a move, the risk is in not doing something about it," Kelly says.

Both UPS's Teri Plummer McClure and Gap Inc.'s Michelle Banks had to confront what Kelly has called "the unknown" as their careers progressed. As they've described it, their mind-sets regarding risk—reputational, personal, and relationship-based—evolved with each step and helped drive their careers forward.

Worlds Apart

"Becoming a lawyer, let alone a general counsel, was not really on my radar screen early on," says Michelle Banks, who grew up in California, the daughter of first-generation Italian-Americans. "It was my love of reading and writing that just naturally led me to law school." Graduating from UCLA School of Law in 1988, Banks' "third-wave" experience there contrasts dramatically with the trials of her first-wave predecessors. "My class was evenly divided between women and men, and as far as I knew, there were no real issues in terms of women leaving or quitting," she says. "We all had equal opportunity." Graduating into a boom market, the story was the same on the job front. "Becoming a lawyer struck me as a relatively easy thing. It was a different world from today's economic reality."

That's an apt description for much of what would follow. Quickly leaving her first firm because of a poor cultural fit, Banks joined Morrison & Foerster as a corporate associate. The hours were crazy, especially during her years in the New York office supporting transactional work from South America; she broke off an engagement; she barely saw her family—but she was realistic: "I understood that putting in your time was what you had to do, and besides, I loved the firm." Soon, though, came her career's first risk-inflection point. "While I did not feel that gender necessarily dictated the effectiveness of mentors and role models," says Banks, "it was hard for me to relate to most women at the firm, because few seemed to share my life priorities, including having a family."

What had seemed so equal in law school struck her as imbalanced in the workplace. This disconnect with her fellow women, growing clearer over time, was a taste of the first wave in her otherwise third-wave world. Lacking female role models, she realized she had to invent her own path: "I knew I had tough choices to make. I just did not like how my life felt." Banks took a decisive step: having worked hard to establish a good reputation at the firm and confident in her latitude there, she risked some political capital to achieve personal change.

"This was more than an opportunity to do something different—this was a major stretch. I decided my career was to be what I made of it."

—BANKS

"A wisdom imparted by my male mentors was to identify who was doing great work," relates Banks, "and then to go for it."

Right here, we see the development of her risk mind-set, comprised of two elements: her sense of self as a female lawyer, and her willingness to stake her professional reputation for a liberating move. "The question I faced was how to move my career in the way I wanted to go," Banks recalls. "I had always wanted to expand my horizons, and I wanted the experience of living and working abroad. I jumped at an opportunity to transfer to Japan." The result: She was sent to Morrison & Foerster's Japan office and seconded there for one year as U.S. counsel to the Itochu Corp., a client of the firm. Unexpectedly perhaps, a go-getter named Kazutoshi Maeda, who later became the head of Itochu's legal department, proved to be a devoted mentor, giving her great work and inspiring her to pursue working in-house, closer to a business.

After reaping the rewards of working internationally, Banks decided it was time to go home. She wanted to change her lifestyle—and soon after arriving back in California, she was introduced to an opportunity at a law firm to work primarily for the NBA's Golden State Warriors.

"This was absolutely a risk-inflection point for my career," she explains. "Did I stay with the security of Morrison & Foerster and the traditional law firm path, or did I go in-house with a new organization in a field in which I was substantially unfamiliar? Had I been a basketball fan, I would have seen this as a dream job, but really, I had some serious thinking to do. This was more than just an opportunity to do something different—this was going to be a major stretch."

A stretch, but now she had a mind-set flexible enough to accommodate the risk. "I decided that my career was to be what I made of it," she says. "So I took the job."

Signing up originally for a one-year assignment, Banks worked for the Warriors from 1995 to 1998; the experience would be nothing short of transformational. "Joining an executive team as an individual contributor, I found that I loved being a lawyer asked to think about business decisions," Banks says.

In addition to getting a taste of decision making, she also embraced the change-over from niche specialist to generalist, which allowed her to issue-spot across an array of subject matters. "The experience validated my notion that I wanted to be in-house and focus on both legal and business issues," she says. "I had the bug." Her bold moves in taking spots in Japan and New York would also pay future dividends; she credits her international work with helping her land her first job with Gap Inc. in 1999.

Nothing ventured, nothing gained. That approach to risk worked for Edwards and Parent and Banks. And these words guided Teri Plummer McClure as she staked herself, her career, and her family on her way up. When McClure reflects on her career today, her view on the value of risk taking is unequivocal: the sum of the risks that she took directly led her to the general counsel job at UPS.

"It does not pay to be risk-averse or overly conservative. If what you are doing isn't working, there is always another job out there."

—LICHTENSTEIN

Are Women Really "Risk-Averse"?

Writing in the April 2009 issue of *CGO Insights*, a publication of the Center for Gender in Organizations at the Simmons School of Management, SOM faculty members Vipin Gupta, Sylvia Maxfield, Mary Shapiro, and Susan Haas explored the reasons why the media, corporate leadership, and a host of empirical research persist in labeling women risk-averse. "Existing literature exploring the causes of women's risk aversion indicates that 'women appear more fearful of losses' and more 'pessimistic' than men," they wrote.

To test that theory, SOM joined forces with Hewlett-Packard and administered a survey to more than 650 women managers at the Simmons School of Management Leadership Conference in May 2008, asking them to talk about "risks they had taken, the factors that influenced their decisions, and the outcomes of those decisions." The findings: "Women do take risks…and their risk decision making is sensitive to many gender-neutral factors."

When the researchers asked how often respondents pursued such business and professional opportunities as "new jobs, assignments, programs, or change initiatives"—being careful not to label these clearly risky activities as "risky"—they found that 80 percent reported they had sometimes or often pursued a major change initiative, "79 percent a major new program, 77 percent a new job, 56 percent a major business development opportunity, and 40 percent a major investment opportunity." And when asked about "opportunistic" risks—opportunities "whose success was not guaranteed, that required learning by doing, and where you had to take personal responsibility for failures along the way," 82 percent of respondents said they'd pursued such risks—following, in essence, what has characteristically been seen as a "male model."

Given this data, the authors wondered, why are women still seen as risk-averse? They saw two explanations: "first, women's actual risk taking may be invisible [because it is unexpected] and so goes unrecognized; second, women may be enacting role-congruent behaviors that are interpreted, through a male lens, to be risk-averse." In fact, they concluded, because women don't seek such visible measures of successful risk taking as promotions and because women are socialized not to brag about their accomplishments, women may actually be pursuing more risk than they acknowledge.

Front-line Decisions

After she graduated from Emory University School of Law in 1988, Teri Plummer McClure spent eight years in three different law firms, becoming a skilled labor and employment practitioner along the way. However, back from maternity leave after having her second child while at the third firm, McClure found herself at an impasse. "Hearing from management that I would have to kick it up if I wanted to make partner, I realized that billing hours for the rest of my life was not what I wanted to do," says McClure, admitting in fact that she "hated" billing hours. "Then a partner from one of my prior firms called to let me know that UPS was hiring in-house, and off I went."

While the risk involved in this switch may have appeared minimal from the

Making the Grade

In a legal career spanning four decades and four prominent, often turbulent Fortune 500 general counsel assignments, Anastasia Kelly has been at the forefront of sweeping changes to the legal and corporate landscapes. In January 2011, Kelly began teaching "The Evolving Role of the General Counsel in Corporate America" at Stanford Law School. Here she chronicles how risk in particular has sharply transformed the chief legal officer function.

- Twenty years ago, you had to be invited to top meetings as a general counsel, whether you were male or female. It was a limited role, and you were not always at the table. Most general counsel didn't appreciate how important it was for them to understand the business that they were in.

- Even when Enron hit, there was still not a strong grasp of the financial, reputational, and legal risks posed by the manipulation of accounting rules and financial reporting. Soon enough, though, it hit all of us that as general counsel, we could no longer afford not to be in room and at every table, both for the company and for ourselves, personally and professionally.

- Fast forward to the SOX era, and that's when the sea change happened for general counsel. As financial controls and reporting became increasingly disciplined, companies suddenly realized that the associated risks they were facing carried at their core legal, compliance, regulatory, or reputational risk. Where did they put that risk? At the feet of the general counsel.

- Now general counsel are not just in the room and at the table, they are *on* the table, as a sacrificial lamb. With legal, compliance, regulatory, and reputational consequences to so much of what is happening today, the general counsel role has become one of the most vulnerable—and dangerous—in the boardroom.

- Risk has evolved the role to where you need real courage for the job, in the traditional sense of the word. You have to be ready to pick up an issue whether it belongs to you or to someone else, and you must be ready to fall on your sword when you have to. And I think that boards and CEOs in general still don't get it when it comes to hiring "coura-geous" general counsel—there remains too much knee-jerk reacting and bad decision making.

- To end on a positive note, though, the rewards are commensurate with the risk. Today, the general counsel is an incredibly important role, right up there with CEO and CFO—a far cry from five years ago. You can shape the company, you can shape the strategy, you can shape the risk profile and the risk appetite. You can make a difference in how a company is run—and you can be the one at the top.

outside, little could have prepared her for what she found when she arrived at UPS. "There was one employment attorney and I," says McClure, "for a company with 280,000 employees, at a time when legislative and legal forces were lighting up the employment litigation docket. My first day was spent before the board on a brewing race-related class action lawsuit."

Springing into action, McClure presented a proposal for forming a labor and employment group, along with several structural and organizational changes for the law department. While taking this initiative would earn her leadership of the group, gaining acceptance within the company's home-grown culture was a different matter. Realizing she was being seen and treated as an outsider, McClure relied on a mentor-navigator to help her learn the distinct language and political and cultural nuances of the company, which helped her rise in the law department. But between her labor and employment work and administrative responsibilities, McClure was starting to burn out, and she contemplated moving on.

Then, McClure confronted a risk-inflection moment that changed everything. "My boss told me I needed hands-on experience in the business if I wanted to grow within the company," she relates, "and asked if I was willing to shift to the operations side as a district manager."

Unlike many UPS employees, McClure, still the outsider, had not started out loading packages on a truck, but here was a chance to at least partially close the cultural gap by assuming responsibility for some 4,000 employees involved in pickup and delivery operations. "It was a huge risk," she says emphatically. "I would be losing my position as head of the labor and employment group, there was no guarantee of promotion, and I had to move my family to central Florida. My husband had his own business in Atlanta and had just started a ministry. It took a lot of gut-wrenching discussions with my family before we made our decision."

When the soul-searching was over, the family headed off to Florida. "Let's see," muses McClure, "I was a company outsider, a lawyer, a black woman, and I had no operations experience. Walking into that warehouse the first day with all the truck drivers and tractor trailers—that was interesting, to say the least."

In a word, her experience as district manager was "phenomenal." Though business was down after 9/11, by the time she got to Florida, business was picking up again, and this meant tough demands and long hours as the company ramped back up to speed. McClure rose to the challenge, focusing on collaboration to build her team and establish credibility as a leader. Her family met the challenge, too, with the children adjusting well and her husband providing major support. "Had I not taken on that role, I would not even have been considered for general counsel," says McClure. "Taking on that responsibility was what allowed me to become general counsel, and the skills I learned during that year in central Florida, in terms of learning the business from the ground up and understanding how decisions are made on the front lines of the organization, are absolutely invaluable to me now." Another example of an excellent adventure.

"Never defer something you know you want in order to find a perfect moment in a career. There is no such thing as a perfect moment."

—SCHULMAN

The Mind-sets of Risk

> ## "I've never turned something down just because it might not work out."
>
> —KELLY

A rose by any other name may be a rose, but risk can go by different names.

Second-waver Susan Lichtenstein, whose first general counsel posting was with Ameritech Corp. in 2000, offers this advice for young women lawyers: Think of your career as a bowl of spaghetti, not a ladder. "Not every lateral move is a bad idea, and not every career decision has to be life or death," Lichtenstein says. "If what you are doing is not working, there is always another job out there. You shouldn't look at each opportunity in terms of where it will lead you, because, honestly, you don't necessarily know." It's a bold concept, and a defining theme in her own career. Reflecting on such pivotal moments as her decision in 1991 to leave the security of a law firm to work for the City of Chicago as deputy corporation counsel, it was her open-minded approach that would yield unforeseen dividends. "It does not pay to be risk-averse or overly conservative," Lichtenstein says. "Life is short, and rather than staying in an unsatisfying job just because it's good for your career, you should have the confidence that there will be opportunities that are equally good or better for your career—at least because you're passionate about them."

Reflecting her innate lifelong optimism, Amy Schulman, who became general counsel of Pfizer in 2008, calls risk "opportunity." Her bright-eyed view of the law started with her grandfather, a federal judge who conveyed an image of lawyers as "guardians of the public trust" and inspired Schulman with his "legendary" work habits. Schulman's father was also a lawyer; joining him was her mother, who went to NYU School of Law when she was 45 years old—separated by a year from Schulman's husband. "She went in unabashedly and fully committed, and that gave me the confidence that women could do anything," says Schulman, whose family actually suggested that she not be a lawyer, fearing it would stifle her creative side. Motivated by a desire to help people, with half an eye on teaching, Schulman went to Yale University Law School, graduating in 1989.

Embarking on a legal career with an infant in tow is challenging, if not risky; for Schulman having the first of her three children while in law school was simply a matter of finding a balance. "Otherwise," she reasons, "I might still be arguing about whether this is the right time." As she tells young women now, "Never defer something you know you want in order to find a perfect moment for in a career, because there is no such thing as a perfect moment." That's precisely what women have long been asked to be in law—perfect—but, in the spirit of Lichtenstein's risk-positive philosophy, Schulman once shared this perspective: "Don't be afraid to pick yourself up when you do something wrong. Do it again, do it better, do it differently. When you drive to be perfect and yet recognize that no one is, it's important to be open to learning from your mistakes. I've had to learn that consciously. Many women are paralyzed because they are afraid to make a mistake."

Venture Capital

It might sound counterintuitive, but avoiding risk is not an advisable strategy if you want to become a legal leader in the Fortune 500. Quite the opposite, in fact. Whether strategic and calculated or based on gut instinct or a leap of faith, risk taking is currency in hand for venturing along the taxing road to the top—where the tolls of risk rise even higher. Portrayed in great depth by the personal stories of this chapter, here are the three primary areas of risk that aspiring women general counsel must contend with—often all at once.

Reputational and professional risks:
Typically involving decisions regarding new assignments, responsibilities, or jobs, especially those that appear off one's career track in a substantive area or industry different from prior experience.

Relationship risks:
Keeping the career moving forward while not sacrificing family and personal times, including, for some, child-rearing duties and aging parent care.

Risk to sense of self:
Becoming a lawyer is no easy task, let alone shooting for the top. How do you protect your original self, ambition, and vision once you embark on years of exacting—but not always certain—legal education, training, and practice?

After a fairly conventional early track, Schulman says that she really only confronted risk later in her career, first when she left the security of one law firm to pursue an opportunity at another, and then by "taking a brand-new job in a challenging industry" at Pfizer. She believes that in general, women can be needlessly risk-averse. "Men are far freer about collecting political capital and spending their chits," she says. "But women tend to hoard their chits. I think what needs to happen is that women need to help each other take appropriate risks." How? "Like it or not, it starts with being unassailable in areas like quality, integrity, competence, and work ethic," she continues, "and that is what buys you the latitude to spend some of your capital and take the right kind of risks."

True Aims

Just what is the "right" kind of risk? Like toying with a loaded gun, mishandling risk can produce misfires, if not fatal shots; careful sighting of the intended "target" before pulling the risk "trigger" is wise. "Battlefield conditions" aptly describes the risks that Anastasia Kelly took in successive moves to troubled companies, starting with Sears, Roebuck and Co., then struggling in the wake of a bankruptcy scandal, its law department decimated. Here once more is the story of a woman encountering risk on three fronts: professional, personal, and in accommodating her relationship with her family.

"The job meant we had to move to Chicago, and the kids did not want to go," explains Kelly. "My husband, Tom—the only mentor in life I trust—told them to support what he called 'Mom's Excellent Adventure.'" Kelly's tenure as general counsel at Sears had a less-than-excellent ending: despite helping to turn the company around, she was eventually replaced by a new executive team—before she assumed an even riskier post as general counsel of bankrupted, scandalized MCI WorldCom, a job introduced to her by Spencer Stuart recruiter Catherine Nathan. "My friends told me I was crazy," says Kelly. "The company and the entire telecom industry were in distress, and things could have turned out really badly. The more stressed the company, the greater the unknown, you know."

Knowing little about the telecom industry, Kelly saw opportunity, not risk. "You can always learn what you need to know about an industry at the upper level," she says, "and I've never turned something down just because it might not work out." As it turned out, things worked out just fine at MCI WorldCom. "The company came out of bankruptcy, and more than 60,000 people kept their jobs," says Kelly. The lesson: "Do a good job, and good things happen."

As *Inside Counsel* observed in a 2006 feature on her appointment to her next general counsel role, for American International Group, "Anastasia Kelly has made a name for herself in the legal community as the go-to counsel for companies in trouble." In the aftermath of an accounting scandal at the time, AIG would become a feature player in the notoriety of the recent financial crisis, putting Kelly's skill in managing complex corporate governance and board crisis issues to the test. Kelly, who has shirked from little in her life, resigned from the company in 2009 to pursue another challenge, joining law firm DLA Piper.

Risk taking is not for everyone, Kelly says. "You have to have the adventurous, change-oriented personality for it. Risk is uncomfortable for people who prefer predictability."

Fair enough, but generally speaking, it's those courageous trips into the unknown that produce great career results. When you take risks, you create, enhance, and optimize your options. Add mentors to the equation and the opportunities only improve—but in the uniquely specialized domain of corporate legal leadership, all the open doors in the world won't matter if you don't have the right credentials for admission.

Michele Coleman Mayes:
One of the Best Jobs I Never Wanted

After conducting more than 70 interviews with general counsel, legal recruiters, and others for this book, co-authors Kara Baysinger and Michele Coleman Mayes sat down to get the details of Mayes' own "excellent adventure" on the record.

Baysinger: What first interested you in being a lawyer?

Mayes: Perry Mason. He was an absolute role model and made such an impression on me that at 11 years old, I went around telling everybody that I was going to be a lawyer— and a flight attendant! One of my junior high teachers, who was also a lawyer, pointed out how many women lawyers remain unmarried, but my attitude was, so what, I am doing this.

Baysinger: Was your family more supportive?

Mayes: Yes, and friends, too. They knew I wanted to be a lawyer and helped me interview with law firms and with Legal Aid when I was an undergraduate at the University of Michigan. I also landed a job as a secretary to the university's Black Law School Association, a role in which I reviewed minority applicants for Michigan's law school and thereby learned what helped applicants get into law school.

Baysinger: Did this experience change your impression of becoming a lawyer?

Mayes: The women lawyers I observed during this time were not that inspiring, and some struck me as negative role models. But I did not feel there were insurmountable obstacles.

I assumed I would be a lawyer regardless. The real disconnect happened when I started law school. Having been around practicing lawyers for all those years, I just could not see the relationship between studying the assigned material and practicing law; law school was not that inspiring. Women and minority admissions were on the rise—this was between 1971 and 1974—so I did not feel isolated, but I kept to myself and focused on my work.

Baysinger: Did you have a master plan for the future?

Mayes: I came out of law school wanting to work for the people, and was certain I would work for Legal Aid. Instead, I got married the same week I graduated and followed my then-husband to the University of Illinois, where he worked on his master's and I taught law to undergraduates for nearly two years at Illinois State University. Up to 1982, my story was about following my husband—picking up and relocating, first to Detroit, where I worked in the U.S. Attorney's office, then to the U.S. Attorney's office for the Eastern District of New York, and then back to my original job in Detroit.

Baysinger: That must have been challenging.

Mayes: More like frustrating. I ended up becoming chief of the civil division in Detroit, but I kept recalling a piece of advice I received shortly after joining the U.S. Attorney's office. It happened one day riding the elevator with one of the division's big dogs. I did not know him that well, but after sizing me up and down, he said, "Whatever you do, don't stay too long." Did he mean that day, or in the job? I decided then not to stay. So eight years out of law school, I started interviewing at law firms.

Baysinger: How did that go?

Mayes: It was a very strange experience. Five interviews—and all I got was silence. Not even rejections, but just silence. They didn't know what to do with me. The turning point was when my husband suggested I look in-house. My first response was, "Are there even real lawyers in-house? Do they practice law?" I took his suggestion, though, and after interviewing with one corporation, I was offered a litigation job with Burroughs Corp., a Detroit-based provider of business equipment and computing systems.

Baysinger: How did you manage the transition to the in-house environment?

Mayes: There were few women in the law department, and I was the only minority female, but I had a great female mentor in Bobette Jones, then the company's assistant secretary. It was Bobette who eventually asked if I had ever thought about becoming a general counsel. That planted a seed and opened my mind to the idea. Inspired it as a goal, actually. The position I held was great. I worked with a smart group of lawyers—yes, there are real lawyers in-house, and yes, they do great work—and we took on all kinds of bet-the-company litigation. I eventually be-

came head of litigation, when the company acquired Sperry in 1986 and became Unisys.

Baysinger: What specific steps did you take toward becoming general counsel?

Mayes: I went to the general counsel, Andrew Hendry, and told him that I wanted a job like his.

Baysinger: What was his reaction to that?

Mayes: He did a double-take, and next proceeded to draw up a laundry list of the skills and experiences I was missing. Then, shortly after saying he would think about my aspiration, he left the company for Colgate-Palmolive. I didn't get the job replacing him at Unisys—they brought in an outsider—but the company gave me plenty of positive feedback. As it turned out, my conversation with Andrew Hendry would produce results. In 1991, he called and asked me if I wanted to explore going to Colgate, where he was general counsel—and that if I still wanted to be a general counsel, he would help me get there.

Baysinger: A testament to speaking up for what you want, right?

Mayes: Don't ask, don't get. So I went to Colgate in 1992. The company was very focused on diversity, and in addition to forming a complementary working relationship with Andy, I developed a great relationship with the CEO, Reuben Mark. He became a real mentor to me, and knowing of my aspirations, made that a personal focus. For example, he put on a full-court press to get me to take a job as head of HR for North America, which he saw as important for bolstering my skills to become general counsel. That was a risk for me—I wasn't convinced, and saw this as a lateral move or worse—but I took his advice, and it ended up being the right move, and one of the best jobs I never wanted.

Baysinger: How so?

Mayes: I came into HR as a non-HR person at a challenging time for the company, with plant closings and union and management issues. But we did not have one work slow-down or strike during my tenure—of which I am very proud, and consider a success. The experience taught me that you can be an effective leader without knowing everything.

Baysinger: And why is that a positive?

Mayes: Because I was no longer hung up on thinking I had to know and manage everything in order to become general counsel—and now I knew that I could fully realize my goal. Surrounding yourself with the right smart people is key, but when you lack their expertise, as was the case when I took the HR job, the challenge is to win them over so that they respect you. The experience provided me with a major lesson in how to motivate and inspire people as a leader.

Baysinger: And those are invaluable skills for the GC role.

Mayes: Exactly. It starts with open communications. I never hide the ball; I figure out what people are or could be best at, let them fly, but also challenge them and hold them accountable for the results. The competencies that I developed in that HR role are the ones I use every day.

Baysinger: What were your next steps at Colgate?

Mayes: This is when Andy really stepped up and took charge of my advancement. He

Baysinger (left), and Mayes.

created a co-deputy general counsel job for me in 1996, he got me in front of the board, he saw that I got corporate and international experience, including managing 50 lawyers overseas, which required a great deal of travel and learning different cultures and legal systems. It went back to that laundry list he created at Burroughs—we were literally checking off tasks and competencies one by one. After three years, he put me in charge of legal operations, which included research, patents, and marketing, but by now, it was becoming apparent that I would have to find the brass ring elsewhere. Andy was in the position, not going anywhere and not likely to go anywhere—and why should he?

Baysinger: So what did you do next?

Mayes: It was a bit unusual for folks at my level to leave—but I left. I left to replace Sara Moss as general counsel of Pitney Bowes. Sara, who had met me previously, had called me saying she thought she had the perfect job for me. Reuben Mark completely understood. He knew I wanted to be general counsel and wished me the best of luck.

"It was a matter of breaking down the challenge one piece and one person at a time."

—MAYES

Alan Klehr

So that's when I went to Pitney Bowes and became general counsel for the first time.

Baysinger: At last, the opportunity to put those skills and competencies to the test—but did you see this as a risk?

Mayes: Yes, there were risks in taking a public company position that I didn't fully understand. But I was convinced I could apply all that I had learned to good use—and do it my way. I was not going to go in as a replica of Sara, simply picking up the reins and continuing down the road she had established. I knew I had to establish my own credibility. Everything fell into place, and my plan was just to stay at Pitney and do my thing—until 2007, when a search firm called wondering if I might be interested in taking on a "challenge."

Baysinger: And that was Allstate Insurance?

Mayes: Yes. Tom Wilson, who had recently become CEO, was starting to build his executive team. Most of the incumbent team had been there many years, and he was looking to add a "change agent." He told me flat out that we were not going to agree on everything if I came on board, but he was looking for a new voice, different from his, and was completely open to changing things and rewriting the rules. So I made the move, joining a new industry and a veteran management team. Again, risk taking combined with confidence in my leadership skills and abilities.

Baysinger: Still, it must have been a bit daunting joining such an established senior team as an outsider.

Mayes: The team was puzzled by Tom's choice of me at first. A former prosecutor?

They probably expected a different profile, someone from the industry.

Baysinger: How did you deal with that?

Mayes: It was a matter of breaking down the challenges one piece and one person at a time. I met individually with each executive and asked the tough questions: What is your view of change management? What would you do differently? What needs to be fixed? What is working well? And lots of whys. We downloaded all the issues, and soon the dynamic changed from suspicion to trust and respect. It remains a point of pride for me that Tom observed that I was making changes and doing things differently without tearing the place apart.

Baysinger: Such as?

Mayes: I institutionalized my approach through a program called Conscious Choice. Adopted company-wide, it guides the safe testing and challenging of business decisions, while helping to define each team member's accountability. It encourages debate. We strive to avoid group-think in reaching the best decision.

Baysinger: The running theme of your professional advancement, it seems.

Mayes: For anybody in the general counsel role. I truly believe in fostering a culture of communication, listening, and debate in an open forum. You can be a leader and a change agent without also being a radical. You have to be willing to empower individuals to make their own decisions and make their own calls—and then you have to be willing to hold them accountable. And you must take smart risks, which, in my experience, is how you create competencies and the next leaders.

Chapter 4

ATTRIBUTES:

legal tender

Essential attributes for legal leadership in the corporate world build upward from core foundations, starting with substantive expertise and keen self-awareness.

hrough their stories in the preceding two chapters, the women general counsel we interviewed were able to clearly articulate the ways in which mentoring and risk taking truly helped their development and advancement as both lawyers and leaders. Their situations varied greatly, of course, but whether they were crediting the people who made a difference for them or describing the leaps of faith they needed to take in tackling a "hot potato" project, relocating to a new city, shoring up their expertise in an unfamiliar practice area, or making what appeared to be lateral or downward career moves, they were able to point to concrete examples of mentoring and risk taking in action, and provide some keen insights into the impact of these experiences on their lives and careers. These examples, in turn, serve our ultimate purpose with this book: to help women in law, in business, in any dimension, understand, map, navigate, and manage their career and leadership development paths.

Have we learned how many mentors one should have, what types of mentors these should be, or how long mentorships should last? Do we really know how many and what kind of risks one should take? In both instances, the answer is no, because those are not the sort of questions we are trying to answer. Mentoring and risk taking do not come with a threshold, or a quota, or a prescribed length, and they cannot be measured. Everyone's path is both individual and unique. Nonetheless, we know these are integral components of success. How do we know this? Because across four generations, a spectrum of industries, and a wide array of age groups, backgrounds, and motivations, a large portion of the women who have served as the leading lawyers of the Fortune 500 have told us that without guiding mentors and flying leaps into the unknown, they would not be where they are today.

However, despite their clarity regarding mentors and risk taking, when we asked about the specific attributes—talent, skills, competencies, strengths, qualities, characteristics—that the general counsel and other leadership roles require, the picture clouded up. The problem was not in identifying the various attributes that had contributed to their career success—all the women with whom we spoke were quite clear and articulate about their respective strengths and qualities, even their weaknesses.

Who's in Charge Here?

It was a Sunday afternoon in 1999, and **Pamela Strobel** had just started as CEO of Chicago utility subsidiary Exelon Energy Delivery. The phone rang; the power grid was down again, a problem plaguing the company at the time. With crisis brewing—the Bears were home that day—and her operations guy unreachable, Strobel, in jeans and a leather bomber jacket, headed downtown to face a rabid media. Goaded by one reporter who repeatedly asked who she was and when would the parent company CEO show up, Strobel finally stood up and said, "Sir, I'm in charge. I am responsible." Strobel reflects on the aftermath with a smile. "Believe me, it was not meant to be a rah-rah for women, but the response was incredible. Women came up to me in the supermarket, men called my secretary asking about where they could buy the same leather jacket for their wives, DJs dedicated songs to me on the radio. For me, though, it was about the leadership."

But when it came to interpreting and then articulating how those attributes actually worked in their careers they became cloudy. For us, this was a red flag: without a detailed understanding of the critical attributes, the career and leadership road map we want to impart would be missing some key coordinates.

That said, it is not that the stories that follow in this chapter lack informational, instructional, or inspirational value—there is much insight to mine here. So we decided to devote this chapter to our women general counsel talking about the attributes that they identify as critical to success in these roles (which are boldfaced), with additional insight and commentary from several legal search specialists and outside sources. Then, in the next chapter, we hand the microphone over to a group of career and leadership development experts to translate these stories into tools and action items, relevant to anyone reflecting on their career path's future trajectory.

But before we get there, there's one truth, one key attribute that became evident to us from the start: Women looking to become legal leaders in business must have **courage.** This is not a goal undertaken lightly. Sara Moss, for one, says the office of general counsel can be a "lonely place." Rebecca Kendall warns, "Be careful what you wish for." And Andrea Zopp reflects, "I used to measure success externally, by what I had achieved. At the top, though, there's really nobody there to pat you on the back, so my definition now is more self-focused, in terms of how I feel personally engaged."

It is also a goal requiring a specialized set of attributes. Dorian Daley, senior vice president, general counsel, and secretary of Oracle Corp., calls the 24/7, always switched-on role of the general counsel "one for which you have to possess enormous capacity." To be sure, today's chief legal officers must be able to stretch. Pamela Strobel reaches back a generation or two for stretching advice to young lawyers when she suggests, "As my grandmother always used to say, if your plate is too full, get a bigger plate." The point: If having the right mentors and taking the right risks pave the way and open the door to the movable feast that is the job of the Fortune 500 general counsel, there is still the matter of actually digesting and doing the job itself without choking on it—which is where professional skills and attributes come in.

Having been a practicing lawyer for 15 years before she became an executive recruiter, Spencer Stuart's Catherine Nathan says she can tell exactly which women are "right" for today's general counsel job. Not surprisingly, her definition pretty much defines the history of women striking forth in the legal profession. "What we are talking about is not the pool of women at large," she explains, "but a group of fearless, courageous, uniquely grounded women who stand up and go to law school, who deal with the drama and politics of law firms, and who advance undaunted by the challenges ahead of them. What you are really looking at is a very self-selected group of women." And if this elite circle shares one trait, Nathan continues, it is an attitude of real **optimism**. "What unifies these women, and men general counsel, too, is that they see the world as a positive place," she says. That's exactly what has carried Moss, a Nathan placement, to the top. Whether facing adversity or the unknown, her glass has always been half-full. "Accompanying my every professional move," Moss says, "is the relentless belief that everything is going to work out."

An integral part of general counsel DNA, optimism animates other core attributes for the role—which in Daley's view begin with three elemental skills that cannot be taught: **judgment, integrity,** and above all, **humility.** "Humility impacts how you form relationships and how you establish and maintain trust," she says, noting that women, generally considered the more nurturing gender, can impart vital humility to the general counsel role, such as in their selflessness in recognizing the contributions that others make. For Daley, it's enough to have her hand on the rudder as long as the whole enterprise is headed in the right direction. "My satisfaction is in seeing the executive team and the board make good, ethical judgments based on the work my team has done in leading them to understand what the right decision is," she says. Calling good judgment "the linchpin for the right people for these jobs," Nathan says that "women in general bring less arrogance to the role, and in their ability to listen well and be more charismatic and empathetic, they are able to fulfill the important likeability quotient. After all, true leaders are people others want to work for."

Consider how optimism's antithesis, pessimism, would affect legal leadership. Think of the executive presence of a pessimist: when grave replaces gravitas, how could this person inspire and influence others? The impact on cross-group collaboration would minimize, not maximize, buy-in and productivity. A negative actor is not

"We are talking about a group of fearless, uniquely grounded women undaunted by the challenges ahead of them."

—NATHAN

securing external networks and important relationships any more than she or he is making good strategic decisions or properly evaluating outcomes. And questions will be asked about the integrity and values of a pessimist: What is wrong with this person? What is she or he hiding?

Now flip the coin back to optimism, and consider how a positive, can-do outlook makes all other attributes come alive. For women especially, it's valuable legal tender for the toll road to and then within the office of general counsel.

Growth Capital

Essential skills for legal leadership in the corporate world build upward from core foundations, starting with **substantive expertise** and keen **self-awareness**. In fact, these were the baseline anchors articulated most frequently by our interviewees, along with the **empathy** that derives from and accompanies knowing yourself.

"The most important thing is to be a great lawyer and have as your primary goal not dollars or status but learning," says Laureen Seeger, who recommends investing time early in a career in a law firm rather than going in-house right away. "The broader your legal experience, the better," she continues, adding that "there was no substitute for the 14 years I spent as a litigator researching, working with, and arguing against other brilliant attorneys." (One note of caution from Heidrick & Struggles' Lee Hanson: Don't spend too much time in a law firm if you want to be general counsel. "By and large, today's chief executives are looking for candidates with public company experience either as deputy or full general counsel," she says. "If you are in a law firm, the best scenario is to go in-house at the mid-level, ideally when you have reached junior partner. Wait much longer, and you will be too specialized and probably make too much money.")

Substantive excellence in the law is one half of the equation; the other, says Korn/ Ferry International's Julie Goldberg Preng, is to have a working, if not a commanding, **knowledge of business-side issues**. "Know the basic language of how business works, such as how to read financial statements," Preng says. "If you are coming out of a law firm or even an in-house job and have not been in touch with the business side of the operation, you are at a huge disadvantage compared to people who have." The quest for knowledge does not stop once you're in-house, adds Hanson. "Make yourself indispensable, and not just as a lawyer," she says. "It's about demonstrating a passion for the business and a dedication to understanding what makes the business tick." In other words, grab that bigger plate and help yourself liberally to the multiple tasks at hand.

While becoming a subject-matter expert is largely a function of hard work and self-application, self-awareness can be something of a trickier asset to acquire and cultivate. During her tenure as a professor at the Texas Tech University School of Law, noted lawyer and teacher Daisy Hurst Floyd (former dean and now professor of law and ethical formation at Mercer University's Walter F. George School of Law) in

> **"Humility impacts how you form relationships and how you establish and maintain trust."**
>
> **—DALEY**

Finding Strength "I Did Not Know I Had"

For **Francesca Maher**, executive presence was an essential component of her challenging job as general counsel of United Airlines. Hired in 1993 for her government relations and regulatory work with the Illinois Securities Department and her skills as a strategic thinker, Maher was thrown feet first into a massive labor reorganization deal. Balancing her job with raising children, she recalls it as an "incredibly demanding and stressful time." Promoted to general counsel in 1997, she went through "unbelievable times" at the company, including complex governance issues and the ill-fated 2000 attempt to acquire U.S. Airways. Then, two unthinkable events. In June 2001, Maher's husband unexpectedly succumbed to an aneurysm; three months and one day later, two United flights were lost on 9/11. "Jim Goodwin [then the CEO] was fine with me stepping off, but I told him that if I did not stay, the terrorists will have won." Finding strength "I did not know I had," Maher shepherded the company through the aftermath, including readying the company for bankruptcy.

Macon, Georgia), wrote a paper about how law school affects students' transformation into lawyers. She discovered a troubling truth: too often, students becoming lawyers, trained to be logical, rational, and objective in their thinking, were losing their sense of vision, meaning, and purpose. In response to these findings, developed over three years, she created exercises in self-awareness for her students to help them expand their thinking regarding who they were and what they could be as lawyers, as opposed to what they thought—rationally and objectively—they should be.

The results were generally positive: her students spoke confidently of a "reclaimed sense of purpose." Being self-aware can also go far in developing a flexible big-picture outlook, which will take you places with far less hindrance and is an essential ingredient for today's general counsel.

"Without self-awareness you will not know your strengths and how to best use them to your advantage and to the advantage of your clients," says Linda Madrid. "Conversely, you won't know your deficiencies and how to overcome them or limit their impact." Self-awareness means accepting that you cannot know everything. Instead, you have the vision, focus, and judgment to align and deploy the right resources around a given issue. "First, I would understand where problems were developing, how serious they might be, and how to head them off," relates Anne McNamara of her time as general counsel of American Airlines. "Then, I would figure out where I could add value and where I should get out of the way so other people could do their jobs."

Knowing your stuff—or as Daley says, knowing more than anyone else—is the first part of having the right stuff, which can start with knowing what you don't know.

Take Andrea Zopp's transition from prosecutor to deputy general counsel at Sara Lee Corp., for example, a move that took her into unfamiliar waters. "It was a little freaky at first," she confesses, "imagining that I was way less knowledgeable than my new colleagues." She proactively took corrective action, though, by "forcing herself" out of her comfort zone by inviting herself to business meetings, and seeking opportunities to present to the board and other key audiences. As a result, she was able to expand her skill set, learn the business, and gain comfort and capability as a corporate in-house counsel. "A key part of the success formula is knowing your strengths and weaknesses and being able to adjust accordingly," says Zopp.

Being self-aware, thinking positively, and taking the big picture view have all helped CIGNA General Counsel Nicole Jones address her initial reticence and move ahead in her career. Considering her rapid rise through a series of increasingly demanding roles and responsibilities in the corporate law departments at Johnson & Johnson, MCI Inc. (where she worked for Anastasia Kelly), and International Paper Co., it may be hard to believe that Jones, by her own admission, once shied from people and feared public speaking. "Left to my own devices, I tended to be an introvert," she relates. "Knowing this about myself, I realized that I had to learn to be comfortable with people, and have them be comfortable with me." Same story for getting in front of a crowd: "It was a matter of not letting fear hold me back, but pushing myself out there and really throwing myself into it."

Jones joined CIGNA in 2006, where she pitched successively into roles as chief counsel of securities, corporate secretary, deputy general counsel, chief compliance officer, and finally, chief counsel for domestic business. Helping her along at CIGNA was then-General Counsel Carol Petren (featured in Chapter 6), who Jones describes as "a great mentor who helped me develop personally and professionally." After a short stint at Lincoln Financial, Jones returned to CIGNA in 2011, and with the departing Petren providing transitional support, became general counsel.

Jones overcame the more reticent parts of her personality to become a leader, one who continues to be seen as possessing an energetic, can-do attitude and who has no trouble attracting people and opportunity. "It's a matter of projecting the right personality and attitude, and taking the time to reach out and ask for help," says Jones, who praises the many people who have been willing to help her in her career. "It may not always be easy, but a mistake people make is to assume or project negative outcomes. Having a positive attitude is a responsibility—and when things do not work out, people might want to step back from the interaction, look in the mirror, and ask themselves if what they are doing might be affecting the situation."

In fact, according to "The Leadership Gap: What You Need, and Don't Have

> **"Without self-awareness you will not know your strengths and how to use them to your advantage."**
> —MADRID

> **"A key part of the success formula is knowing your strengths and weaknesses and being able to adjust accordingly."**
>
> **—ZOPP**

When It Comes to Leadership Talent," published in June 2009 by the New York–based Center for Creative Leadership, self-awareness is the primary attribute that distinguishes successful leaders. "Self-awareness is one of the keys to acting on your vision," write the authors of *The Female Vision*, citing the CCL report. "Visionary leaders know what they want to achieve, but they also know themselves and have a clear picture of how their actions affect others." In turn, according to *The Female Vision*, self-awareness is something upon which empathy—which the authors see as an indispensable leadership ingredient—thrives. As *The Female Vision* goes on to explain, empathy, "the ability to accurately assess and identify with another person's feelings or point of view," is believed to "operate by means of 'mirror neurons' that pick up signals when other people speak or show emotion, and then simulate a corresponding set of feelings in the observer." Women, in turns out, have "particularly active mirror neuron systems, which may be one reason they are particularly skilled at reading emotional states of others," say the authors. According to a 2008 Pew Research Center survey, women also have **compassion**—a close cousin of empathy, offers Pew—on their side, with 80 percent of Americans believing that women, generally speaking, are more compassionate than men.

Why is this significant for legal leadership in business organizations? In a May 2009 blog titled "Empathy: Not Such a Soft Skill," Katherine Bell, deputy editor of the *Harvard Business Review*, sees "the ability to view situations from the perspective of others" as "a sign of business savvy." She argues that "at all levels of management, empathy is a critical skill. If you can imagine a person's point of view—no matter what you think of it—you can more effectively influence him. Empathizing with your team, your boss, your coworkers, and your colleagues won't make you a pushover—it'll give you more power." Or this, as offered by Lieutenant General William Pagonis, director of logistics during the Gulf War, in his 2001 "Leadership in a Combat Zone" article in the *Harvard Business Review*: "Owning the facts is a prerequisite to leadership. But there are millions of technocrats out there with lots of facts in their quivers and little leadership potential. In many cases, what they are missing is empathy. No one is a leader who can't put himself or herself in the other person's shoes. Empathy and expertise command respect."

For search specialist Marty Africa, of Major, Lindsey & Africa, self-awareness and empathy make a powerful pair of attributes for women general counsel. "Women are more self-aware when it comes to knowing what they don't know and are much more willing to seek coaching or other means to strengthen their deficiencies," she says. "As far as empathy goes, I see that as part of what I call the three C's: courage, **clarity**, and compassion," she continues. "Especially significant is the courage to take on others and have your voice heard, which, taken with empathy, results in good business judgment, imagination, and creativity." Like a reinforced concrete foundation, substantive expertise, self-awareness, and empathy are footings upon which the steel of other attributes can begin to rise.

Moving Parts

In a 2008 story on the changing nature of the general counsel role in a non-U.S.-centric global marketplace, the magazine *Diversity & the Bar* succinctly noted, "The résumé of today's capable general counsel may look very different from that of his or her predecessor." Naming a working knowledge of differences in laws and regulations across countries, a multicultural perspective, and exceptional multilingual communication skills among the "must-haves" in the new global paradigm, the article also chronicles bedrock traits and competencies for any era or economy. Chief among these is the **ability to act as a trusted advisor** to the CEO and the board of directors.

Observing that the role of general counsel today has become far more strategic than in the past, Lee Hanson says that her corporate clients want a *consigliere* for their general counsel; reporting directly to the CEO is considered a best practice.

"The days of calling outside counsel for every single issue are long gone," Hanson says. "CEOs and boards want someone who functions as a business partner." Today's target candidates, she continues, "have impeccable judgment, can think strategically, contextually, and independently, and can issue-spot across a wide variety of practices without having to go outside." No longer playing gatekeeper, today's general counsel is called upon to solve problems at a highly sophisticated level. Strategically speaking, it's one of the job's biggest challenges, boiling down to, as Hanson says, "how do we get it done versus no, you can't do it."

The ability to strategize about how to accomplish things within the organization and for the company is one thing. But then there's the challenge of managing those times when no amount of creativity can save a "yes" from becoming a "no." While SNR Denton's Linda Chaplik Harris says it's important to "go sparingly with the refusals or you will not be successful as general counsel," she concedes that there are times when no is the only right answer, and that "makes being able to distinguish between the 'right' and 'wrong' answer the hardest part of the job." When saying no equals bad news, Bristol-Myers Squibb's general counsel, Sandra Leung, believes in leaving off the sugar coating. "It's about telling the board and the executive team what they need to hear in the context of a given situation," she says. "The challenge is to do this while maintaining respect and authority."

Leung faced such a situation when she had to downsize her company's law department. So did Gap Inc.'s Michelle Banks—as her first order of business after she took the job. "I was responsible for a 20 percent downsizing," Banks recalls. "Being open and direct in communicating the vision and principles behind the realignment allowed me to help guide the department through this difficult process. Not everyone liked the impact, but at least they knew where they stood." This defines Banks's style—no pulling punches, no hiding the ball. As she explains, "If I do not like something, I will say so. It's not about being offensive, it's about being open. Consequently, I feel that that we have a very results- and execution-focused orienta-

> **"It's a matter of projecting the right personality and attitude, and taking the time to reach out and ask for help."**
> —JONES

tion, where it's crystal clear to everyone what the critical path is, and how they're doing, measured against it."

For RR Donnelley General Counsel Suzanne Bettman, what underpins real strategic thinking is the **ability to distill and prioritize,** skills that she developed early on as a corporate associate at Kirkland & Ellis. "My M&A experience, with all its disparate moving parts, has proved invaluable in the general counsel role," she says. "It taught me to never let anything fall through the cracks." Anastasia Kelly concurs. "Distillation and prioritization are very important internally," Kelly says. "In a law firm, clients are prioritized to the attorneys. You only work on what you're going to get paid for, right?" It's a different story inside a corporation. "They're only paying you one salary, and you're going to get inundated with everything," she continues. "So the ability to distill what's important and then prioritize is a critical skill, particularly in the early years of in-house."

Kelly shuns micromanagement. "Part of evolving as general counsel is learning how to delegate, while teaching your subordinates to distill and prioritize and come to you when they need to," she says. Knowing how to manage is a critical part of the job. "You've got to shift your people around and shake things up, as difficult and uneasy as that is for many lawyers," she says, adding that she believes women are better managers than men. "That is just what we do. We are more adept at managing multiple priorities, in terms of seeing what has to be done and then getting it done. Men have a more singular focus—they'll get one thing done and worry about the rest of it later."

Nathan agrees. "One of the gifts that women have is the ability to laser focus on what is important," she says. "Typically confronting a sea of issues in the general counsel role, women by and large are able to hone in on what's really important, as opposed to being overwhelmed by the volume." In this respect, there is no denying the power of the "Mom" factor in the workplace.

Family Ties

In the October 2010 issue of *ABA Journal*, an article titled "Family Ties" provided a compelling look inside the private and public lives of Supreme Court Justice Ruth Bader Ginsburg. "It's ironic that being a parent was what made law school easier for Ruth Bader Ginsburg," the article begins. "For a woman in 1950s America, motherhood was held out as the reason that she shouldn't even have been there." For Justice Ginsburg, though, motherhood provided a happy medium. "I think my life was more balanced," she said of her years as a student at Harvard and Columbia law schools. "I was less apprehensive than my classmates because there was something going on that was more important, frankly, than the law." Of primary importance to her was an insistence on gender equality—which began with her relationship with her husband and with her children. "Their marriage—and the sharing of expectations and parent-

"I attribute to my daughter the responsibility for why I was such a good law student."

—GINSBURG

ing responsibilities—impelled both Ginsburgs to achieve," continues the story. Raising children was a true positive for Ginsburg. "I attribute to my daughter the responsibility for why I was such a good law student," she said. "I went home, played with Jane, had dinner, and then I was ready to go back to the books. It was the pause that refreshes."

While being a mother is obviously by no means a prerequisite to being a successful executive or general counsel, the skills of motherhood can be translated to the job in many ways. In the workplace, mothering can also be the skill set that comforts. "It is not incongruous to be both general counsel and mother, especially when it comes to managing the team," says Avon Products Senior Vice President and General Counsel Kim Rucker, herself a mother. "You have to be able to give people the confidence to make tough decisions, and to leave the comfort of the familiar 'nests.' However, when you see that somebody might need their 'blanky,' you also need to be able to step in and instill a sense of security." Putting on the Mom hat can also be effective when the "kids" are misbehaving. Anastasia Kelly, reflecting on the number of times she has had to smooth out fights between the "kids" at the office, says, "They don't call me Mom for nothing."

Multitasking may be the "thief of time" or, as some of our interviewees expressed in Chapter 1, an essential skill for today's general counsel, but there is little doubt that as mothers, women naturally rise to the multitasking challenge every day. The same prioritization and delegation skills transfer to the office, and keep a pragmatic handle on overall work-life balance. As Kristin van Ogtrop wrote in *Just Let Me Lie Down*, "Working motherhood is nothing if not the ultimate triumph of multitasking over sustained focus. Because I am always doing five things at once, I am never really present. Short of becoming a Buddhist, I'm not quite sure how to change."

Sandra Leung has no illusions when it comes to what she calls the "myth" of balance. "I think most women try to do too much and then feel guilty," she says. "I say just commit to the choices you have made and work and live to the best of your ability." She emphasizes the importance of communications on the home front. "It is important to have a dialogue with your partner so you have some clarity about roles and kids." An interesting side note: Leung cooks meals and does her own housework (on weekends) as part of maintaining her family focus and "to stay humble."

A partner with the Los Angeles-based law firm Alston + Bird LLP, Lisa Gilford is actively involved in many bar, civic, and trade organizations, and has served in a number of leadership capacities, including president (2009–10) of the National Association of Women Lawyers. Routinely moderating panels of women general counsel, Alston says that work-life balance and mothering issues are regular topics of discussion. "Most of the women [general counsel] I've interviewed and interacted with have children and family responsibilities that they have to attend to, so that's a very real dynamic that they have to deal with," says Gilford. "Even when we are talking about substantive work-related information, the subject of families comes up." As in Justice Ginsburg's life, the supporting role of the spouse and the family network—in

"I would figure out where I could add value, and where I should get out of the way so other people could do their jobs."
—MCNAMARA

No Fear of Failing

One key piece of advice that Oracle General Counsel **Dorian Daley** offers younger lawyers is to "look for the challenges and dive right in." In particular, she says, "Don't fear the big uglies." She is referring to the complex litigation that she eagerly sought out as a law firm associate early in her career, distinguishing herself within the firm and establishing a modus operandi that she follows to this day. "I never really had a plan," admits Daley. "It was more a matter of trying new things and learning as much as I possibly could as often as I could." Her method plays especially well at meritocratic Oracle, where taking risks and striving upward are recognized and rewarded, but Daley says that the benefits of taking on substantive challenges are universal. "It obviously helps broaden your skills, while also demonstrating your integrity and sense of responsibility," she says. "Just do your best, and don't be afraid of failing—nobody's perfect."

concert with a woman's enhanced ability to delegate—is indispensable.

"Women general counsel have to meet challenges every day," Gilford continues. "They travel constantly, they oversee global operations, they must be accessible 24/7—all the while having to attend to their families. It becomes more of a juggling act than a balancing one, but just about everyone that I have spoken to, including women law firm partners, has been able to effectively 'network' an extended family to make it all work."

Following a brief stint as general counsel of Enron Global, third-waver Jennifer Vogel joined Continental Airlines as vice president of legal in 1995. In 2001, the carrier named her vice president, general counsel, secretary, and chief compliance officer; like Francesca Maher, then general counsel of United Airlines, Vogel had to deal with a tough post-9/11 regulatory climate and reorganization issues. Interestingly, United would end up merging with Continental, a process in which Vogel was intensely involved before taking early retirement in 2010. Throughout these demanding times, she kept a clear head regarding prioritizing her role as a mother. "Once I had children, I knew I had to make a decision," she says. "Am I going to hide and say I am going to meetings when in fact I am picking up the kids? No. I learned that you just go ahead and state what you are going to do—and you do not apologize for it."

Kim Rucker, when talking about how she took time out of a "hundred-miles-an-hour day" to order the delivery of a Thomas the Tank Engine cake for her son's birthday party, has a different take: "Balance is a work in progress. There's no backing away from the challenging demands and I don't sleep much—but when I do sleep, I sleep well. As my current boss says, I don't make all the kid events, but I make the important ones. I don't make all the work meetings, but I make the important ones. It is about balance and trade-offs." Keeping everything anchored and in perspective is her family—and a mature outlook about what she can and cannot do. "In my twenties and thirties, I had this idea that a superwoman had to be able to do it all by herself," she says. "Now I have learned that you can ask for help."

To Rucker's last point, the willingness—and courage—to ask for help is a classic demonstration of self-awareness and humility. These two essential attributes also go far in underpinning two other vital attributes: **executive presence** and **credibility.**

Working Together

For today's *consigliere* general counsel, being taken seriously is paramount. For one thing, executive presence establishes a level of credibility that can make a big difference when you are delivering hard messages. "Tell an outside lawyer they cannot do something, and they generally get it," says McDonald's Gloria Santona. "Tell a business person inside the company that they cannot do something that is going to make them money, and it is a big deal. I cannot over-emphasize how important it is to learn the skills of influencing and communicating so that when you need to say no, it's respected and accepted." It's also part of why CEOs today are so focused on candidates who have deputy general counsel or at least in-house experience at a public company, says Hanson, because in addition to broad-based, substantive expertise and other skills, CEOs and boards want players with "a proven ability to play in the sandbox with others," something that is often absent from law firm culture. "While most law firms do not require that you collaborate, cooperate, or play nicely with your partners," Hanson adds, "this is very important in companies." And in today's general counsel role, it is not just about playing well but about inspiring, influencing, and leading by example, all of which reinforce the importance of executive presence and credibility as integral parts of the leadership equation.

Now retired, former Washington Mutual general counsel and pioneering first-waver Fay Chapman observed one style of attention-getting early in her law firm career that she knew would not be her own. "These attorneys were table-pounders," she recalls. "If you didn't pound the table enough, you were not being a good lawyer." She encountered a similar problem when she started out at Washington Mutual. "We were in Las Vegas working out loan provisions with this group of table-pounding developers," she says. "They kept telling me how it was going to be and pounding their fists to emphasize their points. I remained firm and polite, telling

> "The ability to distill what's important and then prioritize is a critical skill, particularly in the early years of in-house."
>
> —KELLY

them we would leave if they kept at it. Which they did—and so I gave the signal and walked out with my team. They chased us out into the parking lot, all contrite and apologetic, and then we got the negotiation done. Leadership is not about pounding the table or pushing people away. It is about sticking to your values and drawing people to you."

Leadership is also reflected in **presence of mind**, as Suzanne Bettman learned. Just weeks after becoming an in-house attorney at True North Communications, the company became the target of a hostile takeover attempt. Because she just happened to be standing by a fax machine, Bettman was the first to see the incoming bear hug letter. "I went straight to the general counsel—whom I did not even know yet—and told him that we had to convene the board that afternoon. He thought I was being overly dramatic, but this was a sweet spot of experience for me, and I knew we had to act." As events quickly unfolded, Bettman's swift move was soon validated, and in the aftermath of an intense but successful defense, she had earned the trust and respect of the CEO—key success ingredients for today's general counsel.

Yet, says Hanson, it remains a challenge for women to get the stature and gravitas parts just right. "It's still a matter of walking that fine line between appearing confident and ambitious without being viewed as strident," she says.

For women operating in a man's world, accessing the world of sports can be a strong tool for some in enhancing rapport that can lead to credibility and facilitating cross-group collaboration. In fact, it is a recurrent theme among our interviewees in establishing a collaborative fit with the corporate environment and with male colleagues. Now, as when she was an associate working on deals at Vinson & Elkins, Jennifer Vogel enjoys "marshaling the team and being quarterback." For Pamela Strobel, learning to talk sports was a way of developing her people skills. "I made it a habit to stay connected with what's going on with sports teams and sports in general because I find it a common point of conversation that's helpful in terms of working with other people and, in particular, men," she says. Fay Chapman, who played volleyball at UCLA, subscribes to the time-honored allegory of sports as life: "Participating in team sports gives people skills that are important to carry on into the workplace."

On the other hand, while women have made significant strides in sports at all educational levels in the post-Title IX era, the historical exclusion of women from sports teams may have actually produced a silver lining. As discussed when we spoke with Julie Goldberg Preng, whereas men are anointed leaders within the team setting, women have had to establish their leadership and collaboration skills organically. She comments that "the result is that women have become better accustomed to assessing and deploying people based on judgment and demonstrated results, which are skills that play out especially well in the corporate environment and in the general counsel role."

■

"Just go ahead and state what you are going to do—and do not apologize for it."

—VOGEL

Setting the Stage

As we acknowledged at the beginning of this chapter, our interviewees were able to shed significant light on the various attributes, used individually and in combination, upon which they relied to advance in their careers, and continue to use to flourish and excel as leaders in corporate law departments. While not providing the same depth as their insight into mentoring and risk taking (possibly as a result of humility on their part), their stories gave us some reliable guiding principles about preparing for career and leadership success.

At the outset and in the early days of your career, we could suggest that rather than aiming right for the chief legal officer spot, you will be better served by learning as much as you can, seeking out "transformative" experiences, and generally positioning yourself so that serendipity can find you—and then having the courage and confidence to act when it does. We might also say that one must either possess or acquire a unique set of attributes, and then foster an attitude of constant learning and adaptation by which you enhance, strengthen, and expand those skills. If we were to identify elemental, universal attributes shared by past, present, and future women legal leaders, we might highlight self-awareness and optimism as two premium qualities: the ability to have a rational view of self and surroundings balanced by the confidence and self-assuredness to believe that everything will work out.

The wisdom of embracing mentors, no matter how tangential their support may seem, is all but self-evident. Women (and men) who adopt an openness and vigilance to attracting and nurturing the right types of mentoring relationships with the right people at the right time—or any time—immeasurably improve the number and quality of their advancement opportunities and options. The same goes for networking and fostering outside relationships: inside counsel, outside counsel, business leaders, search professionals, professional associations, industry groups, and more.

Shy from risk, and you can all but forget about becoming a leader or a general counsel. Never to be taken blindly and always to be taken with due calculation, risks, so often synonymous with opportunity, are the gateway to rewards. The successful female general counsel candidate will understand, for example, that while lateral or even downward career shifts may appear riskier than other available alternatives in the short term, such moves often translate into precisely the kind of skills, recognition, and relationships required to move up. To reach the top legal suite today—and then prosper in the role—taking the big-picture view is essential.

Anastasia Kelly has served as general counsel for four different Fortune 500 firms. Save her first posting at Fannie Mae, each of her postings proved monumentally challenging, variously involving Kelly in the triage, surgery, and post-op care of scandals, bankruptcies, and other difficulties. The sum of her experiences has afforded her rare insight into the role that perhaps only peers like Susan Lichtenstein, Christine Edwards, Andrea Zopp, Janet Kelly, and Sara Moss—each of whom has also served

> "Leadership is not about pounding the table. It is about sticking to your values and drawing people to you."
>
> —CHAPMAN

multiple tours of duty—can appreciate. Taking stock of her four decades in law and business, Kelly offers her own set of core career-guiding principles. "First off, you have to know yourself and understand your strengths and weaknesses, just so you can figure out what your skill set is and what you do best," she says.

Risk taking is next, something Kelly is intimately familiar with, having weathered storms at Sears, MCI WorldCom, and most recently AIG. "You have to be willing to take risks," she says. "You've got to be able to look beyond the next day—every little adventure is risk taking." An aspect of personal risk management, she adds, is being able to develop and implement strategies to transcend the fear of failure, which goes with the willingness to admit that you may not know everything. Otherwise, says Kelly, "you make the mistake of trying to act like you know what you are doing."

Important, too, is to constantly expand one's portfolio of competencies and one's professional networks, both inside and outside the company. And then there is the guide that comes entirely from within and cannot be taught: gut instinct, the gatekeeper of good judgment. "That can translate into several things," says Kelly. "Maybe it means leaving a job or finding something else to do. Perhaps it's saying no when everybody else is thinking yes. It goes with integrity, in the sense that it keeps you true to who you are. Whatever the case, it is that inner voice that you listen to and trust."

There you have Anastasia Kelly's way—but will it work for you? Can you copy, emulate, or adapt this particular model to go where she went, or where you think you want to go? Kelly's story offers many actionable clues, insights, and wisdoms, but remember, there is no one path to the top, and Kelly's path, ultimately, is one that she blazed all on her own. To define a variety of models, one or more of which might work for anyone, we spoke with a group of expert front-liners in legal career development, advancement, and transitioning about creating a road map and toolkit that can lead you from the pages of this book to the path of your own success. Their advice starts on page 109. But first, a visit with the Blount sisters.

Courage in Action:
A Conversation with Sally and Susan Blount

When we looked for women general counsel in the Fortune 500 to interview, we found Prudential Financial's Susan Blount. When we looked for outside experts to interview for Chapter 5, we found Susan's sister, Sally, dean of Northwestern's Kellogg School. We sat down with the Blount sisters to discuss courage and careers.

Appointed dean of Northwestern University's renowned Kellogg School of Management in July 2010, Sally Blount is an internationally recognized expert in the fields of negotiation and behavioral decision making, with more than 20 years of experience in higher education. Her sister, Susan Blount, featured in Chapter 1 of this book, has been Prudential Financial's chief legal officer since 2005, having advanced through the company in a series of prominent legal leadership positions.

Sally returned to Kellogg, where she had received her Ph.D. in management and organizations in 1992, from the Stern School of Business at New York University, having served as dean of Stern's undergraduate college, vice dean of the business school, and a professor of management and organizations. Earlier career distinctions included her highly regarded tenure on the faculty at the University of Chicago Booth School of Business and her consultancy role with the prestigious Boston Consulting Group.

A common thread—and abiding passion—that runs through Sally's career is courage. In March 2011, after returning from a Kellogg event in New York that was focused on articulating values critical to the long-term well-being of the U.S. and global economies, Sally posted some thoughts on her Kellogg blog, which included the following reflection on the "nature of courage":

"As I headed back to Chicago on Saturday I reflected on the nature of courage and how it typifies what Pete [Peterson, former Secretary of Commerce, co-founder of the Blackstone Group, and a speaker at the event] and Judy [Samuelson, executive director of the Aspen Institute's Business and Society Program] do. I also reflected on my own career and how becoming a dean, with few direct role models to draw from, had shaped me. And I realized that many times it had forced me to dig deep inside and find a level of courage that I never knew I had.

"Yet I also realized that now, having found that courage, it is not one of those things that stays put. It has to be found again and again—each time I get in front of an audience and take a strong stand, each time I make a tough decision, each time I go home at night wondering if I took too much risk in saying what I said. It pushes me to think hard about how we at Kellogg can create a culture

for our students that makes finding and holding on to courage easier—that makes it easier for each one to learn how to identify and live in a place of personal conviction.

"Equipping leaders with courage matters. Not only is it critical to building business organizations with integrity, it is also critical because the 21st century will need business leaders who will not turn their backs—leaders who will boldly confront unprecedented levels of social and economic inequity, complexity, and uncertainty. Cultivating courage among our students is a mission that we at business schools must take on."

In writing this book, we came to our own perspectives on the nature of courage. It took but a few initial interviews for us to see courage as the dominant—and unifying—theme underlying how the women of this book have been able to reach so far. Well before completing our interviews, we also knew that we had discovered the book's title. Not just our title, "Courageous Counsel: Conversations with Women General Counsel in the Fortune 500" is also our organizing theme and our conclusion, for so profoundly does courage underpin these women's stories and experiences, that it easily announces itself as the foundational characteristic for success in the general counsel role.

Identifying the attribute of courage—any attribute, for that matter—is one thing; translating that attribute into actionable terms is another thing entirely. Therefore, to help codify the anecdotal proof of courage already set forth in this book, co-author Kara Baysinger engaged the Blount sisters, each keenly attuned to the role of courage in her own career, in a conversation about courage in action. From understanding the effect of

power on neural pathways, to interpreting and breaking male schemas, to being curious and gaining the "millimeter advantage," their insight, detailed in the following Q&A, provides a working blueprint of courage for getting to the top—and staying there.

Baysinger: Almost to a woman, our interviewees described confronting opportunities in their careers where risk was involved and where courage was needed to deal with that risk. Noting frequently that opportunity and risk are essentially synonymous, many talked about taking "flying leaps" to move ahead. How does that fit with your view of courage?

Sally Blount: Interestingly, there is not much in the academic literature on courage per se. That said, much has been written on constructs I think we all believe tie into courage. By that I mean the willingness to publicly take risks and, in the process, put yourself in a psychological place of vulnerability, because you could be exposed to failure in a way that other people would observe. In that sense, courage, as you're studying it in this book, is fundamentally social in nature—its success or failure is visible to others. It is the willingness to overcome the status quo and take a stand, or do something in an unexpected or perhaps untraditional way, that is noticed by others and, as a consequence, makes you both materially and emotionally vulnerable.

Baysinger: So could we say that courage is a state of mind?

Sally Blount: That's exactly what Susan and

I have talked about. In order to take a stand that makes you publicly vulnerable, there's an emotional state, a place of confidence, that you need to get to first. It's as though you have to start acting like the person you're becoming before you're quite there. The way you dress, the way you walk into a room, the way you hold yourself, are some of the first steps you take.

Baysinger: Like dressing and acting two jobs ahead of where you are, as a senior advisor told me early in my career.

Susan Blount: A classic example. And another construct I thought of for courage is this: while courage is something you can have too little of, it is also something you can have too much of. To be effective, courage has to be accompanied by good judgment. Rushing headlong at things or acting rashly in the spirit of being courageous can backfire, so it is important to incorporate elements such as balance, patience, fortitude, and perseverance in your "courageous" actions.

Sally Blount: There's courage in the short run, and courage in the long run. You have courageous moments when you speak up and say that hard or uncomfortable or unexpected thing publicly and make yourself vulnerable in a five-minute or 10-minute or hour-long meeting. Then you have actions that require taking risks where you won't see the payoffs for a long time, say weeks or months. That's where perseverance and those other balancing elements tie into it—having the fortitude and grit to stay the course day after day.

Sally (left) and Susan Blount

Baysinger: I understand the vulnerability and the visibility aspects, but especially when we are talking about long-term actions, how do you know you are on the right path?

Sally Blount: That's something Susan and I wanted to talk a lot about—the critical importance of seeking and learning from feedback in career development.

Susan Blount: Itself requiring a certain level of courage and bravery to be effective.

Sally Blount: Right. We often talk about how we both still constantly monitor our environments, because even once you've supposedly gotten the big job, you have to make sure you stay on track. From the psychological literature we know that there's this interesting neural connection to attaining a position of power and how that changes the way you process information. Power, it turns out, can make you less attentive to, and less effective at, the things that got you there in the first place.

Baysinger: Another state-of-mind change, and perhaps not for the better?

FRANK VERONSKY

Sally Blount: There's significant research emerging in neural circuitry showing that certain cognitive capabilities actually get diminished once you attain power, including your ability to be attentive to how you sit in the hierarchy within a room and how you are being perceived.

Baysinger: That's amazing.

Sally Blount: Amazing and stunning, and I believe that it explains some failures that you frequently see in the world. Back to what we were saying before about having too much courage: Susan and I grew up with a very strong father who told us never to overestimate or overthink who we were. He taught us that it is better to be under-calibrated rather than over-calibrated on your talent in the world. To this day, Susan and I both constantly want to be sure that we are never over-calibrated on our effectiveness. While we are actually very different from each other, one thing we absolutely share is actively and continuously monitoring our work performance, seeking feedback on what we are thinking and doing.

Baysinger: From whom do you seek this feedback?

Sally Blount: By cultivating trusted advisors and other people who work with us and are willing to answer us honestly.

Baysinger: And having the self-aware-ness, along with the humility and modesty—all key characteristics iden-tified by our interviewees—to take that feedback to heart, even when it's painful, and adjust accordingly?

Susan Blount: Practically speaking, the dif-ference between getting the top job and not getting the top job is going to be measured in millimeters. Not in inches or feet or yards, but in millimeters. And so if you're getting accurate, insightful, and yes, sometimes painful feedback, that's one way to achieve that millimeter advantage.

Baysinger: Is that millimeter measure even narrower still for women, as compared to men?

Susan Blount: I'm not sure. Interestingly, I remember reading an article about a review of some 10 years' worth of notes from execu-tive coaching assignments which found that the range of acceptable behaviors for women in leadership is narrower than it is for men. For women seeking to be courageous, this makes taking the lessons of good judgment, and under-calibration, and continuous feed-back, especially relevant and important.

Sally Blount: The fact remains that you have to put on the game face to move up, and so back to your comment on self-awareness and changing as you go, I think that's right. One of the things we do know is that one of the key attributes associated with being effective in different cultures—and this goes closely with seeking feedback—is the ability, and the courage, to attune and adjust.

Baysinger: But how does a woman do that when, as Susan said, the range of acceptable behaviors for women is narrower?

Sally Blount: Being an effective leader

means adjusting to the culture in which you find yourself—you have to be able to hear and adjust to feedback. Once you have feedback, the challenge—and this is where the judgment of courage comes in—lies in understanding precisely how to adjust to align with the culture. You have to know on which dimensions you need to match exactly, and which areas are flexible enough to allow for the authentic you. Authenticity is critical—you don't want to become some automaton or replicant of who you really are. Being able to discern the dimensions where matching is critical and others where it is not, and where authenticity is allowed, is very important. It means having a finely tuned scanning ability.

Baysinger: And how do women find that courageous voice and balance in an environment still largely tilted toward men?

Sally Blount: I would characterize the environment—the corporate legal environment—as one where male schemas for interaction remain the dominant model. So for women, the challenge of courage is in understanding and interpreting how to act within and around those implicit boundaries. I do not see it as women trying to be courageous in a male-dominated world. Rather, I think it's a matter of women understanding which of those generally accepted behaviors we must still conform to and which can be let go.

Baysinger: How do you go about breaking down the schemas?

Sally Blount: It's a question of how much you think you can change. I learned early

in my career that there were things that I could change about myself and things that I couldn't. Fortunately, over the past 20 years the world has changed enough that some of the core things about me that didn't match then aren't as important now, and I find that I can be an effective leader while holding on to my core. I'm also very well aware that there are things that I can change about myself and probably should. I'm working on adapting as I move more deeply into this role.

Baysinger: Do you see these schemas starting to soften or break up on their own as today's generation of men and women becomes more aware of and attuned to working together as equals?

Sally Blount: Yes. I think the younger generations are more flexible in how they interact, work together, and get along. They are also better at issues of culture and diversity. So I see the dominant schemas changing over time. Quite honestly, I think one of the reasons that my style works now is that I sit on the cusp. I bridge the generational fault line, where ideas and attitudes about leadership are shifting.

Susan Blount: When I became general counsel almost six years ago, the environment for women was still largely defined by adhering to traditional schemas and behaviors. Looking at the landscape now, though, I would agree that barriers are changing and lowering. That said, women in the legal profession are still dealing with old social habits and unconscious biases, which I think partially explains the 20 percent barrier for

"While [Susan and I] are very different, one thing we share is actively and continuously monitoring our work performance, seeking feedback on what we are thinking and doing."

—SALLY BLOUNT

Sally Blount

Dean, Kellogg School of Management, and Michael L. Nemmers Professor of Management and Organizations at Northwestern University, Evanston, Illinois

Education:
- Ph.D., Organizational Behavior, Kellogg School of Management, Northwestern University
- M.S., Organizational Behavior, Kellogg School of Management, Northwestern University
- B.S.E., Engineering Systems and Economic Policy, School of Engineering and Applied Science and Woodrow Wilson School of International and Public Affairs, Princeton University, High Honors

Previously:
- Advisor to the President and Provost for Global Integration, New York University
- Dean of the Undergraduate College and Vice Dean, Stern School of Business, New York University
- Professor of Management, Stern School of Business, New York University
- Associate Professor of Behavioral Science, Booth School of Business, University of Chicago
- Assistant Professor of Behavioral Science, Booth School of Business, University of Chicago

Other Notable Positions:
- Director of Finance and Planning, Eva Maddox Associates Inc.
- Associate Consultant, Boston Consulting Group Inc.

women general counsel, women equity partners, and so on. I am very involved with the Center for Women in Law at the University of Texas, where this topic is a focal point. The courage quotient aside, women sometimes still face unconscious, unspoken bias in how business, opportunities, and other advantages are handed down. I'd say this is a little more problematic in the law firm environment than in the corporate environment, where we have more structured approach that has helped make this a smaller issue. There is still work to be done before this becomes a non-issue, though.

Baysinger: What do you think it will take to make women the "safe" choice for the top-level, most serious, bet-the-company assignments, and legal leadership in business overall?

Sally Blount: While I think we are still figuring that out, one area I look at very closely in terms of courage is role models of women who are excellent in public speaking. Why? Because that skill is so incredibly important for communicating the implicit sense of gravitas that chief executives and boards look for in their senior male colleagues. What we need to develop in our society are really successful archetypes for what gravitas looks like in older women, and I don't think we are there yet. We need female role models to emerge whom we, as a society, can attach to and associate with the power and the intellectual and political heft that's required for successful

Susan Blount

Senior Vice President and General Counsel, Law, Compliance, and Business Ethics
Prudential Financial Inc., Newark, New Jersey

Education:
- J.D., with honors, The University of Texas at Austin
- B.A., History, The University of Texas at Austin

Previously:
- President and Chief Investment Counsel, Investment Division, Prudential Financial
- Vice President and Secretary, Prudential Financial
- Attorney, Commercial Real Estate Operations, Prudential Financial
- Associate, Kirkland & Ellis

Other Notable Positions:
- Past Chair, Committee of Corporate General Counsel of the ABA's Section of Business Law
- Member of the Board of Trustees, NJ LEEP (Law and Education Empowerment Project)
- Member of the Board of Trustees, Pro Bono Partnership
- Member of the Board of Trustees of Montclair State University
- Member of the New Jersey Commission on Higher Education
- Member of the bars of New Jersey and Illinois

senior leadership in law and business.

Susan Blount: That's right. I don't see that we yet have a model of the senior woman lawyer or senior woman legal leader that can create that association. That's not to say that there are not examples, but given that the number of women who went to law school before, say, 1975, is so small, I don't see that we have a central casting mode in place. We do have outstanding examples, like Judge Judith Kaye, who graduated from law school in the early 1960s and went on to have an incredible career including many years as the chief judge of the New York Court of Appeals, but it's a small group.

Baysinger: What a great example—

Judge Kaye actually provided the foreword for this book.

Sally Blount: That's great. I agree with Susan, though. There is not yet a recognizable, diverse group of archetypes, because many older-generation women still fall within the generation that had to adapt to the fairly narrow range of behaviors that was defined by traditional schemas. It's hard for younger women to identify with those particular archetypes. It's still a narrow band of diversity.

Susan Blount: That brings us back to the importance of courage for women seeking to advance in the profession. In the relative absence of role models, women must have the courage to forge new and different

identities—which is why the feedback and attunement are so very important. How do you adjust and shape yourself to become a leader? It takes courage.

Baysinger: So courage in effect becomes a skill that you learn along the way? What if you are someone who does not necessarily feel that courageous?

Susan Blount: I would suggest that most women lawyers start with a pretty decent dose of courage. They have undertaken a challenging education, they have undertaken a career where they have to learn to say no early on, they have undertaken a profession where you are taught early on in your ethics courses that you're legally required to do very difficult things from time to time. And so yes, I would say that most women lawyers start with the basic tools. But courage is a skill that you have to develop along the way, which may not be easy for everybody, but it's something you have to do. Through a combination of basic components, feedback, reading, and looking at role models both in your organization and in the world at large, you ought to be constantly looking to grow courage as a solid skill—understanding that it is courage with judgment, not recklessness, that you are aspiring to.

Sally Blount: And Susan and I both believe that curiosity is an important part of the courage skill set. Before talking to you, Kara, I spoke with Nick Chabraja, who went from being a great litigator to general counsel to chairman and CEO of General Dynamics. Now retired from that post, he came to Kellogg recently to speak about the benefits of having a legal background in the business world—including the leadership advantage of being an excellent communicator. In our conversation, we got into a long discussion on what it takes to be successful as a lawyer. Curiosity emerged as an important theme, expressed in a number of ways. It means always being willing to get into another person's shoes. It means having a fundamental mind-set of seeking to understand the world around you. It means knowing the client perspective as well as your own, the business issues as well as the legal ones. On the macro-level, it means being well-informed; on the micro-level, it means being self-aware. It means being curious about yourself, in terms of having that finely tuned self-scanning mechanism we talked about before, and how you use feedback to learn from and adjust to your environment. It's about having a fundamental openness to the world while having also deep clarity on who you are, what your convictions are, and what you believe in. And in that, I think, you have your working definition of courage: an amazing capacity for adaptiveness grounded by personal conviction, a skill that does not stay put, but has to be found again and again.

Chapter 5

CONTEXT:

keeping up the pace

What does it take for

a woman to succeed

as a legal leader in the

corporate world? It's the

ability to chart her own

path—and having the

right compass and tools

in hand.

t hirty-three women, 33 individual paths to the general counsel role and beyond, 33 personal success stories, 33 courageous conversations—how will you follow in their footsteps? If we tried to map their 33 individual experiences, we would have cartographic confusion of overlapping and intersecting lines and arrows; if we tried to factor out a formula from the elements of their 33 individual experiences, the result would be positively quadratic.

The fact is that there is no one road map, but rather 33 individual sets of coordinates. With all the illumination and guidance of their experiences and insights, the path to success seems apparent—only to become elusive when you actually try to map it. Creating a map, compass, tools, and action steps that *you* can use is the challenge that we address in this chapter.

Our trove of anecdotal evidence notwithstanding, part of the challenge lies in reconciling the profound changes in the social, corporate, and legal environment over the past four decades. How (and why) women lawyers of the first wave came to the general counsel role is completely different from how their second- and third-wave counterparts arrived at the role, to say nothing of the journey ahead for up-and-comers and future generations.

There are patterns, and consistencies, and immutable truths, of course, along with some unique gender attributes that women bring to the role, but still the conclusion remains: every woman takes her own path to the role.

Defining an accessible, portable, essentially evergreen action plan starts with asking a different question of these 33 life and career stories, as well as the historical antecedents and context in which they exist: What do you need to do to achieve the same results at any time? For this, we asked seven experts versed in legal career and leadership development issues how they would answer the question of what it takes for women to be successful executive-level leaders—and what's stopping them.

Drawn from diverse disciplines, the group of five women and two men includes Ella Edmondson Bell, author, professor, and an authority on career development; Dana Mayer, management consultant and executive performance coach; Jacquelyn Mayfield, career and leadership consultant to the legal profession; Suzanne Peck, executive consultant on managing diversity for competitive advantage; Rayona

Signposts Along the Way

While there is no single path to the corner legal office, the experts we spoke with agree that the following are signposts along the path to leadership, whichever route you choose.

✓ See the big picture	✓ Speak up	✓ Build a strong network	✓ Be flexible
✓ Live the role	✓ Speak out	✓ Identify a sponsor	✓ Be positive
✓ Know yourself	✓ Be seen	✓ Use your sponsor	✓ Be willing to doubt
✓ Be yourself	✓ Know your business	✓ Develop others	✓ Be willing to fail
✓ See yourself	✓ Know the issues	✓ Serve others	✓ Be creative
✓ Sell yourself	✓ Know the landscape	✓ See the "audience's" perspective	✓ Focus
✓ Push yourself	✓ Evaluate the options		✓ Be here now
✓ Let yourself be pushed	✓ Assess the complexities	✓ Be patient	✓ Take control
✓ Toughen up	✓ Enjoy ambiguity	✓ Be persistent	✓ Bounce back

Sharpnack, founder of the Institute for Women's Leadership; Brendan Sheehan, journalist, professor, and former editorial director of the National Association of Corporate Directors; and Richard St. John, author, marketer, and success expert.

These experts readily agree that there is no single path to success. Modestly describing himself as "an average guy who found success doing what he loved," St. John (more on his own remarkable personal record of success later) spent 10 years conducting more than 500 face-to-face interviews with extraordinarily successful people, including Martha Stewart, Bill Gates, and the founders of Google. His interviews were based on one simple question: "What helped you succeed?" After analyzing their responses, St. John found and compiled more than 300 different factors for success. From this database he distilled eight traits that subsequently became the basis for his best-selling book, *The 8 Traits Successful People Have in Common: 8 to Be Great.* Says St. John: "These traits do not represent a formula. Success is still about whatever works for you—it's not like you will be using all eight together. Rather, my aim was to give people an overall guiding structure under which you can build levels up."

The legendary Spanish poet Antonio Machado once wrote, "Wanderer, your footsteps are the road, and nothing more....Wanderer, there is no road— Only wakes upon the sea." For Dana Mayer, this poem is an elegant statement of why it would be foolhardy for any rising woman lawyer to try to emulate any one of the 33 paths described in this book. "The point is you cannot follow in someone else's

> **"Success is still about whatever works for you."**
> —ST. JOHN

footsteps. Every step you take is going to present a whole new realm of options and possibilities for you," says Mayer, who runs her own leadership development consultancy (see sidebar, page 113). "To follow Machado's sea metaphor," she says, "watching a disappearing wake doesn't tell you where the sailor came from."

In our experts' authoritative, multidimensional, and interrelated mix of responses, we found affirmation of practically all of the success attributes and techniques we have come to know from the women featured in this book, along with some surprising redefinitions of what we thought we knew about mentoring and women supporting women. In effect, each shared his or her version of the tools you want to have at your disposal to get the result you want.

We like the image of a toolkit—it's how we ourselves talk about making things work in our professional lives, from opening doors to gaining clients to solving problems. Like Rosie the Riveter—the iconic image of the female factory worker from the World War II era—we are talking about employing real tools of strength and leverage. Becoming a general counsel, or achieving any other significant executive leadership role, and then staying in the job are heavy-duty undertakings.

To put into context the stories shared and lessons learned so far in this book, here are a number of key navigational steps to take and tools to acquire for women wishing to chart their own courageous paths in law, in leadership, and in life.

Being There

What defines a leader? Rayona Sharpnack has been translating this complex question into effective results for women in Fortune 500 companies, government agencies, emerging businesses, and nonprofit organizations for the past two decades. Since founding the renowned California-based Institute for Women's Leadership in 1991, Sharpnack has pioneered an accessible leadership model that has helped thousands of women advance in business. Her groundbreaking work earned her an appointment as chairwoman of Leadership Development for Harvard's Kennedy School, Women's Leadership Board; her accomplishments include contributing to *Enlightened Power: How Women Are Transforming the Practice of Leadership*, and, in 2010, writing her own book, *Trade Up: 5 Steps for Redesigning Your Leadership & Life from the Inside Out*.

The concept of "contextual intelligence" is one of the four essential ingredients Sharpnack cites to help women prepare for success in law, including leadership as general counsel. "This term was coined at the Harvard Business School in partnership with the Kennedy School to name the essential ability of a leader to understand that everything she or he does happens in context," she told us. "That could mean the personal context of their belief system or the macro-context of the economic landscape or the social horizon, but everything is context-sensitive—and preparing leaders with contextual intelligence is a huge wave of the 21st and 22nd centuries."

Dana Mayer:
PolyD Leadership

Dana G. Mayer has interviewed hundreds of C-suite attorneys about how they navigate challenges and make decisions, including the founders of the DuPont Legal Model. She and her team of industrial psychologists, educators, and researchers synthesized the way these leaders' brains work in a multidimensional model, the PolyD Leadership System, which is now used by corporate counsel to develop legal leaders. The following, in Mayer's words, is a preview of that system. For more details, visit www.polydleadership.com.

PolyD Leadership is accomplished by focusing on seen and unseen aspects of a three-part process:

1. **Contextualize:** Both the self and the situation.
2. **Curate:** Including and transcending both public rhetoric and private reality.
3. **Connect:** Making the connections between investment and business outcomes and demonstrating the difference between planning strategy and executing strategy.

The One-Dimensional View of Power focuses only on behavior in decision making, specifically on key issues and essentially only in blatantly observable situations. These often take the form of subjective interests.

The Two-Dimensional View of Power qualifies the First Dimension's critique of behavior and focuses on decision making and non-decision making. It also looks at current *and* potential issues and expands the focus

on observable conflict to those types that might be observed overtly or covertly. But the Two-Dimensional View still only focuses on subjective interests, though those are seen as policy preferences or even grievances.

The Multidimensional View of Power examines how humans think and behave—the complex and often unpredictable aspects of leadership. It concentrates on the decision making in a strategic agenda and control over that agenda. While both current and potential issues are considered, the view is expanded to include both overt and covert observable conflicts, and those that might be latent. Leadership includes both subjective interests and those "real" interests that might be held by those excluded by the management process.

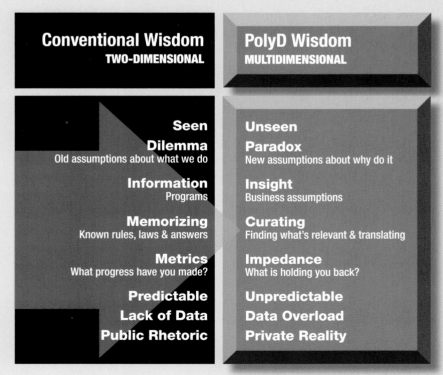

Conventional Wisdom TWO-DIMENSIONAL	PolyD Wisdom MULTIDIMENSIONAL
Seen	**Unseen**
Dilemma Old assumptions about what we do	**Paradox** New assumptions about why do it
Information Programs	**Insight** Business assumptions
Memorizing Known rules, laws & answers	**Curating** Finding what's relevant & translating
Metrics What progress have you made?	**Impedance** What is holding you back?
Predictable	**Unpredictable**
Lack of Data	**Data Overload**
Public Rhetoric	**Private Reality**

While contextual intelligence can be taught (contextual leadership is at the heart of the Institute for Women's Leadership's curriculum) Sharpnack believes that women are more predisposed to the contextual view of life and therefore have the advantage in this area. "Women live more contextually than men do," she says. "It's a more explicit experience for them." By way of example, Sharpnack points to the difference in how women and men talk about training and developing children. "Women will take the systemic, whole-picture view," she says, "while men are likelier to talk about individual activities, like teaching the child how to make a sandwich or drive a car."

What lesson does this provide for those climbing the corporate legal ladder?

"When you hold things in a larger context, you move them from being discrete, separate, disconnected steps or tasks that you stick on a to-do list, into their own independent architecture, their own constellation," Sharpnack told us. "It means being able to think and see in terms of the big picture, which is essential for effective leadership." Contextual intelligence is where stars are born: when you go galactic in the "constellation," you are not just acting like a leader, you are becoming one. "When you see great leaders, they're actually living the role, because they have undertaken to create a leadership context, or identity, for themselves," says Sharpnack, who names business acumen and, as she discusses later in this chapter, the concepts of sales effectiveness and gender intelligence as the other primary ingredients of success.

How does an aspiring leader attain and strengthen these attributes? "First, do a personal diagnostic to assess what you have and what you lack for capabilities," she explains. "Then step back and ask yourself, how am I going to spend my time developing myself? There are 168 hours in a week. How many of those hours are dedicated to self-improvement, professional development, learning, and growing?"

A leader takes personal lifetime responsibility for assessing and upgrading and adjusting herself. As Sharpnack explains, the essential question to answer is, Who am I *being* as a leader? "From kindergarten to graduate school, our educational system is almost exclusively focused on knowing and doing," she says. "Yet I would argue that 'being' is probably the most important critical success factor for any leader, because who you are *being* speaks so loudly and that's what people are attracted to. Yes, there are plenty of smart, capable people, but if who they are *being* is not attractive, people will not follow them, and therefore, they will not be seen as leaders."

"Being" a leader starts with two more essential tools: self-knowledge and self-awareness.

Inner Counsel

As we have seen, getting to the general counsel role is no easy task, and it is not for everyone. While there's the clinical, unemotional version that says you either have what it takes or you don't, it's safe to say that to become a legal leader requires considerable strength—of mind, of intellect, of spirit, of resolve. This is not to say that there is no room for weakness, or deficiencies, or flaws, but whatever the shortcoming—a lack of substantive expertise, a lack of empathy, a lack of courage—a leader accepts the responsibility for fixing it. Leadership, alongside one's career, is a personal obligation—you are in charge of owning, managing, and controlling where and how far you want to go. As Sharpnack noted, it's about being *you*.

From self-knowledge comes self-awareness. It means understanding which strengths you can leverage and which shortcomings you need to address. It means finding your authentic voice and establishing authentic goals, and developing the confidence and courage to know that you have what it takes to be a leader—and if not, if you have what it takes to try. Everybody has different areas where they need more or less work. Only when you know yourself and understand your actions can you gauge how and where you need to concentrate and direct your efforts. Vigilant self-awareness also means you know how you are being perceived and accepted in the workplace by your peers and your superiors.

Ella Edmondson Bell is associate professor of business administration at Dartmouth College's Tuck School of Business and a leading expert in the management of race, gender, and class in the workplace. Founder and president of ASCENT, a national nonprofit organization committed to the professional development and corporate career advancement of multicultural women, Bell co-authored the groundbreaking and critically acclaimed book *Our Separate Ways: Black and White Women and the Struggle for Professional Identity,* followed by her own book, *Career GPS: Strategies for Women Navigating the New Corporate Landscape*, published in 2010.

"Leaders who are truly successful are authentic; they bring their whole selves into the role," she writes on her website. "They have learned to use their cumulative life journey to develop their leadership skill kit, such as courage, empathy, humility, risk-taking, passion, integrity, vision, and most importantly, results. They know the difference between right and wrong." Becoming a leader starts with self-knowledge, which she calls the "first tenet" of leadership. "Knowing yourself builds your confidence and helps ground you. It enables others to trust you and thereby follow you. Knowing, accepting, and liking who you are encourages others to do the same." To know yourself is to know your "special brand of spice," as Bell explains. "It's our spice that fires our creativity, informs our view of the world, facilitates our connections across borders, and enables us to make a difference. What do you bring to the table? Developing yourself will tell you. Besides, you can't develop someone else until you develop yourself. Make no mistake, leadership is about developing others."

Self-awareness is not always easy to manage, though, cautions Bell. "Whether you are busy climbing up the ladder or already in a leadership role, it can be hard to take

> **"Make no mistake, leadership is about developing others."**
>
> —BELL

Joan Williams
Taking Stock

At the forefront of advancing the national discussion on gender, class, and work-family issues, distinguished law professor, legal scholar, and author Joan Williams has unique, multidimensional insights into workplace issues facing both women and men.

In Chapter 1, she discussed how differing gender pressures on men and women, in the context of the requirements of today's business environment, have significantly helped women advance as general counsel. Reflecting on the individual life and career experiences subsequently detailed throughout the book, her key messages for women aspiring to be corporate legal leaders: know the landscape, make astute decisions, persevere—and do not shy away from risk taking.

"As studies show, mistakes are more likely to be noticed and counted against women than they are against men," she says. "This makes women more apprehensive about taking risks that may open them up to mistakes or failures, but as the examples of this book show, you will never get near these top legal jobs if you don't take risks." But one mistake for women to avoid is adopting traditional masculine behavior. "That style does not even work very well for men in legal leadership roles right now," she says.

A resilient mind-set is essential, she continues. "Nobody ever gained one of these jobs without having a string of failures mixed in with their string of successes. If you're going to take your first failure and pack it in, it's not going to work." Women need to think strategically about how to recharacterize a mistake. "Rather than beating yourself up,

think proactively of a mistake as a lesson learned for your company," she says.

With much naturally depending on the given employer, Williams recommends that women clearly understand their work environment. "In some workplaces, the only accepted role for women is as a demure and useful helpmate. If that appears to be the only path to success, maybe it's not the success you want." Acknowledging there are other environments "where women who are politically savvy can survive and strive because competent, assertive women fit just fine," Williams also recommends watching out for workplaces where women are divided into what she calls helpmates—liked but not respected—or "the B-word"—respected but not liked. "This is probably not the place you're going to make your career," she says.

Another red flag is where there are few women—and they are at each other's throats, overtly or in more subtle, behind-the back ways. "One thing to consider is whether they're responding to a message that there's only room for one or a few women and so, of course, they end up fighting with each other," she says. "It's a pattern that exists for women and not for men that is still troublesome."

Cautions aside, her overall view is relatively optimistic. "When I became a lawyer," she says, "I was almost always the only woman, or one of only a few women, in the room. That's no longer the case in many areas of the profession, and while studies show that women have to be more resilient and more politically savvy than men, neither of those is hard to overcome."

that deep breath and actually see what you are doing," she explains. "Self-awareness can go down the tubes and you can lose sight of yourself." Bell adds that women tend to be very critical of themselves, making objective self-analysis difficult. "Focusing on how much you are sacrificing and how hard you are working can also lead to questioning if it is all worth it."

Self-awareness is a career calibration and adjustment tool. "Knowing what your strengths and weaknesses are—and knowing that you can deal with them at least on some level—is very important," says St. John. "Take Chris Anderson for instance, who runs the prestigious TED conferences. He told me he was shy as a kid, and is still shy today. Yet here is a guy who regularly gets on stage and talks to thousands of people. It's an example of knowing yourself—and pushing *through* yourself."

"Push yourself" and "work hard" are two of St. John's eight traits for success, and as evidenced by his own track record, he has been pushing himself all the way. As a member of the scientific team at Nortel Networks R&D labs, St. John masterminded creative production for many of Nortel's largest product launches. In business, he achieved fame, fortune, and high recognition with The St. John Group, his innovative marketing communications company that has long been at the forefront of evolving technology. In life, he has earned a black belt in judo, cycled halfway around the world, run more than 50 marathons on all seven continents, and climbed two of the world's seven summits.

Heady stuff to be sure—but to be an effective leader, St. John says to put the ego aside. "Being self-aware does not mean being self-centered," he says. "I am not saying that many of the people I interviewed for my book do not have big egos, but in a real eye-opener for me, I found most of them to be quite humble." Being too much into yourself is a poor fit for the general counsel or any leadership role. "Success is not just about me, me, me—you have to be able to give of yourself to others."

St. John believes that service is an essential part of how we advance. "In any food chain, you move yourself up by serving whomever is responsible for getting you to the next step," he says. "As a lawyer in business, you are serving both your immediate supervisor and the corporation, so those are the two standpoints that you have to think about—how can I better serve to get to the next step? Face it, people only promote you if you're serving them value. If you're not, you'll stay where you are."

Serving value to others is an elusive concept for today's more self-centered generation, says St. John. "That's the trait that least resonates with young people, who despite seeming to grasp its relevance, still tend to underestimate its practical importance." It's a trait clearly worth adopting, and foolish to ignore. "Many successful, famous people tell me that they willingly put themselves in other people's shoes or bend over backwards to help the people they serve," says St. John. "Those may be uncommon, even uncomfortable practices for lawyers, but law is a service business, and that's how you have to operate."

"People only promote you if you're serving them value. If you're not, you'll stay where you are."

—ST. JOHN

> ### "We don't ask people to cultivate us, and we don't make ourselves available to be cultivated."
> #### —TRAUBER

St. John unreservedly believes that casting egos aside is a lesson for the legal profession as a whole, as well as for would-be leaders, and as we reflected on the personal stories of our women general counsel, it has become clear how "being" and "human" undergird many key success attributes: optimism, humility, empathy, executive presence, and teamwork, as well as self-awareness and leadership.

As St. John acknowledges, however, getting tough is a necessity, if not a prerequisite for leadership. And for women lawyers looking to rise, that means toughening up themselves.

Being Heard

In March 2011, Wharton Women in Business held its second annual Alumnae Conference, in Philadelphia, called "New Models in Women's Leadership: Embracing the Future." Asked one speaker at the event: "What's holding us back? The opportunity is there." In its report on the conference, *Knowledge@Wharton*, the school's online business journal, reported: "The answer—or at least part of it, according to several speakers at the conference—is that women often don't get what they want because they simply don't ask for it."

The report went on to cite studies showing that "women don't negotiate for salaries as often as their male counterparts, they don't network as effectively, and they aren't as skilled in finding or using the essential relationships that would help them successfully climb the corporate ladder. In short, despite more than a century of speaking out, many women in business today still haven't learned to speak up."

"Women don't ask," stated Wharton alumna Priya Trauber, head of women's initiatives at Morgan Stanley and a keynote presenter at the conference. "We don't ask people to cultivate us, and we don't make ourselves available to be cultivated. We have to recognize what our male counterparts have known for years—that relationships matter, asking matters, and you have to make people see you."

That women are "holding themselves back" seems at odds with progress. Women are hardly invisible, with the image of the silenced, socially conditioned woman, at least in the professional world, rapidly fading from view. As we discussed at the end of the first chapter, American women and men are now "overwhelmingly comfortable" with seeing women in the highest positions of leadership in major sectors including law and business. In terms of leadership qualities, women may actually be *more* vocal and visible than men, according to a 2005 joint study from Caliper, a Princeton, New Jersey-based management consulting firm, and Aurora, a London-based organization focused on career advancement for women.

Yet all the studies end up sliding off the end of the equality beam that has 20 percent as its pivot point—the approximate percentage of women general counsel in the Fortune 500 and women business leaders across all major sectors. By that measure alone, women must not hold back at all, but stand up and speak up with greater vigor still. As Mara Swan, then chief people officer for Molson Coors Brewing Co.'s global operations, observed of the Caliper findings, "I believe this study shows that for a woman to become a leader today, she has to fight harder against the status quo, which requires her to be more focused and determined."

Sharpnack offers this spearheading tip: promote yourself. "This may sound funny, but I am willing to fall on my sword by saying that every female lawyer needs training in sales effectiveness," she says. "Whether you are a managing partner in a firm or a litigation lawyer getting parachuted into an array of different situations, understanding sales effectiveness is extremely important." It's a skill for the long run that goes hand-in-hand with career development and advancement. "Can you turn somebody you meet at a cocktail party into a client? Can you sell somebody on hiring you as general counsel? Women lawyers, I believe, should be able to sell themselves and their capabilities over the entire length of their careers."

Having a personal story to tell is important for women advancing against the status quo, especially in dimensions like the public company boardroom, where, in the aftermath of Sarbanes-Oxley and in today's highly scrutinized and regulated world, the role of corporate secretary, especially, has emerged as a new pipeline to the general counsel role. As the former editorial director of *NACD Directorship*, the publication of the National Association of Corporate Directors, Brendan Sheehan has clear insight into the inner workings of corporations and their boards. "The evolving, expanding corporate secretary role in particular is gaining increased attention as a stepping stone to general counsel," says Sheehan, an acclaimed business journalist and expert in governance, risk, and compliance issues.

"The corporate secretary was traditionally a low-profile position, responsible mostly for keeping minutes and certifying corporate documents," he says. "Now, however, it's become more critical and more of an advisory role, focused on legal and governance issues and requiring a level of sensitivity and sophistication that I believe lends itself well to female leadership."

Naming stints in compliance and ethics as other emerging stepping stones to the chief legal officer role, Sheehan acknowledges the growing acceptance of women in senior legal and corporate positions, including in the boardroom. "I think going in-house has become increasingly more appealing to women not only because it can be more interesting and sophisticated than law firms, but because 'the old-boy network' is more alive than ever in firms." To get to the general counsel role—which he sees opening up for women—Sheehan says self-promotion is essential. "First, however, you must have something to promote, so it is important to develop good things to say about yourself," he says. "Be sure to network and develop a strong reputation outside of your organization, and practice talking about yourself, including your life skills."

Affirming some of the key attributes identified by our interviewees, Sheehan also names strong internal and external communications, knowledge of the business, ego-

"You must have something to promote, so it is important to develop good things to say about yourself."

—SHEEHAN

free team- and consensus-building, diplomacy—and simply being a great lawyer—as skills necessary for the general counsel role. "Anecdotal studies show more women becoming board members, which is helping, but only to a point, since typically they are not the ones hiring the general counsel," he adds.

Percentage-wise, women's gains in the boardroom are roughly in line with their leadership in business and law. According to the 2010 NACD Public Company Governance Survey, the average board has 8.3 members; in terms of gender composition, 31 percent of respondents revealed all-male boards, 36 percent had one female director, 22 percent had two female directors, and only 10 percent had three or more female directors. Progress, yes, but in the boardroom and in the C-suite as in the general counsel's office, the need for more courageous conversations remains statistically—to say nothing of culturally—clear.

Having something good to talk about is important, but as credible and compelling as your story may be, and as courageous and determined as you may be in telling it, there remains the pervasive hurdle of how what women say is heard, interpreted, and accepted. It's the subject of Deborah Tannen's best-selling book *You Just Don't Understand*, in which the internationally acclaimed author and linguistics expert explores how and why, as the *Chicago Tribune* put it, "the sexes collide in communication." Tannen provides a vexing view of the complexities of conversation between men and women. For example, when speaking in front of men, women feel that they are "onstage," insofar as they feel they must watch their behavior more. Because men and women regard the landscape from contrasting vantage points, the same scene can appear very different to them, frequently producing opposite interpretations of the same action. Following behavior learned early in life as boys, men establish themselves as individual leaders by giving orders, whereas women, as girls, focus on consensus-building and thereby increase the power of group or community leadership. More perversely, language can be used to keep women in their "place."

How women deal with this issue is what Sharpnack calls "gender intelligence." "It is important for women to understand and know the paradigm, and the language, and the conversation and the dynamics that happen in a man's world versus the woman's world," she says, offering this example of how a woman's vantage point can steer her wrong: "Let's say there's a job opening with five criteria. If a woman feels that she does not have all five, even if she is missing just one, she will typically think that she is not qualified. A man, on the other hand, having just one of the same criteria, will feel qualified and raise his hand. It's an example of this inculcated gender dynamic that can impact career development for women—and why being intelligent about gender dynamics is so important."

That does not mean, however, that women should not assertively define themselves against inculcated societal and gender dynamics, or the status quo. Back in Chapter 1, Linda Madrid replied to a male CFO's snide comment about her pants

There is an "inculcated gender dynamic that can impact career development for women."

—SHARPNACK

suit by saying, "I didn't realize you had to see my legs for me to be dressed appropriately." In Chapter 6, you will read about a comparable return of serve from former CIGNA General Counsel Carol Petren, when as a young litigator, she was addressed as "honey" by her opposing counsel. She quick-wittedly answered back by calling him "turtle dove." For Dana Mayer, these are perfect examples of women shifting from traditional obedience and social conditioning to what she calls "majority citizen" status. "Women need to stop apologizing and explaining why they need that raise, that promotion, that recognition—and expect it, just as men do. We are not an insignificant group still searching for that 'vote and voyce.' We are a majority of the citizens," she says.

Changing from "Jane Doe to majority citizen" is one of the transformational shifts contained in what Mayer calls her "poly-dimensional leadership model" (for more details on PolyD, see sidebar, page 113). It is also a call to action recommended by Jacquelyn Mayfield, founder and president of Boston- and New York City-based Mayfield Consulting. "Women need to stand up and take credit for who they are and what they do, and not just be the peacemaker and moderator," says Mayfield. Built upon a career foundation that includes positions in the U.S. House of Representatives, the White House, and *Time* magazine, Mayfield's business experience includes developing and implementing worldwide marketing communications strategies for Mobil Oil Corp., and as a former executive leadership consultant with the leading executive development organization KRW International. Focused on attorney retention through Mayfield Consulting, her compassionate, custom-designed approach to career development coaching helps lawyers avoid early career attrition and make smooth, effective transitions on their way up.

"It is important for women to preserve their sense of integrity," says Mayfield. "Learning to say no is one way; learning to have fun is another." Again, the emphasis should be on the self and creating the authentic *you*. "It's about defining what is important to you and how you want to spend your time and energy," continues Mayfield, who feels that managing career transitions, including for maternity leave, is one area in need of improvement. "I believe in creating a life dashboard, so you can see, understand, and manage your priorities. It is important to learn how to take care of yourself, have a sense of humor—and not live governed by guilt or social conditioning." Continuous learning is a key tenet of her teaching. "Keep learning so that you always have new ideas and perspectives to contribute." It's an approach shared by Bell. "Nowhere to go right now?" Bell asks. "Even in hard times there are options. Learn a lateral skill, such as accounting, so when the company is firing on all engines again, you will impress through the breadth of your knowledge."

Standing tall and speaking up, achieving independence from inculcation, and moving the social and professional pivot from 20 percent to center, forging ahead and not holding back, learning continuously—all essential steps for women who want to

> **"Women need to stop apologizing and explaining why they need that raise, that promotion, that recognition."**
>
> **—MAYER**

lead. How do you put these into action to get the results you want? It takes patience, persistence, laser focus—and the courage and confidence to change.

Be Here Now

Every conversation about creating success must also talk about dealing with failure. "All successful people fail," says Richard St. John. "Of course it helps to be successful as much as you can, but it does not hurt to fail, either." It's a lesson that St. John learned from his interviews with more than 500 extraordinarily successful men and women across a wide range of fields and disciplines. "A common refrain was the perception that success came quickly and easily to them," he says. "Then they list all of their failures."

It takes time to succeed in anything, leaving plenty of room for failures and setbacks. "It took Einstein 10 years to come up with $E=mc^2$. It took the BlackBerry guys 10 years to develop their technology. It took the Google founders 10 years to get the Google search engine to be a success. The list goes on and on and on," St. John says.

The legal profession is no different. "It probably takes 10 years just to get through law school and then all those internships and clerkships and associate positions before you actually get out there," says St. John. "Then it takes another 10 years before you start becoming eligible for higher-level management-type roles or senior decision-making strategy roles. Whatever their career goals and aspirations, young women entering the profession must ready themselves for a long-term process."

St. John is frequently asked why goal setting is not included in his top eight ingredients for success. "Having a goal, like taking a risk or meeting a challenge, is not a primary attribute," he explains. "It's an option that you can take based on your situation or your environment. Typically, goals, risks, and challenges are just ways that we push ourselves." Pushing yourself, however, is on his list—it's how you drive through and take control of issues and obstacles—and it goes hand-in-hand with another one of his top eight attributes, persistence.

Eligibility for the Fortune 500 general counsel role takes persistence, patience— and the ability to handle failure. "If you fail, make sure you crash and learn. Don't crash and burn," says St. John. "Make failure your school, not your funeral."

Women may possess much hard-won wisdom that provides advantages for leadership, but becoming general counsel is rarely a birthright and never a gift; persistence is what turns raw talent into effective leadership. Didn't win that case? Figure out what went wrong and go tackle the next one. Missed that promotion, even though you were eminently well qualified and had all your ducks aligned? Move on to the next target. Unforeseen consequences got in the way? Chart a new path.

St. John has a word that goes with persistence: CRAP. Actually, it's his acronym for "Criticism, Rejection, Assholes, and Prejudice" (or in some cases, Adversity and

Prejudice), and while drawn agnostically from his many sectors and industries of inquiry, each of these has particular resonance in the legal profession. Criticism is an inherent part of legal training. Rejection looms at every turn. "When you see the very long list of successful people who were rejected more than once in their lives, it makes it a lot easier to take!" declares St. John, noting that "Einstein was rejected three times for a Nobel Prize." "Assholes"? "That's actually more of a joke than anything, but I have plenty of successful leaders who use that term, so it went into my research," says St. John. "Really, though, I am talking about prejudice, which, along with criticism and rejection, is something that people, women more often than not, are going to encounter and have to persist through. Why? Because these are all things that you have no control over. Right or wrong, these are things that come entirely from other people that you have to persist through."

St. John distinguishes between push and persist: "Push is more about dealing with personal, internal obstacles, like shyness or self-doubt, that you have some control over. Persistence covers areas over which you have no control, and which can cause you to fail through no fault of your own. Push is a short-term concept—do it today. Persistence, though, is about the long term."

Another key facet of persistence is one of its more refined parts, and categorically one of the most essential requirements for actually performing the job of general counsel: the ability to focus. In Chapter 1, legal search specialist Marty Africa said that "if you want to do the [general counsel] job properly, you have to be laser-focused and maintain a real clarity of analysis." It bears repeating that Africa was speaking against multitasking in this regard. As defining an aspect of the modern zeitgeist as they come, multitasking is shorthand for doing many things simultaneously in rapid fire. For the effective, successful general counsel, however, multitasking on the job may be anything but a best practice.

"It's a matter of knowing what you can multitask at and what you can't," says St. John, who has "focus on one thing" on his list of ways to be great. "You can be on a nonessential phone call while also looking at a spreadsheet, making a to-do list, and figuring out your weekend plans. But for the things that really matter—the mission-critical work—you need a "Be Here Now" philosophy. This is where you focus intensely on one thing for a short period of time and then are able to quickly shift to another task with the same singular, defined focus."

Being able to put your head down and concentrate on getting things done one at a time is a skill that takes patience and persistence to develop and maintain. It's akin to an intense athletic contest without timeouts where you can stop, catch your breath, and unwind before retaking the field. As Oracle's legal chief Dorian Daley observed, general counsel is a "24/7, always switched-on role." It's why mothering, the ultimate form of short-attention-span theater, interplays so well with being general counsel for women. As described in Chapter 4, it's what allowed Avon Products General Counsel Kim Rucker to twice step out of an intense board meeting, the first time to ensure

> "It helps to be successful as much as you can, but it does not hurt to fail, either."
> —ST. JOHN

Which steps do you take to reach the office of general counsel in the Fortune 500? As the women of this book have taught us, it's many steps along many different paths, with every new set of footsteps different from the last. Same story from the experts who have contributed their perspectives in this chapter—it's a long road to the top, with many possible options and avenues to pursue. But that's ultimately good news, because there's nothing like having opportunities and the power of choice. From their many recommended steps, here are some sure-footed ways to advance as a corporate legal leader.

ELLA EDMONDSON BELL

- Understand company culture and politics
- Know the business
- Develop relationships and a "constellation" of people around you
- Seek out other women for support
- Find a sponsor to advance your career
- See the multicultural context beyond your own experience
- Own your path

DANA MAYER

- Every career path is different. Focus not on following other's footsteps, but on creating your own
- Know that every step forward creates new options and possibilities. The reality you face today is not the same as others have faced in the past
- Shift from traditional social conditioning—women define the talent market just as men do
- Don't apologize for being who you are
- Programs don't develop people; experiences do

JACQUELYN MAYFIELD

- Have a sponsor—someone who will "own" getting you ahead
- Take credit for what you do
- Learn to say no
- Develop relationships and a support network
- Create a life dashboard— define your priorities
- Keep a sense of humor, and don't lose your sense of integrity
- Take care of yourself— and live guilt-free
- Keep learning—always have new ideas and perspectives to contribute

delivery of a Thomas the Tank Engine cake to her son's birthday party, the second to confirm that the cake would be light blue, without skipping a beat in her "hundred-miles-an-hour day."

Perk Up Your Ears

It can get pretty rough out there in business and law. Adept as you may be at shifting that laser focus from one task to the next, unpredictable, unforeseen, and unfamiliar

SUZANNE PECK

- Stand tall, speak up
- Embrace change:
  - Sniff Out the Situation— take a deep breath and take it all in

  - Perk Up Your Ears—listen closely for different and useful perspectives

  - Take a Bite—even a small one, and test new approaches

  - Bark Smart—perfect your pitch for the best possible outcomes

  - Focus on Mutual Success— build up your pack and ways you can help each other succeed

RAYONA SHARPNACK

- Be contextually intelligent—everything is context-sensitive
- Be gender intelligent— women's language and dynamics are different than men's
- Sell yourself—train in sales effectiveness
- Have strong business acumen—know the business inside and out

BRENDAN SHEEHAN

- Be a good communicator, internally and externally
- Be a good team builder and people organizer
- Be diplomatic
- Promote yourself—have a good personal story to tell
- Know the business

RICHARD ST. JOHN

- Be passionate about what you do
- Work hard
- Focus intensely on one thing at a time
- Push yourself
- Come up with good ideas
- Keep improving yourself
- Serve others something of value
- Persist

events, from shareholder lawsuits and market downturns to shifts in job responsibilities and physical relocations, can make you feel like you are a dog chasing your own tail. It is that uncertainty and volatility that author, teacher, and diversity expert Suzanne Peck addresses in her 2011 book *Ruff: A Lost Dog Tale*, a cheerful canine parable about corporate and personal change management, which she co-authored with branding expert Penelope Wong.

As founder and president of Santa Barbara, California-based Peck Consultants, Peck has worked with Fortune 500 companies including General Electric, The Walt

Disney Co., and McDonald's (a client for more than 30 years) on managing diversity for competitive advantage. Her past experiences include 18 years as a principal and diversity practice leader at the global management consulting firm Towers Perrin, where she also managed the human resources and communications line of business for the firm's Chicago office. Peck is also founder of the Corporate Diversity Alliance, a network representing 28 Fortune 500 companies committed to the successful integration of diversity initiatives and promoting diversity in the Chicago area. She's completing Stand Tall, a multimedia package to prevent harassment in schools.

"Lawyers are trained to be conservative and rely on precedent, but as a lawyer in business and in the Fortune 500, you must be open to embracing and creatively working through change," says Peck. "It's about having the ability to think and work through change in a positive and strategic way." Her prescription for change management reads like a synthesis and encapsulation of all the essential attributes shared in this chapter so far—starting with speaking up and standing tall.

"To be an effective leader in the Fortune 500, your voice and ideas must be heard, yet too many women are tentative about engaging in the conversational process in a bold, committed way," she begins, acknowledging that this is not necessarily easy or natural for many women. "Not many women are born psychologically and verbally ready for the corporate environment, so these are strengths you must be prepared to develop, even if it goes against the grain of how you were raised as a girl. An affirmative mind-set is key—stand up for what you believe in, by all means interrupt and take credit where due, know your own strengths, and never let them see you sweat."

Change can be about going with the flow, but more often than not it means getting out of comfort zones and static, frozen, or dead-end scenarios "Sniffing out the situation" is Peck's first strategic step to making a change for the better. "With so many different things happening within an organization at any given time, know the landscape and environment before you jump to a solution," she says. "Take time to assess the complexities of your problem. Perk up your ears to listen for different and potentially useful perspectives—hearing from people with different backgrounds and viewpoints can help you consider different strategies before you make a move, or help you if you are stuck in your thinking or decision making."

Next, take a bite. "This goes with having the courage to speak up," continues Peck. "Women tend to hesitate in expressing a viewpoint if they are not completely sure of themselves. You have to be willing to take some risks, though, so whether it means volunteering for something unfamiliar or trying a new approach to solving a problem, take that bite. Even one little chew can open up a whole new world of possibilities." Like risk taking, though, forethought and calculation are important before speaking up. Peck calls it 'barking smart," her version of how women can effectively negotiate the disparities in how their words and language are interpreted by men.

"Be sure to look at any situation through your audiences' perspective, and frame your pitch to support their priorities," says Peck. "For women especially, this means packaging and modifying your message for the best outcome." Here again, business acumen is an important factor. "Being perceived as somebody who knows the critical issues facing the company is essential. Speaking the language of business—the financials, the marketplace, the customers—will make you appear relevant and credible."

Lastly, don't be a lone wolf—"build up your pack," Peck says. "A focus on mutual success and benefit, I believe, is very important for women. When you build a strong network and team, you are using each other's unique strengths to create positive outcomes for everybody, while also generating sponsors and endorsers who can help advance your career." It's a strong echo of Deborah Tannen's view of women's natural inclination toward group or community leadership over individual power—and whether they be male or female, having that endorser or sponsor is an especially important ingredient of success.

The Last Glass Ceiling?

In the beginning of our chapter on mentoring, we quoted Ida Abbott from her book *The Lawyer's Guide to Mentoring*. "A mentor is a person who helps a lawyer develop professionally to achieve the lawyer's desired professional goals, and mentoring is the process by which the mentor and protégé work together to identify and help the protégé work towards those professional goals," she wrote.

As we also noted, Abbott's classical definition of mentoring as a "one-on-one relationship between an all-powerful elder teacher and a neophyte who is taught, nurtured, and protected" carries a significantly more multifaceted and far less hierarchical meaning today. This is especially true of the super-breed produced by the continuing evolution of the mentor-mentee dynamic: the sponsor.

"A sponsor is someone who will 'own' getting you ahead," says Jacquelyn Mayfield. "Identifying a sponsor is a very strategic undertaking, but it's a must-have if you want to get to the top, and something that more top companies are focusing on." Closest to the traditional definition of mentor as "champion," sponsorship is not a new concept, but it has a hot new relevance in today's environment. Whereas our first- and second-wave women general counsel would have relied all but exclusively on champions and other mentors to get to the top—save those instances where a chief executive or outgoing general counsel provided the sponsorship "push" in their final leg of ascendency—sponsorship has assumed increasing relevance for the third-wave and up-and-coming generation.

According to Rayona Sharpnack, sponsorship is especially critical for women prone to self-limiting thinking. "Let's say a well-intentioned male supervisor informs a female 'mentee' about a job opening in the litigation department, and tells her to go for it," she says. "At that point, the man will consider his job done.

> "Look at any situation through your audiences' perspective, and frame your pitch to support their priorities."
>
> —PECK

What typically follows, though, is that the woman starts questioning her qualifications for the job, or if she even wants the job in the first place, which eventually results in her letting the opportunity languish." When you have a sponsor, however, the outcome is very different.

"Sponsorship has a different orientation than mentorship," continues Sharpnack. "It's much more of an advocacy role, like the old boys' club where somebody took you under their wing and fought for you. They could be your worst critic, but they were also your biggest fan, because they had decided that you were going to make it to the top, and they were going to have your back all the way." Another definition comes from Priya Trauber, head of women's initiatives at Morgan Stanley, as quoted in *Knowledge@Wharton*: "A mentor is someone who advises and helps you think through issues, problems, the good and the bad. A sponsor is someone who helps you get paid, gets you promoted, gets you hired—they're in the room when the decisions are being made."

Richard St. John has his own particular view on the mentoring dynamic. "Many successful people I talked to said they did not have mentors, but instead had what I call tormentors, or people who told them they would not be successful." While seeing both mentors and tormentors as effective, St. John has a reservation about the former. "In all my interviews, I could not find one single instance of somebody praising their mentor for pushing them. I think there is this notion that having a mentor will make your life easier. All you have to do is find a mentor, and then he or she will tell you what to do and where to go and pat you on the back. But people need to be pushed, and so I think the concept of someone who is not necessarily nice to you and pushes you hard when necessary, [what others have referred to as the sponsor model] can be very effective."

Nice and soft is out, and women still hidebound by traditional self-limiting thinking like "I'm not qualified to do that" or "If I do a good job they'll notice and promote me" need to adapt to the more active, aggressive—and, as Mayfield noted, strategic—approach to seeking out and soliciting sponsors. In fact, one of the up-and-coming women lawyers (see page 133) we interviewed for this book told us as much: "I wish I would have been more sensitive to the sponsorship thing and more focused on the politics of getting the job I wanted," she said. "Had I done those things, I probably would have gotten it sooner."

Securing a sponsor is yet another area where women need to speak up; however, like all other equality metrics, access to sponsorship opportunities is not in women's favor.

Published in December 2010, "The Sponsor Effect: Breaking Through the Last Glass Ceiling" is a *Harvard Business Review* report that examined the disparities between sponsored men and women in corporate America. As Sylvia Ann Hewlett, founding president and chairman of the New York City-based nonprofit think tank Center for Work-Life Policy, notes in the executive summary:

> "When you have a sponsor, the outcome is very different."
>
> —SHARPNACK

"Women just aren't making it to the very top. Despite making gains in middle and senior management, they hold just 3 percent of Fortune 500 CEO positions. In the C-suite, they're outnumbered four to one. They account for less than 16 percent of all corporate officers, and comprise only 7.6 percent of Fortune 500 top earner positions. What's keeping them under this last glass ceiling? What we uncover in this report is not a male conspiracy, but rather, a surprising absence of male (and female) advocacy. Women who are qualified to lead simply don't have the powerful backing necessary to inspire, propel, and protect them through the perilous straits of upper management. Women lack, in a word, *sponsorship*."

According to the study, men are 46 percent more likely to have a sponsor than women are. Why? The answer lies in a mix of factors that women can control, and social and attitudinal forces beyond their control. In terms of controllable factors, women are failing to access or make good use of sponsorship. As the report explained, even women "who do grasp the importance of relationship capital fail to cultivate it effectively. While they're happy putting favors into others' banks, they're squeamish about cashing in on those deposits, lest they appear to be self-serving— or for fear they'll be turned down." Furthermore, "many feel that getting ahead based on 'who you know' is an inherently unfair—even a 'dirty'—tactic. Even as they're passed over for a plum assignment, a pay raise, or a promotion, they persist in believing that hard work alone will succeed in turning heads and netting them the reward they deserve."

As for factors beyond their control, women have "ample justification" to be fearful, reluctant, and squeamish. As the report explains, if, for example, a young, unmarried woman spends substantial offsite and after-hours time with a older, married male sponsor, it can look like they're having an affair. Any promotion she then gains becomes the subject of more speculation and gossip, including questions about its integrity and legitimacy. The report concludes, "…because sponsorship can be misconstrued as sexual interest, highly qualified women and highly placed men avoid it."

There are other "traps" as well. As the report notes, because they are subject to greater scrutiny than men, women "must scale a higher bar on a number of fronts… and navigate a minefield of unspoken judgments with regard to their personal lives." Held to the highest standards of "executive presence" in their dress and bearing, women are often simply not told when they "get it wrong." Married with children creates the assumption that women are "less available, less flexible, and less dedicated to their work"; unmarried and childless is equated with "not quite normal" and "threatening." As Dana Mayer points out, the sum of these prejudices and assumptions is devastating: women are invariably branded as "not quite leadership material" for a set of intangible and hard-to-dispel reasons.

On a far more encouraging note, however, as Mayfield mentioned, some of America's leading companies are prioritizing sponsorship. As noted in the "Sponsor Effect" report, such companies as American Express, Cisco, Deloitte, Intel, Morgan

> "Cracking the glass ceiling will give [women] significant competitive advantage in talent markets the world over."
> —MAYFIELD

Stanley, and Unilever are "making significant investments in creating pathways to sponsorship for their standout women." The report adds that these companies "understand that cracking this last glass ceiling will give them significant competitive advantage in talent markets the world over."

This takes us back to Dana Mayer's concept of women shifting their self-definition and actions from "Jane Doe" to "majority citizen" status. As more and more women enter the business and legal professions, and as they continue to rise in greater numbers as leaders across all sectors, not only women, but society itself needs to see that women define the talent market as equally as men do. As Mayer notes, "In her keynote address at the 1976 Democratic National Convention, Barbara Jordan famously said that, 'This country can ill afford to continue to function using less than half of its human resources, brain power, and kinetic energy.' That was more than three decades ago—and when you consider events like the recent economic meltdown, you can only wonder what difference gender equality in the workplace and especially in leadership might have made."

If sponsorship is indeed, as *HBR* has noted, the "last glass ceiling," then women must become more forceful and proactive in asking for sponsors—along with salary raises, promotions, chances to lead, and practically every other category you can think of—to strike the right vocal pitch and decibel level to bring it down for good. Hesitancy born of uncertainty, timidity, and social conditioning, on the other hand, will remain the whisper that needs to be confronted and silenced, and yet another barrier that only courage, the bedrock of success, can bring down.

Shining Examples

When a group of men refused to stop pounding the negotiation table in front of her, former Washington Mutual General Counsel Fay Chapman ushered her team out of the room until the men came outside, apologized, and changed the nature of their interaction. Stuck in a secure but stultifying job as a law firm litigation associate, Louise Parent pulled up stakes and took a bottom-rung job in American Express's legal department. After advancing in the company from there, her next risk-inflection point came in accepting an uncertain-seeming lateral move to a subsidiary and then, further along in her career, taking on a risky hot-potato project that nobody else wanted to touch—the recognition for which saw her appointed as the financial giant's general counsel. Before she became general counsel of UPS, Teri Plummer McClure, frustrated and contemplating leaving the company, relocated her family to take on an unfamiliar non-legal assignment in one of the company's operational centers. One of our interviewees took a stand against a lecherous law firm partner on her way up; another found the strength to overcome sustained sexual harassment in one of her earlier jobs. And when two United Airlines' jets went down on 9/11, the company's then general counsel, Francesca Maher, who had lost her husband to illness just three months earlier, stayed at her post and led with vision through the tragedy's aftermath.

Courage. It's what ties the stories of this book together. It's our title, governing theme, and conclusion—and it's the common bond shared by women counsel who strive to lead. It takes courage to stand tall and speak up, it takes courage to know yourself, it takes courage to persist and push on through, it takes courage to change.

At the beginning of this book, we quoted Clarence Darrow's comment to a group of women lawyers: "You can't be shining lights at the bar because you are too kind. You can never be corporation lawyers because you are not cold-blooded. You have not a high grade of intellect. I doubt you could ever make a living."

How wrong he was. As highlighted throughout this book, women were beginning to shine at the bar even in Darrow's time, and have continued to shine ever since.

Still, ironically, even courage has its limitations.

"There is still the double standard that women who are ambitious are seen as power grabbers and acting outside the confines of good behavior, while men who do that are seen as go-getters," says Sharpnack. "So there's always a chance of getting penalized by being more overt about your ambitions. Imagine how many more women would be in general counsel spots if they were able to make their aspirations and intentions clear from the beginning, as opposed to waiting around to get noticed because they were doing a good job."

In terms of other barriers specific to women in the legal profession, Sharpnack sees the persistence of stereotyping. "Perhaps less so for a general counsel than for a litigator, but the personality preference in hiring seems to be for pit bulls and barracudas who may not have the best social skills but can hammer down defendants and the like," she says. But she also wonders why women, especially those thinking about starting a family, would want the job in the first place. "How many women want to sign up for a 70-hour-a-week job when they're in their child-bearing years, knowing that it's not a sustainable model for getting pregnant and raising a family? I think those are also areas that women have to address for themselves."

Mayfield is encouraged to see more women helping and mentoring women. "Many women do not dedicate enough time to relationship building," she says. "In particular, it is valuable to develop a circle or 'fellowship' of women for mutual support, guidance, and sponsorship."

In her book *The Twisted Sisterhood,* author Kelly Valen comments on the complexities of female relationships, issuing a call for women to "respect, tolerate, support" one another. While she acknowledges that "it's doubly tough to quit behaviors that are routinely encouraged, validated, made light of, and excused or downright rewarded," as both an author and a lawyer, she encourages working women to "start supporting your female colleagues, mentor them, show them the ropes, guide them through….There is really enough pie for you both. And, if there isn't, you can join forces and make more pie."

"There is still the double standard that women who are ambitious are seen as power grabbers and acting outside the confines of good behavior."

—SHARPNACK

Ella Edmondson Bell—who had tormentors rather than mentors as a young girl growing up in the South Bronx, in the form of teachers who told her she would never be good at anything—underscores this point. "Advancing in a corporate structure is all about relationships," she says. "Know the culture and the politics, the business and the clients, the kingpins and the up-and-comers—so you know where the relationships are." Bell says to forget about just working hard and waiting to be recognized. "It's not enough to assume your effort will speak for itself—performance is a given. You have to socialize with the decision makers. It might not mean you have to pick up the golf clubs, but you do have to figure out what works in your own organization."

Barriers aside, courage is a tenacious and determined driver, and the fuel for much optimism as courageous women counsel continue their uphill climb. "My research has proven that women have more integrity and a higher ethical code, which favors their smooth transition into important emerging leadership roles such as the corporate secretary," says Sharpnack. "That's one example of changes in the landscape that plays to a woman's strong suit and, along with the number of women now coming out of law school, a reason I think we are going to see a difference in the profession ahead."

Suzanne Peck is also confident about the future. "The old-boy network is alive and well in corporations, and women still have to adapt to male-dominated parts of the corporate culture, such as on the golf course or in speaking intelligently about sports," she says. "More critical mass in terms of numbers will help women. There is a huge difference between there being one woman in a given situation and having two or more, and while it will still take time, eventually women will have an equal place in these business and legal roles."

Future General Counsel of the Fortune 500:
Women on the Rise

For the top female corporate lawyers in the U.S., 2011 represented a banner year. Women reached an all-time high of 101 general counsel in the Fortune 500, with 82 female chief legal officers at 82 Fortune 500-1000 companies, up nine companies from MCCA's 2010 survey and up four from the 2009 survey. In 2011, reports MCCA, other measurable impacts included women leading the legal departments of 12 of the top 50 most-profitable companies in the Fortune 500, along with two of the 10 fastest-growing companies, most notably Kathleen Mahoney at No. 2 on that list: Nash-Finch.

Reassess these numbers as percentages and the brightness dims a degree or two, but only momentarily, for we are still talking about the math of significant and continuing progress—and for the women lawyers of today and tomorrow, the calculus of continuing hope, perseverance, and courage.

Who are the "up-and-comers" destined to join the current and future waves of women general counsel at America's top public companies, and what does it take to get there in today's environment? We identified 12 women legal leaders at a mix of public and private companies who we think have what it takes to become chief legal officers in the Fortune 500 and asked them for their insights and perspective. True to our overall findings about the women in this book, each found her own path to success, while all agreed on one thing: whether or not you have designs on becoming a Fortune 500 general counsel, you have to take personal charge of your career to make it to the top.

Deborah Bello
Vice President and Chief Legal Officer, Insurance, Prudential Insurance Company of America

As a high-ranking female lawyer at Prudential, Deborah Bello, who joined the financial giant directly from Seton Hall University School of Law in 1979, knows firsthand the complexities of the lead legal role in a large Fortune 500 company. "Creative problem-solving and credibility with internal clients are key," says Bello, who had the opportunity to develop both skills when, early in her career, she took the chief communications role at Prudential Securities. Knowing little about financial public relations or crisis management, she initially hesitated.

"Jim Gillen, who was then general counsel, told me to get over my fear of failing," relates Bello, who did just that and excelled in the role. "It gave me a valuable overview of company operations, and the reputation I developed as a crisis manager helped me stand out as I rose through the ranks."

For Bello, just doing a good job is not enough. "Mentors are important—you risk wallowing in obscurity without that guidance. But moving up ultimately comes down to having a plan, raising your hand, and managing your way forward." Other lessons learned? "Men are bigger risk takers, but women bring the bigger lens when it comes to anticipating and avoiding risk," says Bello, adding that there are certain risky behaviors to avoid. "Don't take things personally or be governed by your emotions," she says, "and know that you have to be more perfect the more you rise. Personality traits can fall in or out of favor depending on the company's leadership. Be self-aware as you go."

Brigida Benitez
Chief, Office of Institutional Integrity,
Inter-American Development Bank

Before joining Washington, D.C.-based Inter-American Development Bank in 2010—where she leads investigations of fraud and corruption in all bank-financed activities, reporting directly to the bank's president—Brigida Benitez spent 16 years as a litigator with prominent international law firm WilmerHale, also based in the nation's capital.

After becoming the firm's first-ever Latina partner in 2001, Benitez gained national attention for second-chairing Wilmer's landmark victory in 2003 for the University of Michigan in a diversity case before the U.S. Supreme Court. Leading the case were founding partner John Pickering and litigation partner and noted civil rights attorney John Payton—both of whom mentored Benitez at the firm.

"I cannot say enough about the importance of how they helped me and of the importance of career-long mentoring," says Benitez. "From friends and peers to lawyers and judges, mentors have been instrumental at every phase of my advancement." Believing in the value of having not one but many mentors, she now willingly mentors others, seeing it as nothing less than an obligation. "I owe it to those who have helped me, and to the community at large, to give back," says Benitez, who also teaches at Georgetown University Law Center and the Washington College of Law at American University.

Her career calculus includes being open to opportunity. "I suppose it was risky leaving the security of a private firm, but it was time to leave my comfort zone and continue honing my skills as a manager," says Benitez, who was recruited to the bank by a headhunter. She was challenged at the outset: her first mandate was to rebuild the bank's integrity team. But like every other step in her highly acclaimed career, she has turned that challenge into reward.

Personal successes aside, Benitez still sees an uphill climb for women lawyers. "I don't think we are where we think we are," she says. "The obstacles may have changed, yet obstacles remain, and for all the strides women have made, the numbers are increasing slowly. It will take more communication and more open dialogue to make things better for us all."

Louise Firestone

Senior Vice President for Legal Affairs and General Counsel, LVMH Moët Hennessy Louis Vuitton Inc.

A leap of faith took Louise Firestone out of an early law firm job into Citibank's legal ranks in the mid-'80s, and she's never looked back. "A partner at the firm told me I was killing my career by going in-house," remembers Firestone, "but I wanted to be on the business side, and it was absolutely the right move." While never setting her sights specifically on becoming a general counsel, Firestone firmly believes in planning ahead, five years at a time. "My motivation was to rise in business, and build and become part of a strong team," she explains, which influenced her next move—becoming one of the first in-house lawyers at Credit Suisse. "That was risky, but I was not afraid to fail, because if things did not work out, I felt there would be another job," she says.

Eventually becoming general counsel of the bank's New York branch, her five-year plan "fell apart" when the bank merged with CS First Boston in 1997, and in 1999, she joined privately held LVMH Moët Hennessy Louis Vuitton Inc. Acknowledging the "hugely" different profile of board-led Fortune 500 companies, Firestone does not see the public company general counsel role becoming less desirable because of risk and governance challenges. "If anything, it stands to be more prestigious and lucrative because of having to meet those challenges," she states. For women on their way up, she believes in full disclosure when it comes to children and family time, and in a job "laden with ambiguity, for which there is no crystal ball," astute career management. "Plan, prepare, and take on as many tasks as you can to enhance your profile. But don't be afraid to take risks. The road to the top is not always a straight path."

Sherry Jetter

Vice President, Intellectual Property and Legal Affairs, Polo Ralph Lauren Corp.

In terms of establishing "brand value" for the general counsel role, Sherry Jetter has a decidedly business-centric perspective. "Get close to your client's business, become valuable to your client, gain the trust of internal clients, and be a business partner," she says, "and be calm, rational, and solution-oriented." It's a point of view shaped by two decades as in-house counsel in the fashion industry, which started with the Donna Karan Co. in 1990. There, Karan's husband, business partner, and co-chief executive, the late Stephan Weiss, was a valuable mentor to Jetter, teaching her and encouraging her in the in-house role. "Finding a mentor who can guide, coach, and encourage you is key," says Jetter, who also sees mentorship as an important part of being a legal leader. "Being a good manager means mentoring, nurturing, and encouraging your people to grow," she says, adding that feedback is also critical. "Watch your senior team members in action, coach them to ask smart questions and not be afraid to learn from mistakes."

Support and encouragement also define Jetter's working experience as a gay woman—both within the company and the fashion industry, she says that her sexuality is neither an issue nor a barrier. As far as women progressing in the general counsel role goes, while she believes that cultural attitudes still need to change—including the perception that men may sometimes be the "safe" choice—her outlook is generally optimistic, her own Fortune 500 aspirations included.

Adrienne Logan

Vice President and Associate General Counsel, Godiva Chocolatier

After law school and a senior district court clerkship in Illinois, Adrienne Logan became assistant general counsel at Avon Products. Her experiences there would define her view of herself as a legal leader and the steps required for her to be successful. "Through mutual contacts, I met Michele Mayes, who became an invaluable mentor in terms of providing real insight into interacting with senior management and other aspects of the general counsel role," says Logan, who says she "makes a point of reaching out to and aligning with people from all areas who can help further my career vision."

Logan's self-focus sharpened considerably when Avon Chairman and CEO Andrea Jung selected her to participate in a CEO advisory council of top 10 performers from business units around the globe to discuss critical matters with senior management. "I was the only attorney and the youngest by far," says Logan. "Those sessions opened my eyes to the fact that having the legal perspective alone was not enough—I knew I needed business acumen, too."

With this impetus, Logan enrolled in the executive MBA program at the Kellogg School of Management. "Business school taught me how to keep the process moving without knowing all the facts, which is different from law school—and crucial for being a legal leader in business," she says.

Logan says that while she has encountered more barriers as an African-American than as a woman, this feeling of isolation has only made her stronger. "You have to believe in yourself when nobody else does, and be your own island when necessary," she says. "Getting buy-in is not always easy. It's about weaving education into the dialogue, and having the confidence and conviction to turn dissension into consensus and agreement."

Sally Narey

Senior Vice President and General Counsel, Firemans Fund Insurance Co.

In her present position since September 2008, Sally Narey's leadership experience reaches back to the 1980s, when she served as general counsel for the U.S. Small Business Administration.

Embarking thereafter on a career in the insurance industry, she successively became general counsel for the National Council on Compensation Insurance (NCCI) and deputy general counsel for CNA Insurance Companies, before leading a team of approximately

225 professionals as general counsel for USAA's property and casualty group. Calling the fast pace and advisory aspect of the role today "appealing," Narey believes that while courage is important for women, the approach does not have to be heavy-going. "You can't be afraid to speak up or make changes, and you have to pick your battles carefully, but as long as you can laugh at yourself, cut down on the drama, and establish rapport, there is room for women to operate in a man's world."

She has the same attitude toward risk taking. "It's rarely as bad as the worst-case scenario you might have imagined," she says, "and it's usually something you can survive." Extolling the virtues of "learning new things at every turn" and finding mentors of either gender who are "open and interested in your career," Narey wonders if the search criteria for women general counsel are sometimes limiting. "When organizations focus on a certain type of experience or a certain number of years of experience, they might be missing the places where women and minority attorneys actually are."

Maureen Phillips

Chief Legal Officer, Allianz Life Insurance Company of North America

Deciding she wanted to be "a great lawyer," Maureen Phillips has made hard work and achievement the focal points of a career that she defines as one of "constant evolution." Prior to Allianz, Phillips spent time in private practice and more than two decades in health care and insurance.

"While I did not have a specific 'GC plan,' I knew I did not have to be in a firm to do great work," she says. "Today, the GC is expected not just to manage legal affairs but to look around corners for risks to come. This is the most significant part of the job—and you have to do it fast."

Naming listening, thinking, and maintaining balance as core attributes, along with diverse substantive knowledge and experience with people, Phillips underlines the decision-making part of the job. "Today's general counsel is a specialist in corporate risk and crisis management," she says, "and it all comes down to judgment."

Part of her own balancing act was freeing herself from the "trained mind-set" facing many women who said that if they worked harder than others they would succeed; another was coming to terms with her role as a mother. "I have gained the confidence that I can do the job and that my family will be fine," she says. In fact, "I feel that my experience as a mother has contributed significantly to my ability to lead."

Juliette Pryor

Executive Vice President, General Counsel and Chief Ethics Officer, U.S. Foodservice Inc.

While in her first year at Georgetown University Law Center, Juliette Pryor learned about how some corporations recruited law graduates directly. "I decided I wanted to go in-house and made that the focus of my career development path," she says. After interviewing with several blue-chip firms, she began her career as in-house counsel for IBM, relishing the company's cultural focus on helping lawyers develop solid business as well as legal skills.

Pryor spent three years as legal advisor to the vice chairman of the U.S. International Trade Commission before going in-house with telecom firm e.spire Communications. Her experience served her well as the company's general counsel sought her help in building the department from scratch. "Our challenge was figuring out how to fit the legal function into other areas of the business," says Pryor, who would face the same challenge several years later, only on a much bigger scale, when recruited to U.S. Foodservice as deputy general counsel. "After e.spire faltered and I guided the company through reorganization, I joined Skadden Arps to 'round-out' my experience," she says. "Then came the U.S. Foodservice opportunity, and I embraced the chance to step into a much larger environment."

Pryor partnered with the company's newly appointed general counsel to help "evolve the department and ourselves as strategic advisors who could help find creative solutions to business-side issues" at the food distributor, the 11th-largest privately held firm in the U.S., with around $20 billion in revenues. That is very much her personal goal, too. "I want people to see me as the go-to person for legal and non-legal matters alike, because they like the way I think," says Pryor, noting that the general counsel role is not for the easily intimidated or faint of heart. "For women in legal leadership, I cannot say enough about being courageous, self-assured, and taking risks," she says. "Absent these qualities, you'll never know if you can succeed."

Laurie Robinson
Senior Vice President and Assistant General Counsel, CBS Corp.

Following stints as a legal intern with the NFL and as an associate with two New York City labor and employment law firms, Laurie Robinson joined CBS Broadcasting Inc. in 2002 as assistant general counsel, representing nearly 150 television and radio stations in labor, employment, and immigration matters. In a leadership role created for her, she also became director of training and development for the broadcast unit. Crediting the devoted mentorship of Louis J. Briskman, executive vice president and general counsel for CBS Corp., Robinson was promoted in 2006 to vice president and assistant general counsel of CBS Corp., reporting directly to Briskman. She was promoted to senior vice president in 2010.

"I went from seeing only one snapshot of the company to having an overview of all CBS operations," says Robinson, "while the addition of executive and managerial responsibilities has greatly enhanced my skills as an in-house lawyer."

Robinson has also earned national recognition—and significantly expanded her skill set—as CEO of Corporate Counsel Women of Color, the nonprofit she founded in 2004. "My inspiration was to create a resource for women of color, whom I saw as isolated in the legal profession, to help and inspire each other." Through her considerable efforts, she now counts over 2,500 members around the globe—along with immeasurable benefits to her career. "From sales and marketing to running a website and organizing conferences, I have learned so many transferable business and leadership skills," says Robinson, her sights set on one day becoming a general counsel or heading up a business unit.

Robinson is unreservedly optimistic about the road ahead for women. "We know where we want to go. And we know that we have the power to control the things within our power to control. Women will be ready when opportunities open up."

Hilary Ware

Managing Counsel, Litigation and Regulatory Affairs, Google Inc.

Influenced in part by her lawyer father, Hilary Ware knew in high school that she wanted to enter the legal profession. After graduating from Harvard Law School, she clerked with a new federal district judge in Miami in what she describes as "a very collaborative and supportive relationship." Other mentors would follow, evenly split between men and women, as Ware spent six years in business litigation at Heller Ehrman in San Francisco. "For mentors, I sought people who understood who I was and where I was coming from, people who had something to contribute to my career, and people who were willing to support me," says Ware. One such mentor was a senior woman partner at the firm, who advised Ware to leave for Google when the opportunity arose in 2004.

Ware quickly established herself alongside Google's other leading litigators, all women themselves. As someone who likes to periodically invigorate her career, Ware is "intrigued" by the idea of becoming a general counsel. "Along with good judgment and business savvy, I see commercial litigation and its insight into deal making as one good path to the role," she says. For now, however, she is happy where she is—which includes having the flexibility to raise her three children in a "two-mom family." Out since high school, Ware says that being gay is a non-issue in San Francisco and at Google. "It's more challenging juggling work and kids than being gay," she says. "Really, it's more a matter of managing how other people perceive me and making their experience comfortable." Ware makes a point of following social cues. "Of course, not everybody is comfortable with gay people, and there are some jobs you will not get because you are gay. Reading and then navigating the social environment is important, in terms of knowing either to pull back from resistance or go comfortably ahead."

Sherry Williams

Senior Vice President and Chief Ethics and Compliance Officer, Halliburton Co.

After spending the first eight years of her legal career working in law firms—and encountering frustrating delays and roadblocks en route to the partnership level— Williams came to a distinct self-realization. "I knew that I was the only one truly accountable for my career," she says. "I saw that I had to get out of the employee mind-set and start thinking like an entrepreneur." Foreseeing greater flexibility by going in-house, she entered into "a joint venture" with Halliburton, taking the view that "as long as the joint venture works for us both, great." It's a "mutual investment" that has paid dividends, as Williams, "fully supported by the general counsel and company senior management," has quickly advanced, levels at a time. While not her goal at first, she is focused on developing the right skill set and "toolkit" so she is ready if the opportunity to become GC arises.

Constant self-improvement is key— she sets aside time each day for learning, documenting her own "lesson plan"—along with nurturing internal and external networks. Mentored by Janet Kelly and most recently by Kim Rucker, two general counsel prominently featured in this book, Williams calls her "Girl Network" a great source of support—while cautioning against "being so out of tune with your political self and in tune with your ambitions that you make other women your enemies." She also believes in keeping a level head. "Being or not being presented the general counsel role does not constitute either ultimate success or failure," she says. "The point is to do your best at the job you have, stay in the present, and don't get caught up in going somewhere just because the wind is blowing you in that direction."

Simone Wu
Senior Vice President and General Counsel, XO Holdings Inc.

At first glance, Simone Wu's career looks like a neatly plotted graph. Columbia University law degree in hand, she started at Skadden Arps in the late '80s and followed that with legal and business roles at MCI and AOL. Then, in 2001, she joined telecom leader XO Communications as senior corporate counsel, and was promoted to vice president and assistant general counsel in 2004, acting general counsel in 2005, and finally general counsel of XO and its holding company in 2006.

In fact, she really did not start with a plan. "It was more about my desire to gravitate toward the business and client side and be more connected to results and outcomes," says Wu. Her decision to "give in-house a try" was unusual in a time when law firms were more popular, but times have changed. "Ideally you reflect more on the direction you want to go and develop a plan to get there," says Wu, "while also being open-minded and flexible to opportunities along the way that may not be part of the plan."

Likening the process today more to a matrix than a ladder climb, Wu does not see the general counsel position as being right for everyone—some prefer specialist roles with highly valuable in-depth knowledge and skills, which would translate to deputy or assistant general counsel roles leading teams within a corporate legal department, she believes.

But regardless of who you are or where you are headed, mentors are essential. "Whether formalized or not, everybody needs mentors," says Wu, and when it comes to characteristics, courage, conviction, and credibility are all essentials. "Decisions you make as in-house counsel carry real consequences," she says. "You have to be able to establish a relationship where the business people listen to you—and trust that you can identify and handle risk without wavering."

PATHS

Chapter 6

SUMMATION:

pay it forward

In a world that "still needs to move forward," women lawyers continue to face a number of challenges. Individual courage alone has gotten them this far—collective courage will power greater advances.

s we've noted time and time again throughout this book, courageous women have a long history in American jurisprudence, dating back to 1648, when Margaret Brent went before the all-male Maryland Assembly and asked for "vote and voyce." Her request was denied, but Brent left an everlasting mark. Recognized as a woman of courage and independence in the annals of Maryland history, most historical accounts identify her as the first woman in America to request the right to vote and the first woman to participate in the U.S. legal system.

Brent did not inspire a female revolution, however, and another two centuries would pass before women of courage began "assembling" to take on the status quo in earnest. Still, she left an imprint as well as an outline of the triumphs that would assume increasingly sharper form and greater dimension.

Along the way, there have also been men courageous enough to recognize women of courage. Take Governor Leonard Calvert, who was so impressed by Brent's business acumen that he made her executor of his estate just before his death in 1647. Imagine what Calvert might have done had he seen Brent in action in court the following year. Yet his example still wants for a popular following. This is one of the essential differences between men and women. When men want to start a revolution, it can seem to happen in an instant, while women—lawyers, for instance—can still be marshalling forces four centuries on. Consider 1972, clearly a watershed year for women (as we noted in the Chapter 1). Katharine Graham was named the first woman CEO of a Fortune 500 company. Catherine Cleary became the first woman director on General Motors' board. Title IX was enacted. And the Equal Rights Amendment was passed (though never ratified). Good things were happening for women—but did it galvanize people and take America by storm? Not at all.

Now, as we were careful to acknowledge when we started, this book is in no way intended to be a proclamation of gender superiority, or a statement of us-versus-them.

Healthy Perspectives

As a young prosecutor in Jackson County, Missouri, **Carol Petren** was trying a rape case with an all-male jury when defendant's counsel, a veteran lawyer, said to her, "Honey, will you approach the bench?" Unflinching in her response—"Turtle dove, I'll be right there"—Petren is all for the defusing power of humor. It's an attribute that served her as well in her early days as an assistant U.S. attorney as in her subsequent 18 years in litigation defense practice, in deputy general counsel roles with Sears, Roebuck and Co. and MCI, and, from 2006 until 2011, as executive vice president and general counsel of health care leader CIGNA. In combination with other key facets including optimism and finding solutions to challenges, Petren has always felt fully equipped for today's risk-laden, crisis-threatened environment. "My view is, the bigger the problem or issue, the bigger the opportunity to solve it," she says. "It's about having the experience, competence, and confidence to make decisions without being able to predict all the factors."

The point is that while so much progress has been made toward women's equal place in the general counsel role, in the legal and business professions, and in society at large, there is still much to do, and we know that it is going to take time. As Richard St. John stated so clearly in Chapter 5, we must be prepared to persist.

Significant Strides

Much has changed in the 32 years since Mary Ann Hynes became the first woman general counsel of a Fortune 500 company. Riding the "waves" we have used to describe Hynes' inaugurating era (1979–96) and the two generations of women who followed (1997 to 2001 and 2002 to the present), their collective journey has been choppy, at times turbulent. When Hynes became general counsel at CCH Inc., she entered untested, uncharted waters for women in an all-male fleet.

If we were to highlight a key change since Hynes's time, it is that women are now generally allowed to function *as* women, and not as women compelled to adapt themselves after men. A proof point: When former National Association of Women Lawyers' President Lisa Gilford speaks with women general counsel on the subject of change and evolution, one of the encouraging themes she has frequently heard is that being a woman today works *for* chief legal officers, not *against* them.

"Women general counsel tell me that they now get to acknowledge their feminin-

> **"Women general counsel tell me that they now get to acknowledge their femininity."**
>
> **—GILFORD**

Mary Ann Hynes
The Banquet of Life

Stretching back to 1648 when Margaret Brent became the first recorded woman in the U.S. legal system, the pantheon of female "firsts" in the law includes Arabella Mansfield, the first woman formally admitted to practice law in the U.S.; Charlotte E. Ray, the nation's first black woman lawyer; and Clara Shortridge Foltz, the "First Woman of California." In 1979, Mary Ann Hynes joined this illustrious group by becoming the first-ever woman general counsel of a Fortune 500 company, the venerable Illinois-based legal and business information publisher CCH Inc.

One of two children, Hynes drew early inspiration from her parents, who came from Europe and worked in U.S. factories, "I was taught to deeply value my education, and I truly appreciated the sacrifices our parents made to afford us that education," says Hynes, naming them, along with her husband, as her "biggest supporters." Excelling in math, debating, and forensic speaking in high school, Hynes found that she "admired lawyers and their unique role as truth-seekers and champions." In 1971, after completing undergraduate and law studies at Loyola University of Chicago, she went to work for CCH.

From day one, Hynes took personal charge of her career—relying on mentoring, risk taking, and skills development all the way. "As a young lawyer, I took risks by taking responsible positions for the company, and worked hard to be sure that the foundations of those positions were rock solid," she says. To make herself "highly relevant" to CCH, Hynes took advantage of tuition reimbursement to earn an LLM in Taxation; through involvement with the Women's Bar Association of Illinois, she expanded her

ity, not only in terms of dress and appearance, but in terms of critical skills such as collaboration and team- and consensus-building," says Gilford. "They say they draw upon the strengths of their community and their team to lead an organization, and they all describe instances in which, for lack of a better phrase, the womanly approach to running an organization has benefited them."

As Gilford also notes, this is a major departure from the early 1980s, when women modeled themselves after men in dress, demeanor, and all other respects, instead of trying to be different and lead on their own terms. Still, the pressure on women to prove themselves endures. "I think we have reached the point where older women lawyers are given the presumption of competence," says SNR Denton senior corporate partner Robin Edwards, who interviewed a number of the women featured in this book, "whereas younger women are still being viewed through the lens of their looks or their relative lack of maturity or the fact that they still have their child-bearing years ahead of them. For them, the question of competency remains."

circle of colleagues and friends; by seeking new responsibilities and exposure to all aspects of the business, she attracted the attention of then CEO and President Robert Bartlett.

"I was blessed to work for Mr. Bartlett," remembers Hynes. "He had confidence in my abilities, and I never wanted to disappoint him or the company." In this Hynes triumphed, for as Bartlett prepared to retire, he and the CCH board made her the company's first vice president and general counsel. Bartlett's introduction of Hynes to CCH's outside counsel would also prove to be the first link in a long chain of professional mentorships and friendships to follow. "Throughout my time at CCH and beyond, mentors and friends were always the source of new opportunities and the key to successful transitions," she states. "The importance of networking and mentors cannot be overstated."

In 2006, Hynes assumed her current position as vice president, general counsel, corporate secretary, and chief compliance officer for Westchester, Illinois-based Corn Products International Inc., a global leader in ingredient solutions. Looking back on the past three decades, Hynes is nothing but upbeat.

"What did I sacrifice along the way?" she asks. "Let's see, wife of 41 years, mother of two, grandmother-to-be, scuba diver, skier, gardener, world traveler—there isn't much I've missed except sleep and self-indulgence. And for that, I've gained a world of excitement that I've cherished." Far from done herself—citing retired federal judge George Leighton (one of Andrea Zopp's mentors), she aspires to work and learn well into her 90s—Hynes believes that today's young women lawyers should go fearlessly ahead.

"Women have made many significant strides in the GC role," she says. "They are comfortable in the C-suite; their opinions are candid, frank, transparent, and trusted; and they should focus and simplify their lives and trust that they have the right stuff to make their future exciting. I would say set your goals high and create opportunities—invite yourself to the banquet of life."

> "Mentors and friends were always the source of new opportunities and the key to successful transitions."
>
> —HYNES

As women adjusted to the role, the nature of the role itself changed, overwhelming some of the key and inherent generational differences. How quaint does the American business landscape of the late 1970s appear in contrast to today's fiercely competitive, scrutinized, and regulated environment? If the American economy was once a bedrock foundation supporting true vertical steel, the go-go '80s, the dot-com mania of the '90s, and the greed of the first decade of this century have conspired to undermine that bedrock and twist those once reliable beams out of shape. Along the way, the risk-taking quotient exploded to the point where today, just about everybody at the company, but particularly the general counsel, finds himself or herself in the hot seat.

The attributes necessary for the general counsel role were naturally altered by these rapid, radical changes. In 2011, if you want to be a general counsel, the things you are going to have wrap your arms—and head—around are going to force you to have bigger and bigger arms, as well as greater powers of concentration, force of will, and capacity to absorb. More than ever, that ability to shift one's laser focus from one thing to the next is paramount.

In an environment more urgent and immediate than during the first wave, today's women general counsel are coming in younger, and on a faster track. The women of the first wave generally arrived at their first general counsel job later in their careers and would typically stay in that one job for an extended period of time, as did Louise Parent, who has spent practically her entire legal career at American Express. This would begin to change in the second wave as women not only started coming to the role earlier in their careers, but then began moving with more frequency and embarking on multiple tours of duty, as in the cases of Susan Lichtenstein, Christine Edwards, and Anastasia Kelly. Come the third wave—when Enron and the global meltdown really rattled the foundations—and volatility entered the picture, creating shorter tenures for both chief executives and general counsel.

Korn/Ferry International's Julie Goldberg Preng believes that the rate of CEO turnover favors the hiring of women general counsel. "Generally speaking, newer-generation CEOs understand how the 'new style' of general counsel works," she says. "Wise to risk and less fearful of change, they recognize that there's much they don't know coming into a new organization, and consequently they tend to be more receptive to hiring what they know to be 'risk-savvy' women general counsel."

Increasing numbers of former general counsel are becoming chief executives themselves, too. In a 2002 *Chief Legal Executive* magazine story called "The Entrepreneurs, The Consiglieri, The Public Servants," Heidrick & Struggles' managing partner Victoria Reese and her former colleague June Eichbaum wrote that "acting as senior legal advisor to CEOs facilitates becoming a CEO." The authors emphasized how "the public sector can provide the context for a transformative experience that activates higher risk tolerance," which becomes part of an overall dissolution of the boundaries between the legal function and the business function. "For those who serve as *consiglieri* to CEOs, becoming a CEO can be the next logical step," they wrote. In particular, they identified "managing a crisis" as "a classic example of an experience that can be transformative." As they put it, "the exigencies of the situation create both the chaos and the opportunity to transcend traditional boundaries."

Case in point: In 2007, WellPoint Inc., the largest U.S. health insurer by membership, named its general counsel, Angela Braly, to replace outgoing CEO Larry Glasscock, a move that made the company the largest in the U.S. with a woman in charge. As Reuters reported, analysts were initially surprised by the choice, but acknowledged that "her experience could help WellPoint navigate a potentially challenging political and regulatory environment."

Crisis and risk have also transformed how management and boards have come to reconsider the value that women can bring to the role. Going from perception

Attention Getter

Nicole Jones gained plenty of notice in her first stint (2006 to 2010) in the legal department of global health care services company CIGNA, earning a series of rapid promotions over five years including corporate secretary and deputy general counsel. What really got management's eye, though, was when she volunteered for a pivotal role during a serious legal matter facing the company.

"It was Christmas Eve, and somebody was urgently needed to act as a point person between the public-facing team and senior management," relates Jones, who now serves as CIGNA's general counsel following her return to the company in 2011. "While outside of my position, I raised my hand and took it on." Her move did not go unnoticed by CIGNA CEO David Cordani. "To this day, he cites my handling of that pressure situation as the reason he has confidence in me and knows I can take on an immediate challenge—essential for today's general counsel role," says Jones.

Her message to young lawyers? "Never turn away a tough assignment or an opportunity—whether apparent or not, the value is always there."

to understanding to embracing, traditionalists saw that women, through such hard-won, culturally forged qualities as heightened sensitivity, heightened intuition, and the heightened ability to make informed judgments in times of crisis, were in fact ideally suited to take on this new corporate and legal paradigm.

In fact, this shift in thinking was developing even before Enron and Sarbanes-Oxley. In 1994—seven years before Enron—*Human Resource Executive* magazine ran an article titled "Shatter the Glass Ceiling: Women May Make Better Managers," in which Bruce Avolio and the late Bernard Bass, two experts in transformational leadership, discussed their findings on the different management and leadership styles of women and men. They found that "the trend in U.S. corporations toward high-involvement work teams, consensus decision making, and empowerment may actually benefit the leadership styles women already exhibit…female managers are seen as more transformational than their male counterparts—a leadership style that has been shown to have a strong positive impact on individual, group, and organizational performance."

More recently, in November 2009, the White House Project's "Benchmarking Women's Leadership" report found that America is unequivocally ready to accept "risk-smart" women as leaders in law and other major sectors and areas of influence.

Advantage women, allowing them to be transformed by their own transformative powers? Well, sort of, but there are still issues to address.

The 30 Percent Solution

On its face, societal acceptance of women as leaders in law and other disciplines is good news, but as the White House Project itself acknowledges, true gains remain elusive. In May 2010, The Glass Hammer, an online community designed for women executives in financial services, law, and business, talked about how "on paper, the numbers look good" for women, citing metrics showing women controlling half of the wealth in the U.S. and representing the fastest-growing group of business owners. However, Linda Basch, president of the National Council for Research on Women, is quoted saying that "the glass ceiling remains virtually shatterproof. We've reached stasis in too many areas."

Is "stasis" also a culprit when it comes to women's advancement in Fortune 500 law department leadership? Since 1999, the Minority Corporate Counsel Association has measured the glass ceiling in corporate law departments via its annual survey of women general counsel in the Fortune 500. Up from 44 in 1999, the 2011 survey recorded 101 women: an all-time high, yes, but still just 20.2 percent of all top legal officers, and far from 50 percent.

Dorian Denburg, president of the National Association of Women Lawyers from 2010 to 2011, has noted that while half of all law school graduates today are women, women still only constitute about 15 percent of law firm equity partners, corporate general counsel, and tenured law professors. At its annual awards luncheon in 2006, NAWL issued this challenge to law firms, corporate law departments, and law schools: By 2015, women should make up 30 percent of all equity partners, 30 percent of all chief legal officers, and 30 percent of all tenured law professors. Modeled after "the 30 Percent Solution," which states that significant progress for women will not happen until the government is comprised of at least 30 percent women, the NAWL Challenge sets forth the same standard for women lawyers in key leadership positions in legal institutions: anything short of 30 percent, in NAWL's view, is progress moving "at a glacial pace."

While that tipping point still seems elusive, Denburg highlights the gender proportionality of the U.S. Supreme Court as the example to follow. "The investiture of Elena Kagan as associate justice of the Supreme Court is significant, momentous, and historic," she said in an interview on the national Women's Radio network. "It means that the U.S. Supreme Court now has three women—33 1/3 percent on the court— and I believe that the United States Supreme Court is an example that law firms, corporations, and law schools would do well to emulate."

Looking down through the glass ceiling from above, several women general counsel see barriers still—for them, that 30 percent, which would be 150 women Fortune 500 chief legal officers, seems far off.

Andrea Zopp, for example, still sees a "huge" glass ceiling. "The ratio of women to men alone tells the story, but there's more," she says. "There's still the issue that not all men are comfortable with strong, powerful women—especially black women."

Rebecca Kendall (formerly Goss), who left Eli Lilly in 2003 after nearly three decades at the pharma giant, believes that while "it now has holes poked in it," the corporate and legal glass ceiling endures—especially at the highest levels. "Women have definitely broken through in areas like human resources, but when it comes to the core functions at the very top, the 'real' ceiling has not moved much," she says. Kendall does feel, however, that many of the outward impediments and the most egregious barriers such as discrimination have largely been struck down, but that "the most insidious and unconscious obstacles, the ones that are much harder to get at," still remain.

Micro-inequities

Gender-based stereotyping is one example. As reported in "New Millennium, Same Glass Ceiling?" there is this bias-filled concept that "women 'don't need' their paycheck because their husbands can support them, whereas men 'really need' their paycheck because they are supporting their families." Bias does not need to be intentional to be harmful, either. Lawyer and leading national expert on legal diversity and inclusiveness Dr. Arin Reeves routinely speaks on the subject of "unconscious bias," or the subtle, gender-based perspectives that pervade thought and action in the legal profession.

In her 2009 article "A New Level of Awareness," Reeves talks about "micro-inequities," a term coined in 1973 by MIT Sloan School of Management professor Mary Rowe to describe "small events which are often ephemeral and hard to prove...often unintentional, frequently unrecognized by the perpetrator...[that]...occur wherever people are perceived to be 'different.'"

Likening micro-inequities to multiple mosquito bites (as opposed to the "shark bites" of macro-inequities such as overt racial discrimination or explicit sexual harassment, where intent is the differentiator), Reeves describes them as "those annoying realities that remind those who are different that they are, in fact, different from the people who have historically been accepted, included, and successful in that workplace." Her examples include Hispanic lawyers mistaken for janitors or black attorneys mistaken for mailroom clerks. It can be far more subtle still, such as a man offering a woman Sweet'N Low instead of sugar because he simply assumes that, as a woman, she's dieting. "Shark bites get news coverage. Mosquito bites get tolerated," writes Reeves. "The perception that a woman is less committed to her career when she becomes a mother is a micro-inequity that is tolerated by women." Soon, though, the micro-inequities can take a toll. "The mosquito bites accumulate, one by one, until the feeling of being the other in the workplace is so tangible and often painful, that it becomes easier to just exit the workplace."

Joan Williams, founding director of the Center for WorkLife Law at the University of California, Hastings College of the Law in San Francisco, prefers the term "unexamined" bias because, as she once commented on an employment law blog, "when you

"You've got to be able to look beyond the next day—every little adventure is risk taking."

—KELLY

use the word 'unconscious' people say, 'How on earth can I be held accountable for something I'm not even conscious of?'" She offers this solution: "You can't control those biases, but you can control whether or not they rule your behavior."

The picture is not entirely bleak, however. Amid the cynicism, there are moderate and indeed some bright outlooks in the forecast.

"The Jobs Are Out There"

"The ceiling is still there," says Jennifer Vogel, "although it seems to be thinning." She also believes that today's higher-echelon women have something that their first-wave predecessors lacked—the power of choice. "I think that women experience varying degrees of success less because they are unable to and more because they choose to," says Vogel. "I think women choose to leave high-powered positions because they are unwilling to live with the demands on their time, and the positions themselves don't have the flexibility to provide balance."

"We see more of a glass ceiling in certain foreign-owned organizations, as well as in certain traditional sectors such as industrial, manufacturing, and energy," says Julie Goldberg Preng. "Even in those sectors, though, women are finding their way, and overall, the ceiling is not what it once was." She attributes the thinning of the ceiling in sectors like high-tech, consumer products, pharmaceutical, and health care both to the corresponding rise of women on the business side and to the younger workforce in these industries. "On the one hand, women still have to overcome presumptions regarding their confidence and competence, along with their ability to sustain in a crisis without getting emotional," she says. "That said, there is not a general counsel search that goes by where the client corporation does not ask for a woman or a minority candidate in the mix."

Spencer Stuart's Catherine Nathan agrees. "What I am seeing now is the opposite of a glass ceiling," she says. "The jobs are out there, and women are in demand for the general counsel role. Why? Boards and chief executives woke up to what is really happening in the corporate world—and what could happen to them—and began to take a real interest in who they were bringing in as general counsel. Women have become attractive candidates in this regard because they are increasingly seen as having mastered the subject matter and skills necessary for the role. We could use more ready women, because the jobs are out there."

Pay It Forward

Individual courage is clearly the most essential ingredient of success for women, but with the road to equality still stretching far out in the distance, it remains a march not for the one, but the many. Wharton alumna Cynthia Schwalm, a consultant in the life sciences industry, offered this wisdom at the 2011 Wharton Women in Business

> "Shark bites get news coverage. Mosquito bites get tolerated."
>
> —REEVES

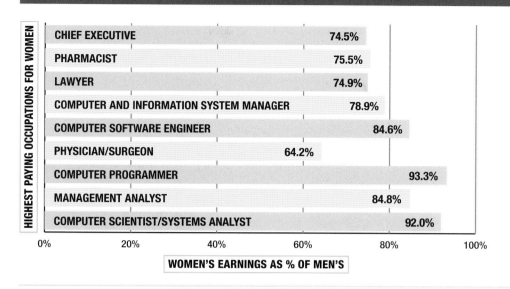

Pay Disparity, Even in Top Professions

HIGHEST PAYING OCCUPATIONS FOR WOMEN

Occupation	Women's Earnings as % of Men's
CHIEF EXECUTIVE	74.5%
PHARMACIST	75.5%
LAWYER	74.9%
COMPUTER AND INFORMATION SYSTEM MANAGER	78.9%
COMPUTER SOFTWARE ENGINEER	84.6%
PHYSICIAN/SURGEON	64.2%
COMPUTER PROGRAMMER	93.3%
MANAGEMENT ANALYST	84.8%
COMPUTER SCIENTIST/SYSTEMS ANALYST	92.0%

WOMEN'S EARNINGS AS % OF MEN'S

According to the White House Project's "Benchmarking Women's Leadership" report from November 2009, women are stalled across the U.S. leadership spectrum, averaging 18 percent across major sectors (lower still for women of color), and behind on compensation, making 78.7 cents to every dollar earned by their male counterparts—a gap only exacerbated by age and the climb up the managerial ranks. Here is a comparative look at women's earnings across a range of major occupations.

Source: IWPR compilation of data from the U.S. Dept. of Labor, Bureau of Labor Statistics, 2009

Alumnae Conference ("New Models in Women's Leadership: Embracing the Future"): "Don't be excited about being the first girl in, or the only woman in the room. I think women aspire to that, or it makes them feel good to be liked, [but] that's not what's important. What is important is to look for organizations that bring on quorums of women…the power in women's leadership, and our unique leadership strengths come when at least 30 percent of the executives at the C-suite table are women…that's when the dynamic changes."

It can be the 30 percent solution, or as Suzanne Peck observed in Chapter 5, "there is a huge difference between there being one woman in a given situation and having two or more." The point is this: For the last four centuries, for the last four decades, women in law have invested themselves heavily in their own progress. The dividends and rewards to date are plain to see—but they are not enough. A unit of courage invested should at least produce a unit of reward, not an average return of around 20 percent. To pay forward the inestimable investment of persistence, optimism, and courage, and for the mission or "excellent adventure" to continue in a world that still needs to move forward, the force that moves the pivot to its rightful place in the center of the equality beam will surely come from courageous women working courageously together. It is then that the observations of Bella Abzug (1920–98), the fearlessly outspoken lawyer, congresswoman, feminist, and women's movement leader remembered as "a glorious role model," will be evident: "Women will change the nature of power, rather than power changing the nature of women."

Green never looked back, steadily assuming control of deals and watching the role of the general counsel change along the way.

Postscript

In September 2010, Maria Green, then the deputy general counsel of venerable Illinois Tool Works Inc., number 156 in the Fortune 500, was celebrated as one of *Profiles in Diversity Journal*'s nine "Women Worth Watching" for 2011. In August 2011, just as *Courageous Counsel* was about to go to press, ITW's board elected Green the company's general counsel—raising the total number of women general counsel in the Fortune 500 to a new all-time high of 102.

To borrow from the legal vernacular, her story serves to uphold and affirm the enduring strength of this book's three main pillars—mentoring, risk taking, and the cultivation of essential attributes—while reminding us that every path to the top is very much an individual one.

Hard work, tenacity, and the highest respect for education were ingrained in Green early by her parents, both professionals in their native Jamaica who worked service-level jobs after emigrating to the U.S. After graduating Boston University School of Law in 1977, Green developed as a real estate and securities practitioner over the 20 years to follow, including serving as regional general counsel for Amtrak. Her "leap of faith" came in 1997, when she interviewed with ITW's then general counsel, Stewart Hudnut. "If I were willing to take a chance and learn M&A, he said he would take a chance on me," recalls Green. "I took a risk and gained an invaluable mentor at the same time."

Like so many of the other women interviewed for this book when faced with similar decisions, Green never looked back, steadily assuming control of deals at the acquisitive company—and watching the role of the general counsel change along the way. "As a multinational with global reach, ITW has a significant risk profile," says Green. "My job is about establishing the right compliance framework, while setting the right ethical tone." Optimistic about the "road to meritocracy" ahead for an increasingly complex GC role that requires "the best people" irrespective of race or gender, Green offers this advice to young lawyers: "Be well-rounded, if not extra-dimensional, take a deep breath and relax—and focus on one thing at a time."

BIOGRAPHIES:

who's who

What does it take to

become a Fortune 500

general counsel? Here's

a look at the credentials

of 80 women who,

at some point in their

careers, have been

there.

Adams

Alexander

Banks

Batcheler

Bettman

Kate Adams

Current Position: Senior Vice President and General Counsel, Honeywell, since April 2009. **Previously:** Vice President and General Counsel, 2008–2009; Vice President and General Counsel, Honeywell Specialty Materials, 2005–2008; Vice President and Deputy General Counsel–Litigation, Honeywell, 2003–2005.

Born: April 20, 1964. **Year Graduated High School:** 1982. **Undergraduate School:** Brown University. Year Graduated: 1986. **Degree:** B.A. with honors, magna cum laude. **Law School:** University of Chicago Law School. **Year Graduated:** 1990.

First Job After Law School: Clerk for then-Chief Judge Stephen Breyer, First Circuit Court of Appeals, Boston, Massachusetts. **Notable Positions Since Law School:** Partner, Sidley Austin, LLP, New York, New York. Law Clerk to Justice Sandra Day O'Connor, Supreme Court of the United States, 1993–1994. Trial Attorney, U.S. Department of Justice, Appellate Section, Environment & Natural Resources Division, 1991–1993.

■

Susan Alexander

Current Position: Executive Vice President, General Counsel, and Corporate Secretary, Biogen Idec, since January 2006.

Born: 1956. **Year Graduated High School:** 1974. **Undergraduate School:** Wellesley College. **Year Graduated:** 1978. **Degree:** B.A. Law

School: Boston University School of Law. **Year Graduated:** 1981.

First Job After Law School: Associate, Bracewell & Patterson (now Bracewell & Guiliani). **Notable Positions Since Law School:** Senior Vice President, PAREXEL International Corp., 2003–2006. General Counsel, IONA Technologies, 2001–2003. Counsel, Cabot Corp., 1995–2001. Partner, Hinckley, Allen & Snyder. Partner, Fine & Ambrogne.

■

Michelle Banks

Current Position: Executive Vice President, General Counsel, Corporate Secretary, and Chief Compliance Officer, Gap Inc., since December 2006. **Previously:** Senior Vice President and General Counsel, 2006–2008; Vice President, 2005–2006; Associate General Counsel, 2003–2005; Senior Corporate Counsel, 1999–2003.

Born: September 1, 1963. **Year Graduated High School:** 1981. **Undergraduate School:** UCLA. **Year Graduated:** 1985. Degree: Bachelor's, Economics. **Law School:** UCLA. **Year Graduated:** 1988.

First Job After Law School: Associate, Morrison & Foerster. **Notable Positions Since Law School:** Legal Counsel, Golden State Warriors, 1995–1998. American Counsel, Itochu Corp., 1992–1993.

Colleen Batcheler

Current Position: Executive Vice President, General Counsel, and Secretary, ConAgra Foods, since September 2009. **Previously:** Senior Vice President, General Counsel, and Corporate Secretary, 2008–2009; Vice President and Chief Securities Counsel, 2006–2008.

Born: January 18, 1974. **Year Graduated High School:** 1991. **Undergraduate School:** State University of New York College at Fredonia. **Year Graduated:** 1995. **Degree:** B.A., magna cum laude, Political Science. **Law School:** Case Western Reserve University School of Law. **Year Graduated:** 1998.

First Job After Law School: Associate, Jones Day, Cleveland, Ohio. **Notable Positions Since Law School:** Vice President and Corporate Secretary, Albertson's Inc. Associate Counsel, The Cleveland Clinic Foundation.

■

Suzanne Bettman

Current Position: Executive Vice President, General Counsel, Corporate Secretary, and Chief Compliance Officer, RR Donnelley & Sons Co., since March 2004. **Previously:** Senior Vice President and General Counsel.

Born: June 23, 1964. **Year Graduated High School:** 1982. **Undergraduate School:** Northwestern University. **Year Graduated:** 1986. Degree: B.A., Economics. **Law School:** University of Illinois College of Law. **Year Graduated:** 1989.

First Job After Law School: Associate, Kirkland & Ellis. **Notable Positions Since Law School:** Partner, Kirkland & Ellis, 1995–1997. Vice President and Associate General Counsel, True North Communications Inc., 1997–1999. Executive Vice President and General Counsel, True North Communications Inc., 1999–2002. Group Managing Director and General Counsel, Huron Consulting Group LLC, 2002–2004.

■

Susan Blount

Current Position: Senior Vice President and General Counsel, Law, Compliance, and Business Ethics, Prudential Financial, since 2005. **Previously:** Vice President and Chief Investment Counsel.

Undergraduate School: University of Texas at Austin. **Degree:** B.A., History. **Law School:** University of Texas at Austin.

First Job After Law School: Associate, Kirkland & Ellis. **Notable Positions Since Law School:** Chair, Committee of Corporate General Counsel of the ABA's Section of Business Law.

■

Paula Boggs

Current Position: Executive Vice President, General Counsel and Secretary, Starbucks Coffee Co., since September 2002.

Born: May 2, 1959. Year Graduated High School: 1977. **Undergraduate School:** Johns Hopkins University.

Year Graduated: 1981. **Degree:** B.A., International Studies. **Law School:** University of California at Berkeley School of Law. **Year Graduated:** 1984.

First Job After Law School: U.S. Army First Lieutenant, Senior Law Clerk, Army General Counsel's Office, The Pentagon. **Notable Positions Since Law School:** Staff Attorney, White House Iran-Contra Legal Task Force. Assistant U.S. Attorney (W.D.WA). Staff Director, Advisory Board on the Investigative Capabilities of Department of Defense (following Tailhook incident). Partner, Preston Gates & Ellis. Vice President, Legal, Dell Computer Corp. Instructor, University of Washington School of Law Trial Advocacy Program. Audit Committee Chair, The Johns Hopkins University Board of Trustees. Washington State Delegate, American Bar Association House of Delegates. Co-Chair, Washington State Campaign for Equal Justice. Executive Committee, Association of Corporate Counsel Board. American Red Cross National Board of Governors.

■

Angelee Bouchard

Current Position: Senior Vice President, General Counsel, and Secretary, Health Net Inc., since December 2009. **Previously:** Vice President, Assistant General Counsel, and Assistant Secretary.

Born: 1968. **Year Graduated High School:** 1986. U**ndergraduate School:** Texas State University. **Year Graduated:** 1990. **Degree:** B.A., Business Administration. **Law**

School: University of Southern California. **Year Graduated:** 1996.

First Job After Law School: Latham & Watkins, LLP.

■

Kim Bowers

Current Position: Executive Vice President and General Counsel, Valero Energy Corp., since October 2008. **Previously:** Senior Vice President and General Counsel, 2006–2008; Vice President–Legal Services, 2003–2006; Managing Counsel–Commercial Law, 2002–2003; Senior Counsel, 1998–2002; Counsel, 1997–1998.

Undergraduate School: Miami University of Ohio. **Year Graduated:** 1986. **Degree:** B.A., Spanish, and B.A., International Studies. **Law School:** University of Texas School of Law. **Year Graduated:** 1991. **Other Graduate Education:** M.A., International Relations, Baylor University, 1987. Stanford Executive Program, Stanford University, 2009.

First Job After Law School: Corporate Law Associate, Kelly, Hart & Hallman, Fort Worth, Texas.

■

Maureen Brundage

Current Position: Executive Vice President, General Counsel, and Chief Ethics Officer, The Chubb Corp., since October 2005.

Born: January 13, 1957. **Year Graduated High School:** 1974. **Undergraduate School:** Fordham

Blount

Boggs

Bouchard

Bowers

Brundage

Campbell

Carter

Chapman

Coleman

McNamara Corley

University. **Year Graduated:** 1978. **Degree:** B.A., Economics. **Law School:** New York University School of Law. **Year Graduated:** 1981.

First Job After Law School: Associate, White & Case, New York, New York. **Notable Positions Since Law School:** Partner and Head of the Securities Practice Group, White & Case, New York, New York.

■

Kristin Campbell

Current Position: Executive Vice President and General Counsel, Hilton Worldwide Inc., since 2011.

Born: 1961. **Year Graduated High School:** 1980. **Undergraduate School:** Arizona State University. **Year Graduated:** 1984. **Law School:** Cornell University Law School. **Year Graduated:** 1987.

First Job After Law School: Associate, Rackemann, Sawyer & Brewster, Boston. **Notable Positions Since Law School:** General Counsel, Staples Inc., 2007–2011. Deputy General Counsel, Staples Inc. Board member, Association of Corporate Counsel–Northeast Chapter.

■

Pamela Carter

Current Position: President, Cummins Inc. Distribution Business, since 2007. **Previously:** President, Cummins Filtration; Vice President, General Counsel and Corporate Secretary, Cummins Inc.

Undergraduate School: University of Detroit. **Year Graduated:** 1971. **Law School:** Indiana University. **Year Graduated:** 1984. **Other Graduate Education:** Masters of Social Work, University of Michigan, 1973.

First Job After Law School: Litigation Attorney, UAW Legal Services. **Notable Positions Since Law School:** Attorney General, State of Indiana. Deputy Chief of Staff, Office of the Governor, State of Indiana. Securities Enforcement Attorney, Office of the Secretary of State, State of Indiana.

■

Fay Chapman

Current Position: Retired.

Born: 1946. **Year Graduated High School:** 1964. **Undergraduate School:** UCLA. **Year Graduated:** 1968. **Law School:** New York University. **Year Graduated:** 1972.

First Job After Law School: Milbrook, Tweed, 1972–1975. **Notable Positions Since Law School:** Foster, Pepper PPLC, 1975–1997. WAMU, 1997–2007.

■

Kristin M. Coleman

Current Position: Vice President, General Counsel and Secretary, Brunswick Corp., since May 2009.

Born: May 24, 1968. **Year Graduated High School:** 1986. **Undergraduate School:** Duke University. **Year Graduated:** 1990. **Degree:** B.A. **Law School:** University of

Michigan Law School. **Year Graduated:** 1993. **Notable Positions Since Law School:** Corporate Attorney, Perkins Coie and Sidley Austin.

■

Kathryn "Kelly" Corley

Current Position: Executive Vice President, General Counsel, and Secretary, Discover Financial Services, since May 1998.

Born: February 2, 1960. **Year Graduated High School:** 1978. **Undergraduate School:** University of Southern California. **Degree:** B.A., Political Science/Slavic Studies. **Law School:** George Mason University School of Law.

First Job After Law School: VP, Government Affairs, Dean Witter Discover & Co., Washington, D.C. **Notable Positions Since Law School:** Managing Director, Morgan Stanley.

■

Dorian Daley

Current Position: Senior Vice President, General Counsel and Secretary, Oracle Corp., since 2007. **Previously:** Vice President, Legal, Associate General Counsel, and Assistant Secretary, 2004–2007; Associate General Counsel and Assistant Secretary, 2001–2004.

Undergraduate School: Stanford University. **Year Graduated:** 1981. **Law School:** Santa Clara University School of Law. **Year Graduated:** 1986. **Notable Positions Since Law**

School: Associate, Landels, Ripley and Diamond, San Francisco.

■

Grace den Hartog

Current Position: Senior Vice President, General Counsel, and Corporate Secretary, Owens & Minor, since February 2003.

Born: January 19, 1952. **Year Graduated High School:** 1970. **Undergraduate School:** Westhampton College of the University of Richmond. **Year Graduated:** 1974. **Degree:** B.A., Psychology. **Law School:** University of Virginia. **Year Graduated:** 1980.

First Job After Law School: Tremblay & Smith, LLP, Charlottesville, Virginia. **Notable Positions Since Law School:** Partner, McGuire Woods, LLP, Richmond, Virginia, 1990–2003. Associate, McGuire Woods, LLP, Richmond, Virginia, 1984–1990.

■

Janet L. Dhillon

Current Position: Executive Vice President, General Counsel, and Secretary, J.C. Penney Co. Inc., since 2009.

Born: April 2, 1962. **Undergraduate School:** Occidental College. **Year Graduated:** 1984. **Law School:** UCLA School of Law. **Year Graduated:** 1991.

First Job After Law School: Litigation Associate and Litigation Counsel, Skadden, Arps, Slate, Meagher & Flom, LLP, 1991–2004. **Notable**

Positions Since Law School:
US Airways Group Inc.: Senior Vice President, General Counsel, and Chief Compliance Officer, 2006–2009; Vice President, Deputy General Counsel, and Chief Compliance Officer, 2005–2006; Managing Director–Legal, 2004–2005. Chairman of the Board of Directors, Retail Industry Leaders Association Retail Litigation Center, 2009–present. Named one of the "Ten Most Influential Lawyers" in Arizona by *Arizona Business* magazine, 2008. Member of the Board of Directors of St. Mary's Food Bank, 2008–2009.

■

Emily Dickinson

Current Position: Senior Vice President, General Counsel and Secretary, PetSmart, since August 2009.

Born: October 3, 1959. **Year Graduated High School:** 1977. **Undergraduate School:** Bowdoin College. **Year Graduated:** 1981. **Degree:** A.B., Government, cum laude. **Law School:** Boston University School of Law. **Year Graduated:** 1984.

Notable Positions Since Law School: Vice President, General Counsel, and Secretary, Hannaford Bros. Co., 2000. Senior Vice President, Delhaize Group, 2002. Vice President, Legal, Delhaize Group, 2006.

■

Carrie E. Dwyer

Current Position: Executive Vice President, General Counsel, and Corporate Secretary, The Charles Schwab Corp., since December 1996.

Born: December 19, 1950. **Year Graduated High School:** 1969. **Undergraduate School:** Santa Clara University. **Year Graduated:** 1973. **Law School:** Santa Clara University. **Year Graduated:** 1976.

First Job After Law School: Legal Department, American Stock Exchange, New York, New York. **Notable Positions Since Law School:** Senior Vice President and General Counsel, American Stock Exchange. Special Counsel to the Chairman, Securities and Exchange Commission.

■

Sheri H. Edison

Current Position: Vice President, General Counsel, and Secretary, Bemis Co. Inc., since 2010.

Born: January 27, 1957. **Year Graduated High School:** 1975. **Undergraduate School:** University of Southern California. Degree: B.A., History and Journalism. **Year Graduated:** 1979. **Law School:** Northwestern University School of Law. **Year Graduated:** 1982.

First Job After Law School: Associate, Thompson, Hine & Flory, 1982–1984. **Notable Positions Since Law School:** Senior Vice President and Chief Administrative Officer, Hill-Rom, 2007–2010. Vice President, General Counsel and Secretary, Hillenbrand Industries, 2002–2007. Associate, Mergers & Acquisitions, Jones Day, 1984–1991. Guest Lecturer, Boler School of Business, John Carroll University, 1996–1999. Member of the board, Appleton Performing Arts Center.

Daley

Dhillon

Dickinson

Dwyer

Edison

Edwards

Fox

Garcia C.

Hightman

Huber

Christine Edwards

Current Position: Partner, Winston & Strawn, since 2003.

Undergraduate School: University of Maryland. **Year Graduated:** 1974. **Degree:** B.A., English and Education. **Law School:** University of Maryland School of Law. **Year Graduated:** 1983.

Notable Positions Since Law School: Executive Vice President and Chief Legal Officer, Bank One Corp. Chief Legal Officer, Morgan Stanley. Chief Legal Officer, ABN AMRO North America.

■

Stacy L. Fox

Current Position: Senior Vice President, General Counsel, and Corporate Secretary, Sunoco Inc., since March 2010.

Born: September 20, 1953. **Year Graduated High School:** 1971. **Undergraduate School:** University of Michigan. **Degree:** B.S. **Law School:** University of Michigan. **Year Graduated:** 1983.

First Job After Law School: Associate, Mintz Levin et al., Boston, Massachusetts. **Notable Positions Since Law School:** Group Vice President and General Counsel, Automotive Systems Group, Johnson Controls. Senior Vice President, General Counsel, and Secretary, Visteon Corp., 2000–2005. Co-Founder and Principal, Roxbury Group.

Elisa D. Garcia C.

Current Position: Executive Vice President, General Counsel, and Corporate Secretary, Office Depot Inc., since July 2007.

Born: November 8, 1957. **Year Graduated High School:** 1975. **Undergraduate School:** State University of New York at Stony Brook. **Year Graduated:** 1980. **Degree:** B.S., Political Science. **Law School:** St. John's University School of Law. **Year Graduated:** 1985. **Other Graduate Education:** M.S., Policy Analysis and Planning, W. Averell Harriman College, State University of New York at Stony Brook, 1980 (joint B.S./M.S. degree).

First Job After Law School: Corporate Associate, Willkie, Farr & Gallagher, New York, New York. **Notable Positions Since Law School:** Corporate Counsel, GAF Corp. Regional Counsel, Latin America, Philip Morris International. Executive Vice President, General Counsel and Secretary, Domino's Pizza Inc.

■

Carrie J. Hightman

Current Position: Executive Vice President and Chief Legal Officer, NiSource Inc., since December 2007.

Born: October 10, 1957. **Year Graduated High School:** 1975. **Undergraduate School:** University of Illinois. **Year Graduated:** 1979. **Degree:** B.A. **Law School:** Florida State University. **Year Graduated:** 1982.

First Job After Law School: Staff Counsel, Florida Public Service

Commission. **Notable Positions Since Law School:** Counsel, Florida Office of Public Counsel, 1985–1986. Partner, Schiff Hardin LLP, 1986–2001. President, AT&T Illinois.

■

Marie Oh Huber

Current Position: Senior Vice President, General Counsel and Secretary, Agilent Technologies Inc., since September 2009.

Born: November 1, 1961. **Year Graduated High School:** 1979. **Undergraduate School:** Yale University. **Year Graduated:** 1983. **Degree:** B.A., cum laude, Economics. **Law School:** Northwestern University School of Law. **Year Graduated:** 1986. **Other Graduate Education:** London School of Economics, 1981–1982.

First Job After Law School: Dewey, Ballantine, Bushby, Palmer & Wood, 1986–1988. **Notable Positions Since Law School:** Hewlett-Packard Co., 1990–1999. Heller, Ehrman, White & McAuliffe, 1988–1990.

■

Mary Ann Hynes

Current Position: Senior Vice President, General Counsel, Corporate Secretary, and Chief Compliance Office, Corn Products International Inc., since April 2006.

Born: October 26, 1947. **Year Graduated High School:** 1965. **Undergraduate School:** Loyola University. **Degree:** B.A., Political Science, Math.

Law School: John Marshall Law School. **Years Graduated:** J.D. 1971; LLM in Taxation, 1975. **Other Graduate Work:** Lake Forest Graduate School of Business. **Degree:** M.B.A. **Year Graduated:** 1993.

First Job After Law School: CCH Inc., Riverwoods, Illinois. **Notable Positions Since Law School:** Senior Vice President, General Counsel, and Corporate Secretary, IMC Global Inc., 1999–2004. Senior Vice President, General Counsel, and Corporate Secretary, Sundstrand Corp., 1998–1999. General Counsel, Wolters Kluwer, 1996–1998; Vice President and General Counsel, CCH Inc.

■

Frances Jones

Current Position: Executive Vice President and Deputy General Counsel, Branch Banking and Trust Co., since September 2010. **Previously:** Senior Vice President and Practice Group Manager, Branch Banking and Trust Co.; Executive Vice President, General Counsel, Corporate Secretary, and Chief Corporate Governance Officer, Branch Banking and Trust Co. and BB&T Corp.

Born: July 28, 1962. **Year Graduated High School:** 1980. **Undergraduate School:** Dartmouth College. **Year Graduated:** 1984. **Degree:** A.B., Distinction in major (Government). **Law School:** Vanderbilt University School of Law. **Year Graduated:** 1987.
First Job After Law School: Associate, Brown, Todd & Heyburn, Louisville, Kentucky. **Notable Positions Since Law School:** Vice President and Counsel, PNC Bank. Senior Vice

President and Corporate Banking Counsel, Bank of Louisville.

■

Nicole S. Jones

Current Position: Executive Vice President and General Counsel, CIGNA Corp., since 2011.

Born: March 11, 1970. **Year Graduated High School:** 1988. **Undergraduate School:** Fordham University. **Year Graduated:** 1992. **Degree:** B.A., Economics and Philosophy. **Law School:** New York University. **Year Graduated:** 1995.

First Job After Law School: Associate, Davis Polk & Wardwell. **Notable Positions Since Law School:** General Counsel, Lincoln National Corp.

■

Anastasia D. Kelly

Current Position: Partner, DLA Piper, since March 2010.

Born: October 9, 1949. **Year Graduated High School:** 1967. **Undergraduate School:** Trinity University. **Year Graduated:** 1971. **Degree:** B.A. **Law School:** George Washington University. **Year Graduated:** 1981.

First Job After Law School: Associate, Carrington, Coleman, Sloman & Blumenthal. **Notable Positions Since Law School:** Partner, Wilmer, Cutler & Pickering, 1985–1995. Deputy General Counsel and Senior Vice President, Fannie Mae, 1995–1999. Executive Vice President and

General Counsel, Sears, Roebuck and Co., 1999–2003. Executive Vice President and General Counsel, MCI/WorldCom, 2003–2006. Executive Vice President, General Counsel, and Chief Compliance and Regulatory Officer; Vice Chairman, Legal, Regulatory Compliance, Human Resources, Communications, Government Relations, AIG, 2006–2010.

■

Janet Langford Kelly

Current Position: Senior Vice President, Legal, General Counsel, and Corporate Secretary, ConocoPhillips, since 2007. **Previously:** Deputy General Counsel and Corporate Secretary, ConocoPhillips.

Undergraduate School: Grinnell College. **Year Graduated:** 1979. **Degree:** B.A., History, with honors. **Law School:** Yale Law School. **Year Graduated:** 1983.

First Job After Law School: Clerk for the Hon. James Hunter III, Third Circuit Court of Appeals. **Notable Positions Since Law School:** Partner, Zelle, Hoffman, Voelbel, Mason and Gette. Adjunct Professor, Northwestern University School of Law. Senior Vice President, Chief Administrative Officer and Chief Compliance Officer, Kmart Corp. Executive Vice President of Corporate Development and Administration, General Counsel and Secretary, Kellogg Co.. Senior Vice President, Secretary and General Counsel, Sara Lee Corp. Partner, Sidley Austin, Chicago. Associate, Corporate and Securities Group, Wachtell, Lipton, Rosen & Katz, New York.

Hynes

Frances Jones

Nicole S. Jones

Kelly

Langford Kelly

Kendall

Kerrigan

Kuper

Lambeth

Lamboley

Rebecca O. Kendall

Current Position: Retired.

Born: January 8, 1948. **Year Graduated High School:** 1966. **Undergraduate School:** Indiana University. **Year Graduated:** 1970. **Degree:** B.S., Education. **Law School:** Indiana University Indianapolis Law School. **Year Graduated:** 1975.

First Job After Law School: Staff Attorney, Eli Lilly and Co., 1975–1978. **Notable Positions Since Law School:** Eli Lilly and Co., 1981–2003: Senior Vice President and General Counsel, 1998–2003; Vice President and General Counsel, 1993–1995; Deputy General Counsel, 1988–1993; General Counsel, U.S. Pharmaceutical Operations, 1983–1988; Staff Attorney, Human Resources Division, 1981–1983.

■

Sylvia Kerrigan

Current Position: Vice President, General Counsel, and Secretary, Marathon Oil Corp., since September 2009.

Born: 1965. **Year Graduated High School:** 1983. **Undergraduate School:** Southwestern University. **Year Graduated:** 1986. **Degree:** B.A., Philosophy, Political Economy and English. **Law School:** University of Texas, Austin. **Year Graduated:** 1990.

First Job After Law School: Private practice as civil litigator, Houston, Texas. **Notable Positions Since Law School:** Texas Supreme Court in Austin. United Nations, Geneva, Switzerland.

Debra E. Kuper

Current Position: Vice President, General Counsel, and Corporate Secretary, AGCO Corp., since January 2008.

Born: March 25, 1965. **Year Graduated High School:** 1983. **Undergraduate School:** University of Wisconsin. **Year Graduated:** 1993. **Degree:** B.S., Political Science. **Law School:** Marquette University Law School. **Year Graduated:** 1997.

First Job After Law School: Civil Litigator, Kenosha, Wisconsin. **Notable Positions Since Law School:** Senior Corporate Counsel, Caterpillar Inc., 2005–2008. Associate General Counsel, Wal-mart Stores Inc., 2004–2005. Corporate Counsel and Assistant Secretary, Tenneco Inc., 2002–2004. Senior Counsel, Corporate Governance and Government Affairs, CNH Global, N.V., 1999–2002.

■

E. Julia "Judy" Lambeth

Most Recent Position: Executive Vice President and General Counsel, Reynolds American Inc., 2006-2010.

Born: June 19, 1951. **Year Graduated High School:** 1969. **Undergraduate School:** Hollins University. **Year Graduated:** 1973. **Degree:** B.A., English. **Law School:** Wake Forest University. **Year Graduated:** 1977.

First Job After Law School: Attorney (general commercial and litigation), DuPont Co., Wilmington,

Delaware. **Notable Positions Since Law School:** Associate General Counsel, DuPont. Deputy General Counsel, Conoco and its successor, ConocoPhillips. Corporate Secretary, Conoco and ConocoPhillips.

■

Catherine A. Lamboley

Current Position: Consultant (self-employed), since July 2007.

Born: September 30, 1950. **Year Graduated High School:** 1968. **Undergraduate School:** University of Wisconsin–Madison. **Year Graduated:** 1972. **Degree:** B.S., Secondary Education. **Law School:** University of Texas at Austin. **Year Graduated:** 1979.

First Job After Law School: Attorney, Shell Oil Co., Legal Department, 1979–1996. **Notable Positions Since Law School:** Shell Oil Co.: Senior Vice President, General Counsel and Corporate Secretary, 2000–2007; General Manager and Associate General Counsel, 1999–2000; Vice President, Commercial Products, Shell Oil Products Co., 1996–1999; Associate General Counsel, 1995–1996; Assistant General Counsel, 1994–1995; General Attorney, 1991–1994.

■

Susan Lanigan

Current Position: Executive Vice President, General Counsel, Dollar General Corp., since July 2002.

Born: May 29, 1962. **Year Graduated High School:** 1980. **Undergraduate School: University of Georgia. **Year Graduated:** 1984. **Degree:** B.A., cum laude, Journalism. **Law School:** University of Georgia. **Year Graduated:** Magna cum laude, 1988.

First Job After Law School: Attorney/Litigator, Troutman Sanders, Atlanta, Georgia. **Notable Positions Since Law School:** Senior Vice President, General Counsel and Corporate Secretary, Zale Corp., 1996–2002. Attorney, Turner Broadcasting System, 1995–1996.

■

Maryanne R. Lavan

Current Position: Senior Vice President, General Counsel, and Corporate Secretary, Lockheed Martin Corp., since 2010. **Previously:** Vice President, Internal Audit, 2007–2010. Vice President, Ethics and Business Conduct, 2003–2007. Vice President and General Counsel, Electronic Systems, 1996–2003.

Born: May 8, 1959. **Year Graduated High School:** 1977. **Undergraduate School:** State University of New York at Albany. **Year Graduated:** 1981. **Law School:** The Washington College of Law, American University. **Year Graduated:** 1984.

■

Theresa K. Lee

Current Position: Senior Vice President, Chief Legal and Administrative Officer, Eastman Chemical Co., since January 2001. **Previously:** Vice President, General Counsel and

Corporate Secretary; Vice President, Associate General Counsel and Secretary; Assistant Secretary and Assistant General Counsel, Legal Department Corporate Group; Assistant Secretary and Assistant General Counsel, Legal Department, Health, Safety and Environmental Group; Assistant Secretary and Senior Counsel, Texas Eastman Division of Eastman Chemical Co..

Born: November 21, 1952. **Year Graduated High School:** 1970. **Undergraduate School:** East Tennessee State University. **Year Graduated:** 1974. **Degree:** B.S., Political Science and History. **Law School:** University of Tennessee. **Year Graduated:** 1977. **Other Graduate Education:** Harvard Business School, Advanced Management Program.

First Job After Law School: Legal Aid Attorney, Legal Services of Upper East Tennessee. **Notable Positions Since Law School:** Senior Law Clerk to the Hon. H. Emory Widener, U.S. Court of Appeals for the Fourth Circuit.

■

Holly E. Leese

Current Position: Senior Vice President–General Counsel and Secretary, Chrysler Group LLC, since 2009. **Previously:** Senior Vice President, General Counsel and Secretary, Chrysler LLC; Vice President, General Counsel, and Secretary, Chrysler LLC; Assistant General Counsel and Assistant Secretary, Chrysler Group, DaimlerChrysler; Senior Staff Counsel and Assistant Secretary, Chrysler Corp.; Senior

Staff Counsel, Corporate Affairs, Chrysler Corp.; Staff Counsel, Corporate and Government Affairs, Chrysler Corp.

Born: November 15, 1955. **Year Graduated High School:** 1972. **Undergraduate School:** State University of New York at Albany. **Year Graduated:** 1976. **Degree:** B.A., Social Sciences. **Law School:** Albany Law School. **Year Graduated:** 1979.

■

Sandra Leung

Current Position: General Counsel and Corporate Secretary, Bristol-Myers Squibb Co., since February 2007. **Previously:** Acting General Counsel, Vice President, and Corporate Secretary, 2006–2007; Vice President and Corporate Secretary, 2002–2006; Corporate Secretary, 1999–2002; Associate Counsel, 1997–1999; Assistant Counsel, 1996–1997; Senior Staff Attorney, 1994–1996; Staff Attorney, 1992–1994.

Born: April 19, 1960. **Year Graduated High School:** 1978. **Undergraduate School:** Tufts University. **Year Graduated:** 1981. **Degree:** B.A., Political Science. **Law School:** Boston College. Year Graduated: 1984.

First Job After Law School: Assistant District Attorney, N.Y. County District Attorney's Office, 1984–1992.

Lanigan

LaVan

Lee

Leese

Leung

Lichtenstein

Lione

Maher

Majoras

Marco

Susan R. Lichtenstein

Current Position: Senior Vice President, Corporate Affairs, and Chief Legal Officer, Hill-Rom Holdings Inc., since May 2010.

Born: January 4, 1957. **Year Graduated High School:** 1974. **Undergraduate School:** University of Minnesota. **Year Graduated:** 1978. **Degree:** B.A. **Law School:** Northwestern University Law School. **Year Graduated:** 1981.

First Job After Law School: Associate, Schiff Hardin & Waite. **Notable Positions Since Law School:** Corporate Vice President and General Counsel, Baxter International, 2005–2009. Senior Vice President and General Counsel, Tellabs Inc., 2001–2002. Senior Vice President and General Counsel, Ameritech Corp., 2000–2001. Partner, Schiff Hardin & Waite. Deputy Corporate Counsel, City of Chicago. General Counsel to the Office of the Illinois Governor.

■

Gail Lione

Most Recent Position: President, The Harley-Davidson Foundation, 2006-May 2011.

Born: October 22, 1949. **Year Graduated High School:** 1967. **Undergraduate School:** University of Rochester. **Degree:** B.A., Political Science, magna cum laude, Phi Beta Kappa. **Law School:** University of Pennsylvania. **Year Graduated:** 1974.

First Job After Law School: Morgan, Lewis & Bockius, Philadelphia. **Notable Positions Since Law School:**

Executive Vice President, General Counsel, and Secretary, Chief Compliance Officer, Harley-Davidson Inc., 2007–2010. General Counsel, U.S. News & World Report, 1990–2007. Senior Vice President, Corporate Secretary, and General Counsel, Sun Life Group of America Inc., 1986–1989.

■

Francesca M. Maher (Edwardson)

Current Position: Chief Executive Officer, American Red Cross of Greater Chicago, since January 2005.

Born: October 27, 1957. **Year Graduated High School:** 1975. **Undergraduate School:** Loyola University. **Year Graduated:** 1978. **Degree:** B.A., Economics, cum laude. **Law School:** Loyola University. **Year Graduated:** 1981.

First Job After Law School: Associate, Mayer Brown Rowe & Maw, Chicago. **Notable Positions Since Law School:** Special Counsel, Mayer Brown Rowe & Maw, 2003–2004. Senior Vice President, General Counsel and Secretary, UAL Corp., 1998–2003. Vice President, General Counsel and Secretary, UAL Corp., 1997–1998. Vice President, Law and Corporate Secretary, UAL Corp., 1993–1997.

■

Deborah Platt Majoras

Current Position: Chief Legal Officer and Secretary, Procter & Gamble, since February 2010. **Born:** August 10, 1963. **Year**

Graduated High School: 1981. **Undergraduate School:** Westminster University. **Year Graduated:** 1985. **Degree:** B.A. **Law School:** University of Virginia Law School. **Year Graduated:** 1985.

First Job After Law School: Judicial Clerk, The Hon. Stanley S. Harris, U.S. District Court for the District of Columbia. **Notable Positions Since Law School:** Chairman, U.S. Federal Trade Commission. Principal Deputy Assistant Attorney General, U.S. Department of Justice Antitrust Division. Partner, Jones Day.

■

Lori J. Marco

Current Position: Vice President–External Affairs, General Counsel, Hormel Foods Corp., since 2011. **Previously:** Senior Attorney, 2007–2011. Corporate Attorney, 2004–2007.

Born: August 30, 1967. **Year Graduated High School:** 1985. **Undergraduate School:** University of Minnesota, Morris. **Year Graduated:** 1989. **Degree:** B.A., Biology. **Law School:** University of Minnesota Law School. **Year Graduated:** 1997.

Notable Positions Since Law School: Attorney, Briggs and Morgan, P.A. Registered patent attorney.

■

Elizabeth Markowski

Current Position: Senior VP, General Counsel, and Secretary, Liberty Global Inc., since 2005.

Born: October 26, 1948. **Year Graduated High School:** 1966. **Undergraduate School:** Fordham University. **Year Graduated:** 1970. **Degree:** B.S., Psychology **Law School:** New York University. **Year Graduated:** 1978.

First Job After Law School: Law clerk to Hon. Edward Weinfeld, SDNY. **Notable Positions Since Law School:** Senior Vice President, General Counsel, and Secretary, Liberty Media International Inc., March 2004–present; Liberty Media Corp., 2000–2004. Senior Vice President, Public Affiliates, 1992–2000. Partner, BakerBotts, LLP.

■

Siri Marshall

Current Position: Retired **Undergraduate School:** Harvard University. **Year Graduated:** 1970. **Law School:** Yale Law School. **Year Graduated:** 1974.

Notable Positions Since Law School: Senior Vice President, General Counsel, Secretary, and Chief Governance and Compliance Officer, General Mills. Senior Vice President, General Counsel, and Secretary, Avon Products Inc.

■

Michele Coleman Mayes

Current Position: Executive Vice President and General Counsel, Allstate Insurance Co, since November 2007.

Born: July 9, 1949. Year **Graduated High School:** 1967. **Undergraduate School:** University of Michigan. **Year Graduated:** 1971. **Degree:** B.A. **Law School:** University of Michigan Law School. **Year Graduated:** 1974.

First Job After Law School: Assistant Professor, Illinois State University. **Notable Positions Since Law School:** Senior Vice President and General Counsel, Pitney Bowes, 2003–2007. Vice President, Legal and Assistant Secretary, Colgate-Palmolive, 1992–2003. Staff Vice President, Burroughs/Unisys, 1982–1992. U.S. Attorney's Office, Eastern District of Detroit, 1979–1982. U.S. Attorney's Office, Eastern District of New York, 1979–1979. U.S. Attorney's Office, Eastern District of Detroit, 1976–1979.

■

Teri Plummer McClure

Current Position: Senior Vice President of Legal, Compliance & Public Affairs, General Counsel, and Corporate Secretary, UPS, since 2005.

Born: December 31, 1963. **Undergraduate School:** Washington University. **Year Graduated:** 1985. **Degree:** B.S., Business Administration, Marketing and Economics. **Law School:** Emory University School of Law. **Year Graduated:** 1988.

First Job After Law School: Ford & Harrison. **Notable Positions Since Law School:** Troutman Saunders, 1993–1995. Currie Smith & Hancock, 1990–1993.

Margaret B. McLean

Current Position: Senior Vice President, Chief Legal and Compliance Officer and Corporate Secretary, CH2M HILL Companies, Ltd., since February 2007.

Born: April 10, 1963. **Year Graduated High School:** 1980. **Undergraduate School:** University of Arizona. Year Graduated: 1983. **Degree:** B.S., Computer Science, magna cum laude. **Law School:** University of Michigan. **Year Graduated:** 1992, cum laude. **Other Graduate Education:** M.B.A., University of Colorado, 1985.

First Job After Law School: Holme Roberts & Owen, Denver, Colorado. **Notable Positions Since Law School:** Partner, Holme Roberts & Owen, Denver, Colorado. Also: Director of Management Information Systems, Science Applications International, 1986–1989.

■

Anne McNamara

Current Position: Retired.

Born: October 18, 1947. **Year Graduated High School:** 1965. **Undergraduate School:** Vassar College. **Year Graduated:** 1969. **Degree:** B.A. **Law School:** Cornell University. **Year Graduated:** 1972.

First Job After Law School: Associate, Shea & Gould. **Notable Positions Since Law School:** AMR Corp.: Senior Vice President and General Counsel, 1989–2003; Vice President, Personnel, 1989–1989; Corporate Secretary, 1979–1988; Attorney, 1976–1979.

Markowski

Mayes

McClure

McLean

McNamara

McWatters

Moss

O'Meara

Parent

Petren

Denise McWatters

Current Position: Vice President, General Counsel, and Secretary, Holly Corp. and Holly Energy Partners, since May 2008. **Previously:** Deputy General Counsel, 2007–2008.

Born: 1959. **Year Graduated High School:** 1977. **Undergraduate School:** Southern Methodist University. **Year Graduated:** 1980. **Degree:** B.S., Psychology, Phi Beta Kappa. **Law School:** University of Texas at Austin. **Year Graduated:** 1984. **Other Graduate Education:** M.A., Psychology, Southern Methodist University, 1981.

First Job After Law School: Associate Litigation Attorney, Sharp & Morse, Austin, Texas. **Notable Positions Since Law School:** Shareholder, Cox & Smith, Dallas, Texas. Counsel, Citigroup Inc. Shareholder, Lock Lord Bissell & Liddell. General Counsel, The Beck Group.

■

Sara E. Moss

Current Position: Executive Vice President and General Counsel, The Estée Lauder Companies Inc., since September 2003.

Born: November 13, 1946. **Year Graduated High School:** 1964. **Undergraduate School:** University of Massachusetts. **Year Graduated:** 1968. **Degree:** B.A., History. **Law School:** New York University Law School. **Year Graduated:** 1974.

First Job After Law School: Law clerk, the Hon. Constance Baker

Motley, U.S.D.J., S.U.N.Y. **Notable Positions Since Law School:** Senior Vice President and General Counsel, Pitney Bowes Inc., 1996–2003. Senior Litigation Partner, Howard, Smith & Levin (now Covington & Burling), 1984–1996. Litigation Associate, Davis, Polk & Wardwell, 1981–1984. Assistant U.S. Attorney, Criminal Division, United States Attorneys Office, Southern District of New York, 1978–1981. Litigation Associate, Davis, Polk & Wardwell, 1975–1978.

■

Vicki O'Meara

Current Position: Executive Vice President and President, Pitney Bowes Services Solutions, since July 2010. **Previously:** General Counsel, 2008–2010.

Born: May 13, 1957. Year **Graduated High School:** 1975. **Undergraduate School:** Cornell University. **Year Graduated:** 1979. **Degree:** B.A. **Law School:** Northwestern University. **Year Graduated:** 1982.

Notable Positions Since Law School: General Counsel, Chief Compliance Officer, and President, Supply Chain Solutions, Ryder System Inc., 1997–2007. Jones, Day, Reavis & Pogue, 1993–1997. Assistant Attorney General, U.S. Department of Justice, 1992–1993. Jones, Day, Reavis & Pogue, 1988–1992. Deputy General Counsel, U.S. Environmental Protection Agency, 1987–1988. White House Fellow, 1986–1987. Captain, U.S. Army, 1982–1986.

Louise M. Parent

Current Position: Executive Vice President and General Counsel, American Express Co., since May 1989.

Born: August 28, 1950. **Year Graduated High School:** 1968. **Undergraduate School:** Smith College. **Year Graduated:** 1972. **Degree:** A.B. **Law School:** Georgetown University Law Center. **Year Graduated:** 1975.

First Job After Law School: Donovan, Leisure, Newton & Irvine.

■

Carol Ann Petren

Current Position: Executive Vice President and General Counsel, MacAndrews and Forbes Holdings Inc., since 2011.

Born: 1952. **Year Graduated High School:** 1970. **Undergraduate School:** Boston College. **Year Graduated:** 1974. **Degree:** B.A. **Law School:** University of Missouri School of Law. **Year Graduated:** 1977. **Other Graduate Education:** University of Missouri School of Law, LLM—Trial Practice, 1978.

First Job After Law School: Assistant Prosecutor, Jackson County Prosecutor's Office, Kansas City, Missouri. **Notable Positions Since Law School:** CIGNA Corp.: Executive Vice President, General Counsel, and Corporate Secretary, 2010–2011; Executive Vice President and General Counsel, 2006–2010. Senior Vice President and Deputy General Counsel, MCI

Inc. (Verizon Business as of January 2006). Vice President and Deputy General Counsel, Sears, Roebuck and Co. Managing Partner, Wilson, Elser, Moskowitz, Edelman & Dicker. Partner, Jordan Coyne & Savits. Counsel, Committee on Standards of Official Conduct, U.S. House of Representatives. Assistant United States Attorney, Western District of Missouri.

■

Jennifer W. Pileggi

Current Position: Executive Vice President, General Counsel, and Corporate Secretary, Con-way Inc., since December 2004.

Born: July 27, 1964. **Year Graduated High School:** 1982. **Undergraduate School:** Yale University. **Year Graduated:** 1986. **Degree:** B.A., Art History. **Law School:** New York University Law School. **Year Graduated:** 1990.

First Job After Law School: Heller, Ehrman, White & McAuliffe, San Francisco, California. **Notable Positions Since Law School:** Vice President and Corporate Counsel, Menlo Logistics, 1999–2004.

■

Helen P. Pudlin

Current Position: Executive Vice President and General Counsel, The PNC Financial Services Group Inc., since February 2009.

Year Graduated High School: 1967. **Undergraduate School:** University of Pennsylvania. **Year Graduated:** 1970. **Degree:** B.A.

Other Graduate Education: University of Pennsylvania, Masters in Education, M.S., 1971. **Law School:** University of Pennsylvania Law School. **Year Graduated:** 1974.

First Job After Law School: Associate, Ballard, Spahr, Andrews & Ingersoll, 1974–1981. **Notable Positions Since Law School:** Partner, Ballard, Spahr, Andrews & Ingersoll, 1981–1989. Lecturer, University of Pennsylvania Law School, 1983–1987. Co-Vice Chair, Board of Trustees, The Wistar Institute, 2001–present.

Awards and Recognition: National Diversity Council, 2011 Pennsylvania Most Powerful and Influential Women Award; 2011 Girls Inc. New York Luncheon Women of Achievement Honoree; Women Worth Watching in 2010, The Legal Intelligencer; Women Worth Watching in 2008, Diversity Journal; Alumni Award of Merit, University of Pennsylvania Law School, 2005.

■

Teresa Rasmussen

Current Position: Senior Vice President, General Counsel and Secretary, Thrivent Financial for Lutherans, since March 2005.

Born: October 9, 1956. **Year Graduated High School:** 1973. **Undergraduate School:** Minnesota State University Moorhead. **Year Graduated:** 1981. **Degree:** B.S., Accounting. **Law School:** University of North Dakota Grand Forks. **Year Graduated:** 1984. **Other Graduate Education:** A.A., Dental Hygiene, NDSSS, 1977. **First Job After Law School:**

Trial Attorney, U.S. Department of Justice, Tax Division, Washington, D.C. **Notable Positions Since Law School:** American Express, Minneapolis, Minnesota, 1990–2005.

■

Carter M. Reid

Current Position: Vice President, General Counsel and Corporate Secretary, Chief Compliance Officer, Dominion, since 2011. **Previously:** Vice President–Governance and General Counsel, 2007–2011; Director–Executive Compensation, 2003–2007; Managing Counsel, 2000–2003; Assistant General Counsel, 1996–2000.

Undergraduate School: James Madison University. **Law School:** T.C. Williams School of Law, University of Richmond.

Notable Positions Since Law School: Associate, Hunton & Williams and McGuireWoods.

■

Christine P. Richards

Current Position: Executive VP, General Counsel and Secretary, FedEx Corp., since 2005. **Previously:** Corporate VP-Customer and Business Transactions.

Undergraduate School: Bucknell University. **Year Graduated:** 1976. **Law School:** Duke University. **Year Graduated:** 1979.

Notable Positions Since Law School: Assistant Secretary, Board of Trustees, The Dixon Gallery and

Pileggi

Pudlin

Rasmussen

Reid

Richards

Rivera

Rucker

Santona

Schulman

Schumacher

Gardens. Member, Board of Visitors, The Fuqua School of Business at Duke University.

■

Kim Rivera

Current Position: Vice President, General Counsel, and Secretary, DaVita Inc., since January 2010.

Born: November 4, 1968. **Year Graduated High School:** 1985. **Undergraduate School:** Duke University. **Year Graduated:** 1990. **Degree:** B.A., Interdisciplinary Studies. **Law School:** Harvard Law School. **Year Graduated:** 1994.

First Job After Law School: Associate, Jones Day, Cleveland, Ohio. **Notable Positions Since Law School:** Vice President, Law, Rockwell Automation. Vice President, Associate General Counsel, The Clorox Co.

■

Kim K. W. Rucker

Current Position: Senior Vice President, General Counsel, and Corporate Secretary, Avon Products Inc., since March 2008.

Born: January 4, 1967. **Year Graduated High School:** 1985. **Undergraduate School:** University of Iowa. **Year Graduated:** 1989. **Degree:** B.B.A., Economics. **Law School:** Harvard Law School. **Year Graduated:** 1993.

Notable Positions Since Law School: Senior Vice President, Sec-

retary and Chief Governance Officer, TXU Corp., 2004–2008. Counsel, Corp. Affairs, Kimberly-Clark Corp., 2001–2004. Partner, Sidley Austin Brown & Wood, 1993–2001.

Gloria Santona

Current Position: Executive Vice President, General Counsel, and Secretary, McDonald's Corp., since June 2001. **Previously:** General Counsel, 2001–present; U.S. General Counsel, 1999; Corporate Secretary, 1996.

Born: June 10, 1950. **Year Graduated High School:** 1968. **Undergraduate School:** Michigan State University. **Year Graduated:** 1971. **Degree:** B.S., Biochemistry. **Law School:** University of Michigan Law School. **Year Graduated:** 1977.

First Job After Law School: Attorney, McDonald's Corp.,

■

Amy Schulman

Current Position: Executive Vice President and General Counsel, Pfizer, since 2008, and Business Lead, Pfizer Nutrition, since 2010.

Undergraduate School: Wesleyan University. **Law School:** Yale Law School. **Year Graduated:** 1989. **Notable Positions Since Law School:** Partner, DLA Piper.

■

Laura J. Schumacher

Current Position: Executive Vice President, General Counsel, and Secretary, Abbott, since February 2007.

Born: 1963. **Year Graduated High School:** 1981. **Undergraduate School:** University of Notre Dame. **Year Graduated:** 1985. **Degree:** Business Administration. **Law School:** University of Wisconsin Law School. **Year Graduated:** 1988.

First Job After Law School: Schiff Hardin, LLP, Chicago, Illinois. **Notable Positions Since Law School:** Abbott: Senior Vice President, General Counsel and Secretary, 2005; Vice President, Deputy General Counsel and Secretary, 2003.

■

Teresa M. Sebastian

Current Position: Senior Vice President, General Counsel and Corporate Secretary, Darden Restaurants Inc., since October, 2010.

Born: November 11, 1957. **Year Graduated High School:** 1975. **Undergraduate School:** University of Michigan. **Year Graduated:** 1978. **Degree:** B.A. **Other Graduate Education:** University of North Florida, M.B.A., 1983. **Law Schools:** Michigan State University College of Law, J.D., 1993; Wayne State University Law School, LL.M., 2003.

Notable Positions Held Since Law School: Vice President, General Counsel, and Corporate Secretary, Veyance Technologies. Senior Vice President and General Counsel, Information Resources Inc. Assistant General Counsel and Assistant Corporate Secretary, DTE Energy Corp. Senior Corporate Counsel, CMS Energy Corp.

Laureen Seeger

Current Position: Executive Vice President, General Counsel, and Chief Compliance Officer, McKesson Corp., since March 2006. **Previously:** General Counsel, McKesson Provider Technologies, 2000–2006.

Born: October 25, 1961. **Year Graduated High School:** 1979. **Undergraduate School:** University of Wisconsin–Eau Claire. **Year Graduated:** 1983. **Degree:** B.A., Business Administration. **Law School:** University of Wisconsin–Madison. **Year Graduated:** 1986.

First Job After Law School: Commercial Litigation Associate, Jones, Day, Reavis & Pogue. **Notable Positions Since Law School:** Partner, Morris, Manning & Martin, LLP, 1994–2000.

■

Karen Shaff

Current Position: Executive Vice President and General Counsel, Principal Financial Group, since May 2004 (General Counsel since 2000).

Born: October 26, 1954. **Year Graduated High School:** 1972. **Undergraduate School:** Northwestern University. **Year Graduated:** 1976. **Degree:** B.A., Political Science. **Law School:** Drake University Law School. **Year Graduated:** 1979.

First Job After Law School: Associate, Austin & Gaudineer, **Notable Positions Since Law School:** President, Association of Life Insurance Counsel, 2006–2007.

Lauri Shanahan

Current Positions: Board of Directors, Charlotte Russe, since 2009; Principal, Maroon Peak Advisors, since 2009.

Born: August 24, 1962. **Year Graduated High School:** 1980. **Undergraduate School:** University of Colorado, Boulder. **Year Graduated:** 1984. **Degree:** B.S., Finance. **Law School:** UCLA. **Year Graduated:** 1987.

Notable Positions Since Law School: Chief Legal and Administrative Officer, Gap Inc.; Associate, Thelen, Marrin, Johnson and Bridges.

■

Paula J. Shives

Current Position: Retired.

Undergraduate School: Western Kentucky University. **Law School:** University of Kentucky.

Notable Positions Since Law School: Senior Vice President, General Counsel, and Secretary, Darden Restaurants, 1999–2010. Senior Vice President, Secretary and General Counsel, Long John Silver's.

■

Victoria Silbey

Current Position: Senior Vice President and Legal and General Counsel, SunGard Data Systems, since January 2005. **Previously:** Vice President, Legal and Assistant General Counsel, 2004–2005.

Born: November 12, 1963. **Year**

Graduated High School: 1981. **Undergraduate School:** Cornell University. **Year Graduated:** 1985. **Degree:** BA, History. **Law School:** Cornell Law School. **Year Graduated:** 1990. **Other Graduate Education:** University of Oxford, M.Phil, History, 1987.

First Job After Law School: Clerk for Judge John G. Davies, U.S. District Court for the Central District of California, 1990–1991. **Notable Positions Since Law School:** Lawyer, Morgan, Lewis & Bockius, LLP, Philadelphia, 1991–1997.

■

Maura Abein Smith

Current Position: Executive Vice President, Government Affairs, General Counsel, and Corporate Secretary, PepsiCo, since 2011.

Undergraduate School: Vassar College. **Degree:** B.A., Economics. **Other Graduate Education:** Oxford University, Oxford, England, Master of Philosophy, Economics. Rhodes Scholarship recipient, Oxford University. **Law School:** University of Miami School of Law.

Notable Positions Since Law School: Senior Vice President, General Counsel, Corporate Secretary, and Global Government Relations, International Paper. Senior Vice President, General Counsel, and Corporate Secretary, Owens Corning. Vice President and General Counsel, General Electric Plastics Division. Partner, Baker & McKenzie. Associate, Steel Hector & Davis (now part of Squire Sanders). Commissioner, Tennessee Supreme

Sebastian

Seeger

Shaff

Shanahan

Shives

Smith

Strobel

Vespoli

Walker-Lee

Zopp

Court Access to Justice Commission, 2009–present.

■

Laura Stein

Current Position: Senior Vice President and General Counsel, The Clorox Co., since 2005.

Undergraduate School: Dartmouth College. **Law School:** Harvard Law School.

Notable Positions Since Law School: Senior Vice President –General Counsel, H.J. Heinz Co.. Assistant General Counsel– Regulatory Affairs, The Clorox Co. Attorney, Morrison & Foerster.

■

Pamela Strobel

Current Position: Retired.

Undergraduate School: University of Illinois. **Law School:** University of Illinois College of Law.

Notable Positions Since Law School: Executive Vice President and Chief Administrative Officer, Exelon Corp. Chairman and CEO, Exelon Energy Delivery. Executive Vice President, Unicom Corp. General Counsel, ComEd. Partner, Sidley Austin. Partner, Isham, Lincoln & Beale.

■

Leila L. Vespoli

Current Position: Executive Vice President and General Counsel,

FirstEnergy Corp., since March 2008. **Previously:** Senior Vice President and General Counsel, 2001–2008; Vice President and General Counsel, 2000–2001; Associate General Counsel, 1997–2000.

Born: July 24, 1959. **Year Graduated High School:** 1977. **Undergraduate School:** Miami University (Ohio). **Year Graduated:** 1981. **Degree:** B.S., Business Economics. **Law School:** Case Western Reserve University. **Year Graduated:** 1984. **Other Graduate Education:** Reactor Technology Course for Utility Executives, Massachusetts Institute of Technology, 2009.

First Job After Law School: Associate Attorney, Ohio Edison, which merged with Centerior Energy to form FirstEnergy in 1997.

■

Jennifer Vogel

Most Recent Position: Senior Vice President, General Counsel, Secretary, and Chief Compliance Officer, Continental Airlines Inc., 2001–2010.

Born: September 29, 1961. **Year Graduated High School:** 1979. **Undergraduate School:** University of Iowa. **Year Graduated:** 1983. **Degree:** B.B.A. **Law School:** University of Texas. **Year Graduated:** 1987.

First Job After Law School: Associate, Vinson & Elkins. **Notable Positions Since Law School:** General Counsel of NYSE-traded subsidiary, Enron, 1994–1995.

Robin Walker-Lee

Current Position: Executive Vice President, General Counsel, and Secretary, TRW Automotive Holdings Corp., since February 2010.

Born: March 25, 1954. **Year Graduated High School:** 1972. **Undergraduate School:** University of Kansas. **Year Graduated:** 1976. **Degree:** B.A., French and English, with honors. **Law School:** Michigan Law School. **Year Graduated:** 1985, magna cum laude.

First Job After Law School: Judicial clerkship, Hon. Cornelia G. Kennedy, U.S. Court of Appeals for the Sixth Circuit. **Notable Positions Since Law School:** Assistant General Counsel, General Motors Co. General Counsel and VP, Public Policy, Latin America, Africa & Mideast, General Motors Co.

■

Andrea Zopp

Current Position: President and CEO, Chicago Urban League, since 2010.

Undergraduate School: Harvard University. **Degree:** Bachelor's, History and Science. **Law School:** Harvard Law School.

Notable Positions Since Law School: Executive Vice President and General Counsel, Exelon Corp. Senior Vice President, General Counsel and Corporate Secretary, Sears Holdings Corp. Vice President, Deputy General Counsel, Sara Lee Corp. Assistant U.S. Attorney, Chicago.

WOMEN GENERAL COUNSEL IN THE

Fortune 500

In 1999, MCCA began

charting the rise of

women general counsel

in the Fortune 500.

Here's the 2011 list, in

which women GCs hit an

all-time high of 101.

2011 RANK	2010 RANK	COMPANY	GENERAL COUNSEL	INDUSTRY
4	6	ConocoPhillips	Janet Langford Kelly	Utilities: Gas and Electric
15	14	McKesson	Laureen Seeger	Wholesalers: Healthcare
24	26	Valero Energy	Kim Bowers	Petroleum Refining
26	22	Procter & Gamble	Deborah Platt Majoras	Household and Personal Products
29	41	Marathon Oil	Sylvia Kerrigan	Utilities: Petroleum Refining
31	40	Pfizer	Amy Schulman	Pharmaceuticals
32	32	Walgreen	Dana Green	Food and Drug Stores
43	50	PepsiCo	Maura Abeln Smith	Food Consumer Products
48	43	United Parcel Service	Teri Plummer McClure	Mail, Package, and Freight Delivery
52	44	Lockheed Martin	Maryanne Lavan	Aerospace and Defense
54	39	Goldman Sachs Group	Esta Stetcher**	Commercial Banks
59		Chrysler Group	Holly Leese	Motor Vehicles
64	65	Prudential Financial	Susan Blount	Insurance: Life, Health (Stock)
68	78	Sunoco	Stacy L. Fox	Petroleum Refining
69	75	Abbott Laboratories	Laura Schumacher	Pharmaceuticals
71	64	New York Life Insurance	Sheila Davidson	Insurance: Life, Health (Mutual)
72	61	Northrop Grumman	Sheila Cheston*	Aerospace and Defense
73	60	FedEx	Christine Richards	Mail, Package, and Freight Delivery
78	100	Amazon.com	Michelle Wilson	Internet Services and Retailing
80		Enterprise Products Partners	Stephanie C. Hildebrandt*	Pipelines, Natural Gas Processing
81	74	Honeywell International	Katherine Adams	Aerospace and Defense
89	68	Allstate	Michele Coleman Mayes	Insurance: Property & Casualty (Stock)
91	88	American Express	Louise Parent	Commercial Banks
96	105	Oracle	Dorian Daley	Office Equipment
103	91	CHS	Lisa Zell	Wholesalers: Diversified
105	104	International Paper	Sharon Ryan	Forest and Paper Products
108	101	Staples	Kristin Campbell	Office Equipment
111	108	McDonald's	Gloria Santona	Food Services
119	119	TJX	Ann McCauley	Specialty Retailers
122	129	CIGNA	Nicole Jones**	Health Care: Insurance and Management
127	118	Nationwide	Patricia Hatler	Insurance: Property & Casualty (Stock)
131	114	Bristol-Myers Squibb	Sandra Leung	Pharmaceuticals
135	124	Nike	Hilary Krane	Apparel
146	133	J.C. Penney	Janet Dhillon	General Merchandisers
151	123	PNC Financial Services Group	Helen Pudlin	Commercial Banks
154	137	Altria Group	Denise Keane	Tobacco and Other Products

* New to list   ** Replaced a woman on last year's list   Source: Minority Corporate Counsel Association; first published in *Diversity & the Bar,* Sept/Oct 2011

2011 RANK	2010 RANK	COMPANY	GENERAL COUNSEL	INDUSTRY
162	153	Dominion Resources	Carter Reid	Utilities: Gas and Electric
165	274	Bank of New York Mellon Corp.	Jane Sherburne	Commercial Banks
167	162	Gap	Michelle Banks	Specialty Retailers
171	201	TRW Automotive Holdings	Robin Walker-Lee	Motor Vehicles and Parts
179	146	Health Net	Angelee Bouchard	Health Care: Insurance and Management
183	179	FirstEnergy	Leila Vespoli	Utilities: Gas and Electric
184	175	Consolidated Edison	Elizabeth Moore	Utilities: Gas and Electric
185	176	Chubb	Maureen Brundage	Insurance: Property & Casualty (Stock)
186	218	Cummins	Marya Rose	Construction
188	195	Dollar General	Susan Lanigan	General Merchandisers
190	191	Community Health Systems	Rachel Seifert	Health Care: Medical Facilities
191	180	Sara Lee	Paulette Dodson	Food Consumer Products
200	178	ConAgra Foods	Colleen Batcheler	Food Consumer Products
205	229	Southwest Airlines	Madeleine Johnson	Airlines
211	192	Office Depot	Elisa Garcia	Office Equipment
226	228	Avon Products	Kim Rucker	Household and Personal Products
229	241	Starbucks	Paula Boggs	Food Services
230	259	CSX	Ellen Fitzsimmons	Railroads
247	240	R.R. Donnelley & Sons	Suzanne Bettman	Publishing, Printing
255	210	Liberty Global	Elizabeth Markowski	Telecommunications
268	266	Principal Financial	Karen Shaff	Insurance: Life, Health (Stock)
273	284	Whole Foods Market	Roberta Lang	Food and Drug Stores
284	272	Reynolds American	E. Julia "Judy" Lambeth	Tobacco and Other Products
289	431	Holly	Denise McWatters	Petroleum Refining
291	286	Discover Financial Services	Kelly McNamara Corley	Commercial Banks
295	283	Owens & Minor	Grace den Hartog	Wholesalers: Healthcare
307	308	Estee Lauder	Sara Moss	Household and Personal Products
310	310	VF	Candace Cummings	Apparel
312	299	Campbell Soup	Ellen Oran Kaden	Food Consumer Products
318	342	Thrivent Financial for Lutherans	Teresa Rasmussen	Insurance: Life, Health (Mutual)
325	340	Hormel Foods	Lori Marco**	Consumer Food Products
327	297	Eastman Kodak	Laura Quatela**	Photo Control Equipment
332	311	Darden Restaurants	Teresa Sebastian**	Food Services
340	357	AGCO	Debra Kuper	Industrial and Farm Equipment
342	456	Las Vegas Sands	Gayle Hyman*	Hotels, Casinos, Resorts
348	415	Eastman Chemical	Theresa Lee	Chemicals

* New to list   ** Replaced a woman on last year's list   Source: Minority Corporate Counsel Association; first published in *Diversity & the Bar*, Sept/Oct 2011

2011 RANK	2010 RANK	COMPANY	GENERAL COUNSEL	INDUSTRY
353	352	AECOM Technology	Nancy Laben*	Transportation, Logistics
356	362	Avery Dennison	Susan Miller	Chemcials
359	355	DaVita	Kim Rivera	Health Care: Medical Facilities
361	327	Commercial Metals	Ann Bruder	Metals
362	336	NiSource	Carrie Hightman	Utilities: Gas and Electric
367	394	Reliance Steel & Aluminum	Kay Rustand	Wholesalers: Diversified
381	480	Spectrum Group International	Carol Meltzer	Global Collectibles
384	507	Expeditors Intl of Washington	Amy Tangeman*	Global Logistics
387	389	Advance Auto Parts	Sarah Powell	Motor Vehicles and Parts
400	393	PetSmart	Emily Dickinson	Specialty Retailers
405	401	Pacific Life	Sharon Cheever	Insurance: Life, Health (Stock)
411	384	Clorox	Laura Stein	Household and Personal Products
419	461	Agilent Technologies	Marie Oh-Huber	Scientific, Photographic and Control Equipment
422	381	CH2M Hill	Margaret McLean	Engineering, Construction
423	453	Lubrizol	Suzanne Day*	Chemicals
434	380	SunGard Data Systems	Victoria Silbey	Software, Technology Services
436	445	St. Jude Medical	Pamela Krop	Medical Products and Equipment
443	448	Wesco International	Diane Lazzaris	Wholesalers: Diversified
445		Avaya	Pamela Craven*	Telecommunications
449	400	Nash-Finch	Kathleen Mahoney	Wholesalers: Food and Grocery
462	564	Bemis	Sheri Edison*	Specialty Retailers: Toilet Seats
469	451	NCR	Jennifer Daniels	Telecommunications
470	455	Washington Post	Veronica Dillon	Publishing, Printing
476	471	Biogen Idec	Susan Alexander	Pharmaceuticals
482	540	J.M. Smucker	Mary Anne Harlan*	Food Consumer Products
487	458	Genzyme	Karen Linehan	Pharmaceuticals
490	487	Sealed Air	H. Katherine White	Packaging, Containers
491	465	Charles Schwab	Carrie Dwyer	Securities
494	492	Host Hotels & Resorts	Elizabeth Abdoo	Hotels, Casinos, Resorts

* New to list   ** Replaced a woman on last year's list   Source: Minority Corporate Counsel Association; first published in *Diversity & the Bar,* Sept/Oct 2011

READ MORE ABOUT IT:

bibliography

In developing this book,

we spoke with many key

sources and consulted

many books, journals,

and magazine articles,

most of which are listed

on the following pages.

Selected Bibliography

ABA Commission on Women in the Profession. "Unfinished Business: Overcoming the Sisyphus Factor: A Report on the Status of Women in the Legal Profession." American Bar Association, December 1995.

Abbott, Ida O. *The Lawyer's Guide to Mentoring.* National Association for Law Placement, Inc., 2000.

———. "Mentoring Plays a Key Role in Retaining Attorneys of Color." *Law Governance Review*, Spring 1998.

———. *Women on Top: The Woman's Guide to Leadership and Power in Law Firms.* West Publishing, 2010.

Barbara Allen Babcock, review of *Sisters in Law: Women Lawyers in Modern American History,* by Virginia Drachman (1998). 50 Stan. L. Rev. 1689, May 1998.

Barnes, B. Kim. *Exercising Influence: A Guide for Making Things Happen at Work, at Home and in Your Community.* Pfeiffer, 2006.

Barsh, Joanna, Susie Cranston, and Geoffrey Lewis. *How Remarkable Women Lead.* Random House, 2009.

de Beauvoir, Simone. *The Second Sex.* French Trade Publisher (unknown), 1949.

Bell, Ella L.J. Edmondson and Linda Villarosa. *Career GPS: Strategies for Women Navigating the New Corporate Landscape.* Amistad, 2010.

Bell, Ella L.J. Edmondson and Stella M. Nkomo. *Our Separate Ways: Black and White Women and the Struggle for Professional Identity.* Harvard Business School Press, 2001.

Bell, Katherine. "Empathy: Not Such a Soft Skill." *HBR Blog Network*, May 28, 2009. http://blogs.hbr.org/cs/2009/05/empathy_not_such_a_soft_skill.html.

Bruce J. Avolio and Bernard M. Bass. "Shatter the Glass Ceiling: Women May Make Better Managers." *Human Resource Executive*, December 1994.

Catalyst. "Damned If You Do, Doomed If You Don't." Catalyst, 2007.

———. "Women in the Law in the U.S." Catalyst, 2010.

Collins, Gail. *When Everything Changed: The Amazing Journey of American Women from 1960 to the Present.* Little Brown & Co., 2009.

Coughlin, Linda, Ellen Wingard, and Keith Hollihan, eds. *Enlightened Power: How Women Are Transforming the Practice of Leadership.* Jossey-Bass, 2005.

Drachman, Virginia G. *Sisters in Law: Women Lawyers in Modern American History.* Harvard University Press, 1998.

Eichbaum, June. "Globalization and General Counsel." *Diversity & The Bar*, July/August 2008.

Eichbaum, June and Victoria Reese. "The Entrepreneurs, The Consiglieri, The Public Servants." *Chief Legal Executive*, Fall 2002.

Friedan, Betty. *The Feminine Mystique.* W.W. Norton & Co., 1963.

Friedman, Lawrence M. *A History of American Law.* 3d ed. Touchstone, 2005.

Gupta, Vipin, Sylvia Mayfield, Mary Shapiro, and Susan Haas. "Risky Business: Busting the Myth of Women as Risk Averse." *CGO Insights,* April 2009.

Harris, Barbara J. *Beyond Her Sphere: Women and the Professions in American History.* Greenwood Press, 1978.

Helgesen, Sally and Julie Johnson. *The Female Vision: Women's Real Power at Work.* Berrett-Koehler Publishers, Inc., 2010.

Hewlett, Sylvia Ann, Kerrie Peraino, Laura Sherbin, and Karen Sumberg. "The Sponsor Effect: Breaking Through the Last Glass Ceiling." *Harvard Business Review*, December 2010.

Kouzes, James M. and Barry Z. Pozner. *Encouraging the Heart: A Leader's Guide to Rewarding and Recognizing Others.* Jossey-Bass, 2003.

————. *The Leadership Challenge.* 4th ed. Jossey-Bass, 2008.

Lapovsky, Lucie and Deborah Slaner Larkin, eds. "The White House Project Report: Benchmarking Women's Leadership." The White House Project, November 2009.

Leslie, Jean B. "The Leadership Gap: What You Need, and Don't Have, When It Comes to Leadership Talent." Center for Creative Leadership, June 2009.

Martin, Renee and Don Martin. *The Risk Takers: 16 Men and Women Share Their Entrepreneurial Strategies for Success.* Vanguard Press, 2010.

Pagonis, William G. "Leadership in a Combat Zone." *Harvard Business Review,* December 2001.

Peck, Suzanne and Penelope Wong. *Ruff: A Lost Dog Tale: 5 Great Strategies to Manage Change at Work and Beyond.* Blue Point Books, 2011.

Reeves, Arin N. "Diversity: A New Level of Awareness." *The Docket*, March 2009.

Richardson, Veta T. and Joan C. Williams. "New Millennium, Same Glass Ceiling? The Impact of Law Firm Compensation Systems on Women." The Project for Attorney Retention and Minority Corporate Counsel Association, July 2010.

Sharpnack, Rayona. *Trade Up!: Five Steps for Redesigning Your Leadership & Life from the Inside Out.* Jossey-Bass, 2007.

St. John, Richard. *The 8 Traits Successful People Have in Common: 8 to Be Great.* Train of Thought Arts, 2010.

Tannen, Deborah. *Talking from 9 to 5: Women and Men at Work.* William Morrow & Co., 1994.

————. *You Just Don't Understand: Women and Men in Conversation.* Ballantine Books, 1990.

van Ogtrop, Kristin. *Just Let Me Lie Down: Necessary Terms for the Half-Insane Working Mom.* Little, Brown and Co., 2010.

Ward, Stephanie Francis. "Family Ties." *ABA Journal,* October 2010.

Wellington, Sheila and Betty Spence. *Be Your Own Mentor: Strategies from Top Women on the Secrets of Success.* Random House, 2001.

Williams, Joan C. *Reshaping the Work-Family Debate: Why Men and Class Matter.* Harvard University Press, 2010.

————. *Unbending Gender: Why Family and Work Conflict and What to Do About It.* Oxford University Press, 2000.

CONVERSATION STARTERS:

interview questions

Here's how we started

our conversations

with women general

counsel and executive

recruiters. The answers

the questions sparked

are evident throughout

the book.

GENERAL COUNSEL QUESTIONNAIRE

OVERVIEW/OBJECTIVES

Chronicling the history of women general counsel in Fortune 500 companies from 1979 to 2011, the overall objectives of this book are to explore, determine, and establish the individual and common attributes, behaviors, critical decision points/actions, and influences/environmental factors (collectively, the "factors") that have distinguished and contributed to the ascendancy of women to the level of assistant general counsel and then on to general counsel and beyond.

Critically, we're seeking to understand which factors were most helpful at various points along these women's career paths.

In addition, we're looking to demonstrate how these factors may have evolved from 1979 to 2011, changing or evolving from the first wave to the second wave to the third wave.

And, as we seek to understand why certain women advance while their peers do not, we expect to ultimately reveal the relevancy, influence, and impact of **mentoring, risk taking,** and **attributes** as the principal forces of career advancement to the general counsel role.

INTERVIEW QUESTIONS

A. GROWING UP/PRE-LAW

Covering the period of your life from early childhood through college and up to the point of entering law school, this section is focused on understanding and revealing, from every relevant angle, the influential, deciding, and ultimately cementing factors that set you on the road toward a legal and business career.

Simply put, we want to organically understand why and how you came to the law and then moved up professionally—and how your aspirations, ambitions, convictions, and all other feelings/emotions (doubt, fear, anxiety, too, if applicable) coalesced and evolved around the vision that guided you in that direction.

MENTORING

■ Who (and what) most influenced your decision to become a lawyer? Thinking broadly and extensively (e.g., family, friends, professors, neighbors, lawyers, authors, businesspeople, others), how exactly did they influence you?

■ How did you go about approaching people during this period of your life? And when did you awaken to the role that a "mentor" could play in your life?

■ In the same vein, what events most influenced you and shaped your world view? Think social, societal, historical, environmental, cultural, more.

ATTRIBUTES/SELF-UNDERSTANDING

■ Growing up, what moved you? Who did you want to be? What was important to you?

■ Thinking about the evolution of your self-image, as a person, but also as a woman, describe your evolving sense of yourself as a woman in the world, how you would make your way, and what the future looked like to you.

■ In going through high school, entering college, and choosing to go to law school, what skills, attributes, talents, and personality traits would you say defined you? This can include intellectual prowess, leadership skills, personal achievements, and so on.

■ All along the way, how did you identify your strengths, and in what areas did you know or suspect you had work to do? What self-improvement steps did you take?

RISKS

■ Was the beginning of your road to the law a linear one—well-mentored, informed, confident, certain—or was your experience one of climbing up hills, navigating around obstacles, dealing with doubts—and taking risks? If the latter, describe the major challenges you had to overcome.

■ If you had not chosen the legal path, what else would you have done?

B. ENTRY LEVEL
(Law school plus 5–8 years)

Covering your law school experience and subsequent first work experiences, this section is focused on understanding and revealing, from every relevant angle, the shaping and sharpening of your professional vision and ambitions. From outer influences to deliberate choices to risks confronted to sheer good luck, we want to distill the essence of your first steps up the professional ladder.

MENTORING

■ As before, who were your major mentors, consults, and way-makers during this part of your life? Which classmates, law professors, men or women ahead of you, colleagues, and/or clients made the difference?

■ Did you seek out people, or did they come to you? How did you attract attention? What were you doing—or what did you think you had to do—to make yourself a worthy "investment" in people's eyes?

ATTRIBUTES/SELF-UNDERSTANDING

■ What were your expectations going into law school, and what effect did your law school experience (socially, academically, work experience) have on defining where you wanted to go afterward?

■ How did your sense of self as a woman evolve during law school? What was your sense of gender dynamics at this time, including your outlook on your post-graduate future?

■ You've just graduated from law school—now what? Talking through the key professional and personal moves you made over the next eight years, what drove your choices? Where did you work, and why? And how did you change along the way? What did you discover about yourself, in terms of your capabilities and attributes?

■ What did you to do to prepare for and effectuate each successive transition to the next level/phase of your career? Describe the major transitional events that moved you forward.

RISKS

■ Now making career and life decisions in earnest, how did you come to terms with the concept of risk taking? What was your definition of risk taking at this time—and how willing were you to test the boundaries, if not stretch the limits, of your professional and personal comfort zones?

■ What was your definition of "opportunity" at this time? Would you say you were opportunistically minded, or cautious, or deliberate, or what?

■ Give examples of where you were confronted by decision-making circumstances involving risk—how did you respond? Did you find such moments unnerving or emboldening? What did you learn from these instances?

■ To what extent, if at all, did you feel you had to "defeminize" yourself to be competitive with your male peers, in terms of dress, attitude, and demeanor? Was this something you encountered or observed among any female peers, either inside or outside of your own working environments?

■ What frustrations do you remember from this time? Conversely, what rewards and assurances?

■ What risks did you confront at this time?

C. MID-LEVEL
(Law school plus 8–15 years, now managing others as a supervising or managing attorney)

No turning around now: you are well up the ladder, ascending into the upper atmospheres. Did you now take hold of your destiny—or were there still rungs to climb?

MENTORING

- Where did mentoring fit into your professional life now? Again, who were the people making a difference for you?

- Were you now evolving into a mentor? If so, who did you take under your wing?

- At this point, what stock did you take of women helping women up the ladder? Had this been prevalent in your own experience, or from your observation of the experiences of other women?

- Did you encounter examples of women being resentful of other women in the workplace, and if so, why?

- What was your sense now of climate changes for the advancement of women in law and business?

ATTRIBUTES/SELF-UNDERSTANDING

- Describe your professional self at this point—what had you done, and what did you do, that made you who you were as a legal/business professional? What were your strengths, and what, if any, still needed some work?

- What had you done to advance ahead of your female peers? Your male peers?

- At what point did your vision for becoming in-house corporate counsel begin to materialize?

- As before, what did you to do to prepare for and effectuate each successive transition to the next level/phase of your career? Describe the major transitional events that moved you forwar. Did you seek out openings or were search firms involved?

RISKS

- At this advancing point of your career, what constituted risk and risk taking for you?

- What risks did you face, which risks did you take on, and what were the payoffs?

D. SENIOR LEVEL
(From assistant general counsel to general counsel)

Atop the ladder, and now on board at the executive level, you have arrived. One eye on the past and one looking ahead, what ultimately did it take to get here, and where do you go from here?

ATTRIBUTES/SELF-UNDERSTANDING

- Describe the circumstances by which you first became a GC. What made you the winning candidate for the job, what was expected of you, what were your responsibilities, and how did you manage? How did you evolve in the job?

- In which of the following attributes were you strongest, and in which did you need improvement? If the latter, how did you go about improving?

  - Strategic thinking and problem solving
  - Executive presence
  - Distillation and prioritization
  - Contextual intelligence
  - Ability to inspire others (oratorical skills, leadership skills, and presence)
  - Cross-group collaboration
  - External networks and important relationships
  - Integrity
  - Flexibility, agility, self-starting
  - Influencing skills

MENTORING

■ When you first ascended to the GC role, did you have the benefit of a mentor to help you transition into the job or was it a trial by fire?

■ Reflecting on all the mentors and way-makers who helped guide your journey, what would you say about the importance of mentoring to today's young women lawyers?

■ What have you done, and what are you doing now, to mentor women?

RISKS

■ How does the concept of risk change in the GC role? And, to the extent appropriate, describe risky situations you have faced as a GC, and how you dealt with them?

■ What are the risks facing you in the future?

E. IN CONCLUSION

■ What did you have to sacrifice along the way? Conversely, what have you gained?

■ What is your take on the evolution of the "woman as corporate counsel and GC" over the past three decades, and what progress do you see being made in the near term?

■ What would you say to the present and future generations of women aspiring to the GC role? What advice would you give them in terms of seeking and providing mentorship, confronting, evaluating, and taking (or avoiding) risk, and establishing the requisite attributes for the optimal positioning and presentation of their candidacy?

■ Reflecting on the sum of your experiences and journey to the GC role/executive suite, is there a formula for success that today's women lawyers can follow?

■ How do you define success? What qualities does a woman

bring to decision making and leadership at that nexus where law and business meet?

■ Why do certain women advance while their peers do not?

■ What is your perspective on gender dynamics in law and in business? How high is today's glass ceiling—or is this really on the wane?

■ Lastly, where do you go from here? Can you say you have finally arrived, or is there still a climb ahead?

EXECUTIVE RECRUITER QUESTIONNAIRE

OVERVIEW/OBJECTIVES

Chronicling the history of women general counsel in Fortune 500 companies from 1979 to 2011, the overall objective of the book is to understand the individual and common attributes, behaviors, critical decision points/actions and influences/environmental factors (collectively, the "factors") that have distinguished and contributed to the ascendancy of women to the level of assistant general counsel and then on to general counsel and beyond.

Evolution is a governing theme, which we are seeking to understand in two major ways.

First, there is the concept of charting three distinct waves of women rising to the general counsel role:

FIRST WAVE: The pioneering women who became GC from 1979 to 1998—those who were a minority in law school, who had few peers or mentors along their road to the C-suite, and who had few peers they could reach out to as GCs.

SECOND WAVE: Those who became GCs from 1999–2002, before women represented a critical mass.

THIRD WAVE: Those from 2003 to the present, increasingly less anomalous in the role.

Second, we are focusing on the personal evolution of our women GC interviewees, toward understanding which factors were most helpful at various points along their career paths.

Keeping both of these frameworks in mind, the following questions are designed to prompt your experience with and understanding of the evolutionary forces and factors that have shaped, and will continue to shape, opportunities for women general counsel in the Fortune 500.

INTERVIEW QUESTIONS

- What precluded/excluded women from the general counsel role prior to 1979?

- What critical events/conditions/forces began opening the door and raising the ceiling?

- How has the GC role changed from 1979 to the present? How would you compare today's GC job description with 1979's, and in the intervening years?

- What core attributes were required for the GC role in 1979, and how have they evolved since? Specifically for women, how have they evolved?

- What characteristics distinguished the ideal GC candidate in 1979, and how have they evolved since? Again, specifically for women, how have those evolved?

- For each wave, what were the keys to success for women aspiring to the GC role? Can you describe or characterize personality types for women GCs in the three waves?

- From 1979 to the present, discuss the evolution of a woman's self-identity in the GC role. Covering everything from credentials and accomplishments to appearance, manner, and conduct, what was required of a woman to be competitive, to be taken seriously, to be authoritative and influential, and to gain power in the law profession and the GC role?

- What sacrifices and trade-offs have women made along the way to ascendancy and permanency in the GC role? What sacrifices should today's woman be prepared to make?

- There are cases where "macho bluster" has backfired for male GCs. Does a woman possess qualities that might make her better suited to the role than a male counterpart?

- How have women GCs met the challenge of an increasingly stringent regulatory environment, and the additional visibility, demands, and pressures this has brought to the GC role?

- Power, visibility, accessibility and influence are all attributes accompanying and necessary for GC success. How is each different between a female GC and a male GC, and how have these concepts/definitions evolved through the waves?

- What professional experience do you bring to judging women GC candidates? What do you look for, and how has that evolved?

- Why do certain women advance while their peers do not?

- What is your perspective on gender dynamics in law and in business? How high is today's glass ceiling—or is this really on the wane?

- Reflecting on the sum of your experiences in this realm, what guiding principles would you offer to today's women lawyers and GC aspirants?

- What have we learned from the last 32 years? And what will it take to develop transformative leaders in a more systematic way in the future?

acknowledgments

"no one goes it alone"

For our second chapter in this book, on mentoring, we chose the title "The Rose Trellis" to depict women lawyers blossoming on the framework set for them by champions, sponsors, guides, and other life and career mentors. It's an image that extends to the people who made this book possible, starting with the 46 past, present, and future women general counsel who shared with us their individual journeys to the top. When we first conceived of and then embarked upon creating this book, we never imagined just how open and willing our "sisters in law" would be to talk about their lives as women and as lawyers. Courageous in every way, they give this work, the first of its kind, its singular heartbeat and soul.

From the outset, the team at Leverage Media, our publisher, a custom content provider specializing in thought leadership, was our indispensable ally in bringing *Courageous Counsel* to life. Over the course of a nearly two-year-long journey, Michael Winkleman and Jeff Heilman (an exceptionally gifted writer who proved invaluable in his way with words) helped us mold our interviews, notes, ideas, and ultimately our vision into the book you are about to read. They, and we, were also supported by the talented designer and art director Carole Erger-Fass; project manager, researcher, copyeditor, and proofreader Sue Khodarahmi; and production manager Rose Sullivan.

We also extend our special thanks to a number of people who were instrumental in creating and organizing the book. In founding the Minority Corporate Counsel Association in 1997, Lloyd Johnson envisioned a national organization dedicated to achieving lasting diversity success in the legal profession. His work continues to inspire positive change.

Just as our women general counsel were generous with their time and insight, so too were the leading women legal search professionals who contributed their frontline views of what it takes to secure the top corporate legal spot today: Martha Fay (Marty) Africa and Natasha Innocenti of Major, Lindsey & Africa; Lee Hanson of Heidrick & Struggles; Catherine Nathan of Spencer Stuart; and Julie Goldberg Preng of Korn/Ferry International. These remarkable women, many of whom we consider our friends and confidantes as well, were incredible sounding boards on this project, as they have been otherwise.

For their insight into the attributes and characteristics of successful women lawyers and women in general, we also thank our esteemed experts of Chapter 5: Ella Edmondson Bell, Dana Mayer, Jacquelyn Mayfield, Suzanne Peck, Rayona Sharpnack, Brendan Sheehan, Richard St. John, and Joan Williams. These great minds have spent extraordinary time and effort getting to the bottom of many of the questions we had about what it takes to make it to the pinnacle of the in-house legal profession and, in fact, any profession.

We give our full-fledged salute to a group of unsung heroes who were critical to our ability to complete this project. To the five SNR Denton women partners who assisted with the general counsel interviewing—Robin Edwards, Leslie Davis, Peg Hall, Linda Chaplik Harris, and Natalie Spears—and to a special group of "right-hand" women—our assistants Eleanor (Ele) Kuntzi and Lily Smith, along with Lloyd Johnson's assistant, Tinnie Easter-Smith—we are indebted for your time, dedication, and invaluable support.

And finally, a special thank you to SNR Denton for the firm's support of this project and its commitment to diversity in the practice of law.

—Michele Coleman Mayes and Kara Sophia Baysinger

■ ■ ■

No one gets ahead alone in this world, and as I have extended an open hand to others, many people have helped me, starting with my family. To my mother and father, Geraldine and Wilbert Coleman, my sister Greta Pitts Moore, my aunts Mattalyn Pitts and Katherine House, my uncle Robert Pitts—and my former husband, Jean A. Mayes—thank you for being there for me in your vital respective ways. For all the promise they provide for the future, I also want to recognize my nephews Jack N.E. Pitts Jr. and Jean Coleman Pitts, my goddaughter Torya Beard, and my cousin Ivanetta Rivers—and, celebrating all our good times together, my close friends Francois Djenohan and Valerie Moon.

Early in my career, it was a female mentor, Bobette Jones, who inspired me to become a general counsel. From there, I have Andrew D. Hendry, Ed Fogarty, and Lois Juliber to thank especially for giving me the room I needed to grow, along with Michael Critelli, for his faith in hiring me for my first general counsel job at Pitney Bowes; Murray Martin, for continuing to have faith in me after Mike stepped down; and my current boss at Allstate Insurance, Thomas Wilson, for believing in me even when my career background did not make me the obvious choice for this position.

Along the way, there were bosses, colleagues, outside counsel, and friends who helped guide me and were willing to clear a path for me in the workplace. In the final analysis, they often pushed me to reach for greater heights because they "surrounded and supported" me. The men in this group include the following: Michael Wicks, David Wilf, Scott Bass, Rick Pacynski, Thomas Woods, James Robinson, Leonard Gilman, John Lowell, Jay Brant, James Olson, Reuben Mark, Bob Joy, Cyril Hyman, Daniel McClellan, Robert Alston, Lawrence Byrnes, Bruce Owens, Dennis Archer, Mauricio Boscan, Franki Iturbe, Steve Blaske, Kim Brunner, John Nestico, Dennis Hickey, Harvey Pitt, Richard Rossman, Saul Green, Judge Henry Heading, Judge Louis F. Simmons Jr., Judge Damon Keith, Judge Ralph Guy, Judge Edward R. Korman, Bruce Aitken, Steve McCormick, Joseph Zammit, John Schwolsky, John Harkins, Alan Gilchrist, Kenneth Frazier, Rick Palmore, Ram Charan, Owen James, LeRoy Williams, David Wilcox, Henry (Hank) Ruth, Benjamin Wilson, Arthur Bowman, John Masty, Curtis Mack, and Ziggy Johnson. Equal in their guidance and support are the following women: Marty Africa, Catherine Nathan, June Eichbaum, Judge Judith Kaye, Lynn Hecht Schafran, Jean Otte, Kathy Rodgers, Cathy Higgins, Sara Moss, Renée Baruch, Magistrate Judge Marilyn Go, Leah Simms, Yvonne Johnson, Gail Burroughs, Zenola Harper, Judge Jacqueline Allen Baity, Jax Lowell, Eileen Letts, Dana Freyer, Sheila Birnbaum, Beth McQuillan, Dineen Garcia Weinberg, Mary-Joe Raidy, Bertha Walker, Johnna Torsone, Laurel Bellows, Judy Perry Martinez, Julie Daum, Julie Johnson, Veta Richardson, Susan Hackett, Sherrie Baidoon, and Magda Kristoff.

And, of course, there is my good friend Lloyd Johnson, for providing the original spark of inspiration to share my story and the stories of a very special group of fellow lawyers with women everywhere in the pages of this book—and to Aja, his daughter, the very essence of the joy, reward, and sheer vitality that comes from mentorship.

Finally, I want to give special mention to Doreen Triano and LuAnn Moccia, my administrative assistants at Colgate-Palmolive and Pitney Bowes, respectively, and my invaluable right hand here at Allstate, Eleanor (Ele) Kuntzi. She has been with the company for more than four decades—her entire career—and from making sure I did not run into any invisible walls when I first arrived here to inspiring me with a giant amount of confidence and an infectious sense of humor, I can happily say that she, too, is one of my mentors. For her dedication to writing this book, I also give heartfelt thanks to my co-author, Kara Baysinger.

—Michele Mayes

■ ■ ■

Success in any endeavor is a team sport—and this project and my career as a whole are no exception. First and foremost, my dear husband, Eric, deserves my unending gratitude for his unflinching support, love, and encouragement. No matter what I dream up, he asks the right questions and then does everything he can to help me accomplish it. My precious twin daughters, Rebecca and Julia, who inspire me to make this world a better place and to leave a legacy on my profession that benefits those who come to it next and later. And truly, to my parents, Keith and Josephine Kischer, for teaching me that if I could dream it and believe it, I could achieve it. My sister Noelle Kischer-Lepper, brother Alex Kischer, cousin Bivan Kischer, nephew Gregory Kischer, and father-in-law John Baysinger play a role in defining my wonderful experiences of the grounding and launching power of family.

My experience as a lawyer and a businessperson was framed and fostered by my dear mentor, partner, and friend, the late Harold Shapiro, who taught me more about being a lawyer and partner than he could have possibly known—starting with when I was his client and not yet a lawyer.

I owe immense gratitude to my co-conspirator, ally, teammate, colleague, and friend, the late Gary Hernandez, who remains in my heart and mind every single day. His encouragement and counsel brought me to law firm life and to California. We built our practices together. Without him, I would never have the truly blessed life I have now.

I am a strong believer in the power of a strong personal network (an extended personal board of directors, in a sense) of amazing and inspirational colleagues, friends, and confidantes, including far too many to list, but starting with Dana Kaufman, Kim Stricker, Phoebe Pierson Carleton, Michael Davis, John Kramer, Maggie Kavalaris, Myrtle Potter, Elizabeth Gaynes, Elizabeth Tosaris, Sarah Postyn, Carl Goldberg, Sara Holtz, Kelly Valen, Kelly Spencer, Karen Gray, Karen Fang, Barbara Hughes, Kathleen Bissell, Delia Chilgren, Mary Cranston, Holly Hanke, Sue Saperstein, Duane Quaini, Elliott Portnoy, Jim Klenk, Phyllis Solomon, Laura Favinger, Jackie Darrah Knapmiller, Marlene Nations, Cynthia D'Amico, James Daly, Rick Baum, Pat Carmody, Shelly Canter, Natasha Innocenti, Marty Africa, Merle Vaughn, Ann Strayer, Marla Brady, Jessi Dunne, Catherine Wendel, Len Karpowich, Mary Nader, Betsy Romweber Sullivan, Melissa Skoog Dunagan, Matt Orwig, and Sally King. I have known some of you forever it seems, and some for a much shorter time, but you all influence and inspire me, and I am grateful for your presence in and impact on my life.

And certainly not least, to Michele, my co-author, whom I have come to know better, and respect immensely, through this project. You are a fabulous, wise, wonderful person, and I am honored to have created this with you.

—Kara Baysinger

index

Note: **Bold** page numbers refer to individuals in profiles, interviews, and special features.

about the authors

Michele Coleman Mayes

Michele Mayes is executive vice president and general counsel for Allstate Insurance Co. and a member of the senior leadership team. Mayes is responsible for guiding Allstate's strategy to foster sound compliance of governance practices a healthy legal, political, and regulatory environment. She joined Allstate in November 2007.

Mayes brings extensive legal, corporate, and government experience to Allstate. From 1976 through 1982, she served in the United States Department of Justice as Assistant United States Attorney in Detroit and Brooklyn, eventually assuming the role of chief of the Civil Division in Detroit.

In 1982, Mayes entered the corporate sector as managing attorney of Burroughs Corp. As Burroughs and Sperry Corp. merged, creating Unisys Corp. she was appointed staff vice president and associate general counsel for Worldwide Litigation. In 1992, she joined Colgate-Palmolive Co. as vice president and associate general counsel U.S. In 1993, she was promoted to vice president of Human Resources and Legal for North America then transitioned to vice president, deputy general counsel, and assistant secretary. In 2001, she was promoted to vice president, legal and assistant secretary, and elected a corporate officer. In 2003, she joined Pitney Bowes as senior vice president and general counsel.

Mayes is the recipient of numerous awards, including American Bar Association Commission on Women in the Profession—The Margaret Brent Award and the Minority Corporate Counsel Association Trailblazer Award. She was named one of America's top black lawyers by *Black Enterprise* in 2003. In 2009, Mayes was recognized as one of the most Influential General Counsel in America by *The National Law Journal* and by Ethisphere Institute in *2011 Attorneys Who Matter*.

Mayes is a member of the board of Legal Momentum, RAND Corp., and Leadership Counsel for Legal Diversity.

Kara Sophia Baysinger

Kara Baysinger is a San Francisco-based partner at SNR Denton US LLP, where she heads the firm's Insurance Regulatory practice and is co-chair of the firm's Global Insurance practice. She serves on the firm's U.S. Policy and Planning Board, its Global Advisory Committee (executive committee), and its Women's Business Development Group.

Baysinger began her career working in-house for insurance companies for almost 10 years, responsible for product and contract development, regulatory compliance, agent licensing and contracting, reinsurance, corporate contracting, market conduct practices and examinations, insurance department complaints, and government relations for all 50 states. She joined SNR Denton (then Sonnenschein Nath & Rosenthal LLP) in 1998.

Baysinger has served on numerous state and National Association of Insurance Commissioners advisory groups and is a frequent speaker, author, and cited authority on insurance regulatory issues and trends.

Admitted to practice in California as well as Illinois, Baysinger is consistently named a "SuperLawyer" by *Super Lawyers* (a peer survey of 52,700 Northern California attorneys), a "Leader in California" by *Chambers USA: America's Leading Lawyers for Business Client Guide* (2004–2010), and is listed in the 2011 *Legal 500* for her capacity to "handle difficult and politically sensitive issues."

Baysinger is passionate about issues relating to diversity and women in the law, and about mentoring and coaching women lawyers to be leaders, both in-house and in law firms.

She studied at Northwestern University (Kellogg Executive Education), in the Women Directors' Program, and received her law degree from Loyola University School of Law in Chicago, and a B.A. in political science from the University of Michigan.

what they're saying about
COURAGEOUS COUNSEL

"*Courageous Counsel* is a compelling, well-organized testament to the ingenuity, resourcefulness, and formidable horsepower of women in the law. Whether you are a Fortune 500 general counsel, an "up and comer," still in law school, or really, any woman interested in tracing our gender's ascent in the legal arena, this book will speak to you. It highlights just how far we've come, but isn't afraid to remind us that women still have work to do in order to reach true parity within the profession. The book's historical framework, laced with complementary statistics, graphics, biographies, and fascinating personal journeys (or "conversations") of some of our most esteemed female practitioners, makes this a highly readable, informative, and even entertaining work. It's plain that the authors put a great deal of sweat and toil into this book. I'm left feeling proud, grateful, and inspired."

—KELLY VALEN,
California-based attorney and author of
The Twisted Sisterhood: Unraveling the Dark Legacy of Female Friendships (Random House, October 2010)

This is an essential career guide for women lawyers—or any ambitious woman—whether or not they aspire to the general counsel's role. Told through the inspiring voices of women general counsel and refreshingly free of platitudes and generalities, this book places their stories in a broad historical and empirical context and distills important career lessons and choices that other women can replicate.

Whether discussing the pivotal importance of optimism or the essential role of risk taking, it is a treasure trove of mentoring advice from women who have already been there, tried that, succeeded, and offered wise and practical counsel to help other women learn from their experiences.

Congratulations and thanks to the authors and the interviewers who put together such an extraordinary book for all of us. I can't wait to share it with my women clients, colleagues, and friends.

—RACHELLE J. CANTER, PH.D.,
Executive coach and author of
Make the Right Career Move (Wiley, 2006)